LAW AND ORDER

Critical Issues in Crime and Society

Raymond J. Michalowski, Series Editor

Critical Issues in Crime and Society is oriented toward critical analysis of contemporary problems in crime and justice. The series is open to a broad range of topics including specific types of crime, wrongful behavior by economically or politically powerful actors, controversies over justice system practices, and issues related to the intersection of identity, crime, and justice. It is committed to offering thoughtful works that will be accessible to scholars and professional criminologists, general readers, and students.

LAW AND ORDER

Images, Meanings, Myths

Mariana Valverde

Rutgers University Press
New Brunswick, New Jersey

First published in the United States 2006
By Rutgers University Press
New Brunswick, New Jersey

First published in Great Britain 2006
By Routledge·Cavendish
2 Park Square, Milton Park, Abingdon, Oxon OX14 4RN

Routledge·Cavendish is an imprint of the Taylor & Francis Group, an informa business

Library of Congress Cataloguing in Publication Data
Valverde, Mariana, 1955–
Law and order: images, meanings, myths/Mariana Valverde
p. cm.—(Critical issues in crime and society)
Includes bibliographical references and index.
ISBN-13: 978–0–8135–3879–2 (hardcover : alk. paper)
ISBN-13: 978–0–8135–3880–8 (pbk. : alk. paper)
1. Crime and the press.   2. Crime in mass media.
3. Criminal investigation in mass media.
4. Mass media and crime.   5. Mass media and criminal justice.
6. Fear of crime.   7. Law enforcement.   8. Crime—Sociological aspects.
I. Title.   II. Series.
HV6168.V35   2006
364—dc22   2005035876

Manufactured in Great Britain

Contents

Acknowledgements |

Beverley Brown commissioned this book and gave invaluable support and substantive suggestions on the first draft. Rosemary Gartner, Nicole Rafter and Colin Perrin gave much support and help along the way. Sandra Jones did a fabulous job copy-editing and correcting citations, and Karen Carew-Carswell provided excellent and enthusiastic research assistance. Students taking my WDW385 course over the past few years were unwitting guinea pigs for most of the ideas contained in this book, and I thank them for tolerating me and helping me to be a little less uninformed about popular culture. Finally, the book is dedicated to my children, Nicky and Ming, who have helped this text-centred academic better to appreciate the power of images.

Chapter 1
Introduction

The problem of 'sensation'

Academics studying criminal justice, including media representations of criminal justice, generally believe more in social solutions than in harsh retribution. The hard-line, law-and-order policies followed in recent years by governments in the UK and in the US are not overly popular in the academy, and in most programmes students are trained to critique these policies as simple-minded. The critique is not usually presented as one political approach or preference versus another, however: it is generally presented as a question of 'good facts' or 'good research' versus mere opinion and prejudice. Occasionally academics will join journalists and activists in explicitly ethical or political attacks on right-wing policies on crime and safety; but on the whole, academics prefer to speak in the name of the facts. Thus, criminologists typically try to counter law-and-order sentiments with research showing that higher sentences and the criminalization of minor public order offences do not actually deter people from committing serious crimes. For their part, media studies scholars write articles and books showing that television cop shows present a totally misleading picture both of crime and of law enforcement work.

In this way, academics attempt to turn political and ethical debates about what to do with evildoers or how to best ensure community safety into an argument about who has the facts, meaning the social science facts, the research facts. And not surprisingly, researchers – who after all produce virtually all of the social science facts about crime and criminal justice and who are the main consumers of such facts – always feel justified in claiming superiority in regard to facts. Researchers wring their hands and complain, usually to one another but sometimes to the media as well, that if anybody listened to 'the' facts – meaning 'our' facts – we wouldn't have such heavy sentences for minor or victimless crimes; if anybody out there read the research, very young people would not be put in prison; and so on.

Why do politicians, the media and the public appear to be deaf to researchers' facts? This is the key question that this book will address, albeit indirectly. The most commonly mentioned explanation for the lack of fit between research and policy runs something like this: politicians and the public are ignorant of the real facts (the social science facts), partly because they are simply uneducated (not having attended our classes, or not attentively at any rate) and partly because they are far too influenced by populist mass media. Hollywood, the tabloids and commercial television fill people's heads with false fears, myths and misleading, simplistic solutions. In this context, one often sees the word 'sensationalism' used to dismiss huge amounts of material that contains information as well as 'sensation'. But what exactly is sensationalism? And why is sensation so bad?

It is important to note at the outset that the right-wing, law-and-order views propounded by the tabloids and by many American films and television programmes are certainly questionable on a number of dimensions, including fit with empirical research findings, but on other dimensions as well. When tabloids encourage public (council) housing tenants to form vigilante squads and drive sex offenders out, for instance, criminologists should indeed intervene to point out that such solutions do nothing but cause more problems. An ex-offender who is made to feel like a monster is unlikely to have the incentive to behave well, and, regardless of rehabilitation goals, driving people with criminal records underground only makes supervision more difficult. But are the tabloid views bad public policy because they are impractical and short-sighted (as I would argue) or are they bad because they allow for the venting of half-conscious emotions? Are all emotional responses to crime necessarily bad from a public policy point of view? Why are criminologists (with some notable exceptions [Young, 1996; Katz, 1988; Garland, 1990]) so afraid of emotion?

The Enlightenment as a knowledge revolution

The academic's hand-wringing tale of ignorant publics and vote-seeking politicians in thrall to the lowest common prejudices and emotions is not a new one. Whether knowingly or not, today's researchers on crime and criminal justice are enacting a time-honoured intellectuals' kneejerk response to being ignored by the masses – a response most famously associated, historically, with the Enlightenment *philosophes*. Toward the end of the eighteenth century, as the United States was becoming the world's first more or less democratic republic, while in France the groundwork for revolution was being prepared, intellectuals across many countries formed common cause to denounce superstition, prejudice, commonsense views and tradition. 'Dare to know! Have the courage to use your own reason!' exhorted the famous philosopher Immanuel Kant, in a popular essay he published in 1784 under the title of 'What is Enlightenment?' He elaborated: don't just do what your priest or what your parents tell you; mistrust tradition; mistrust received opinion; exercise your critical faculties and question everything you were trained to believe. What we have inherited from the past, from tradition, from authority, is unexamined and probably wrong.

Reason, meaning the individual capacity to examine, question, gather information and evaluate it in a dispassionate manner, was central to the Enlightenment's truth project. Neither logical reasoning nor scientific inquiry was new, and they were certainly not uniquely European (contrary to the claims made by most *philosophes*). But what was arguably new was that the ability to reason critically for oneself was presented, perhaps for the first time in history, as the rightful inheritance of humanity as such, rather than as the esoteric capacity of a few scholars. Although initially certain highly educated European men were the only authorized spokespersons for reason, logic and science, what made the Enlightenment a powerful political movement was the belief that as time went by, more and more people would become enlightened, and thus the whole world would become gradually rational. In England, Mary Wollstonecraft argued, more or less at the same time that Kant was writing his famous essay on enlightenment, that women too had the potential to shed their culturally induced preferences for sentimentality and frippery and become serious rational thinkers. And shortly after the French

Revolution, in the Caribbean, Toussaint L'Ouverture led a rebellion of African slaves against the French imperial forces, arguing that if reason was the foundation of the rights of Man that were being preached in France, black people too were endowed with rationality and were thus agents of Enlightenment, potentially at any rate.

Although some influential thinkers, such as Jean-Jacques Rousseau, tried to combine the Enlightenment interest in science and rational knowledge with a validation of feelings and sentiments, overall, and especially in the long run, rationality was regarded as better, and higher, than passion, emotion and 'sensation'. More typical and lasting than Rousseau's sentimentalism was Mary Wollstonecraft's contempt for traditional feminine culture, including her contempt for the sentimental romance novels so popular at the time. Her own publications were far more serious-minded, including the ground-breaking polemic *A Vindication of the Rights of Woman* (1792). There is a certain historical irony here, since her daughter, Mary Shelley, would later publish the Gothic novel par excellence, *Frankenstein*, which in many ways is characteristic of the sensational literature disparaged by her mother.

The powerful narrative that began in the eighteenth century suggested that the darkness of superstition, emotion and tradition, unable to withstand the scrutiny of scientific and philosophical reasoning, would give way to a new sunlit world in which policies would be decided upon on a purely rational basis, rather than being based on tradition, emotion or prejudice. Here we see the beginning of intellectuals' longstanding contempt for 'sensation'.

The knowledge revolution of the Enlightenment can be characterized as twofold. First, debates about which facts were true, while not disappearing, were overshadowed by a more theoretical focus on the process, on the question of *how we come to know*. The way information was generated, communicated, tested out and justified greatly preoccupied thinkers. In the political realm this translated into a new concern for process, and especially for representativity – 'no taxation without representation', the American revolutionary slogan, was one political manifestation of this focus on the process rather than on outcomes. What taxation monies were used for was not as important as the process of representation. Kant's essay on enlightenment, mentioned above, similarly defined 'enlightenment' as the process of questioning authorities and using one's own individual light of reason. That for him was the key. Believing a true fact merely on authority was to him not enlightened – an approach that is still very current in today's academy. This first aspect of the Enlightenment knowledge revolution can thus be described as the concern about *method*.

We can see this emphasis on method and process in the way in which science experiments are performed in school. The point of making you struggle with beakers and Bunsen burners is to let you see, with your own eyes, how a particular scientific truth emerges. It would be much quicker to make students memorize the chemical elements of this or that substance. But then the great enlightenment ideal of having people see for themselves how truths are generated would have been defeated. In time, this approach came to dominate the social sciences as well. This has been particularly true of sociology, which remains to this day obsessed with what is called 'method' – that is, the rules governing the production and the verification of scientifically reliable knowledge.

The focus on following certain set rules of knowledge production and verification – rules making up what is known as the scientific method – is one of the key legacies of the Enlightenment. It underlies today's set-piece academic critiques of government crime policy and of popular media representations of crime, whether or not the criminologists who speak the language of Enlightenment have ever heard of Immanuel Kant or Mary Wollstonecraft. The privilege of scientific method is assumed without discussion by academics as they/we dismiss journalistic accounts of crime and victimization as 'merely' journalistic, however insightful they might be. This same privilege, again assumed without much if any discussion, lies behind the dismissal of people's personal experiences as 'merely anecdotal'.

The placing of the pejorative term 'merely' before 'anecdotal', 'journalistic' and 'sensational' is shorthand not only for a certain theory of knowledge production and its rules but also for a whole theory of what counts as a legitimate *format* for communicating information. This is the second important legacy of the Enlightenment's knowledge revolution. The dating here is different from that applying to the first dimension, the focus on method. It was only in the late nineteenth century, with the rise of social science university departments, that a particular format came to dominate intellectually respectable communications about urban dangers such as crime. The most respected thinkers in late eighteenth-century Europe and North America – people like Voltaire, Benjamin Franklin, David Hume, Diderot, Rousseau, etc. – did not write anything like refereed journal articles. They wrote philosophical treatises, novels, educational booklets, political pamphlets, encyclopedia entries and, in Rousseau's case, popular operas. One of the most influential intellectuals of the eighteenth century, the baron of Montesquieu, became famous not because of his learned treatise *The Spirit of Laws* but rather owing to the immense popularity of his sociological novel, *Persian Letters*, a more or less journalistic account of European law and customs attributed to two fictional Persians travelling in Europe. Similarly, Jean-Jacques Rousseau was better known in his own day for his moral/social novel *Julie, on La Nouvelle Héloïse* than for his political theory treatises.

But by the late nineteenth century, 'fiction' had emerged as a distinct way of writing practised by novelists. Alongside a professional class of fiction writers there developed a separate quasi-professional body of social researchers. Many of the early pioneers of social research – Charles Booth and Beatrice and Sidney Webb in the UK, Jane Addams and her co-workers in Chicago – were not university based. However, with the success of the 'Chicago School' of sociology, which defined its endeavours as 'scientific' partly by rejecting the more community-based work of Jane Addams and the early pioneers of social surveys as 'merely social work', certain kinds of research on social issues such as crime and poverty acquired the prestige of 'science'. As we shall see in Chapter 8, studies claiming the status of social science were characterized as much by their format and their rhetorical choices as by the quality and quantity of research carried out by their authors.

The story of the professionalization of research on social issues cannot be told here in any detail, however. The point that really matters is that it was only at a particular point in time that a certain way of collecting information about social problems and a certain way of organizing texts purporting to give scientific information became dominant. Research methods and the formats used to present scientific communications became largely standardized in the first half of the twentieth century.

Academic formats

Although media scholars have spent much time critiquing various popular formats (e.g. tabloid news; Hollywood movies) and analysing their implications, few if any communications scholars have turned their critical gaze onto academic communications, the communications we ourselves produce. Undergraduates reading this may say: 'But that's the thing about academic journal articles: they have no format!' Grey pages with no illustrations, however, do not indicate an absence of formatting: they indicate a particular choice of format. This choice may not be one that the authors make consciously – but then, neither does the morning television newsreader necessarily reflect on or consciously choose the format choices made within his or her institution. The academy has as many conventions about what is 'proper' formatting as the tabloids or the TV news. But what is specific to the academy is that the conventions regarding format and style are all designed to leach out colour, eliminate personal opinion, get rid of any lively prose, ban all illustrations (other than scientific graphs or charts), and generally create the impression that the article was not written by a living breathing human being with feelings and an imagination, but rather by some kind of impersonal collective machine that churns out facts and communicates them with as few adjectives as possible.

Academic formats seem peculiar to those not used to it. First-year university students sometimes complain, 'Why does the lecturer say that we can't use "I" in an essay?' 'Why do we have to say, "research has shown"?' And law students have to suppress any desire to write in elegant English as they are taught to write 'It is submitted that . . .' where ordinary mortals would use 'I think that' or 'I argue that . . .'

First-year textbooks are usually illustrated, often with colour photographs, for it is thought that youngsters need some kind of transition from school texts to proper academic prose. But readers with some experience of university courses will know that illustrations grow scarcer the closer one approaches graduation. Similarly, publishers of introductory textbooks usually push reluctant academic authors to put in reader-friendly boxes containing anecdotes, cartoons or newspaper articles. These boxes relieve the boredom of the main scholarly text. But again, these are regarded as crutches for beginners and are eliminated from 'real' scholarly publications. Social science, including criminology, presents itself to its consumers in uniformly grey texts that appeal strictly to the reader's cold logical faculties.

Why this uniformity of format choices? What does the grey page and the impersonal prose without adjectives communicate to consumers of social science? In a word, the format tells the consumers that this is real science, proper scholarship, 'just the facts'. These days even low-budget television shows can afford some snazzy graphics, even if they can't afford a foreign correspondent. The proliferation of sophisticated technologies for livening up and formatting textual as well as visual and oral communications makes the academic insistence on grey formatting stand out more than it did some decades ago. It is as if social science were constantly shouting, 'We are not populist', 'We are not emotional'. When criminology lecturers complain about or ridicule the tabloid's coverage of this or that crime, what is often being ridiculed is not so much a particular theory of crime, but rather the very fact that the tabloid highlights emotion and sensation. As Willem de Haan and Ian Loader put it in their introduction to an important special issue of *Theoretical Criminology* (De Haan and Loader, 2002, p 243):

> States of emotional arousal – pleasure, anger, fear, sadness, disgust, remorse, resentment, shame, guilt and so forth – seem somehow deeply and intimately implicated in (and hence vital to an understanding of) numerous fields of criminological inquiry . . . Yet the emotions remain a somewhat peripheral topic within theoretical criminology. Many established and thriving modes of criminological reflection and research continue to proceed in ways that ignore entirely, or at best gesture towards, the impact of human emotions on their subject matter.

The downgrading of anything emotional is not an accident; it is integral to science's self-image. Science's self-appointed task – discovering and communicating the factual truth – seems to be inextricably connected to a certain theory of the relation between truth-seeking and other human interests and capacities. This theory goes something like this: emotions, colour, feelings, pictures and even liveliness are inimical to truth-telling. We may not know what counts as science, in these days of contested paradigms: but we do know what counts as communication that claims the status of science, and we know this by its format. The dispassionately written grey text has the status of scientific discourse by virtue of its anti-emotional format. Its particular content, its claims about the world, may well be overturned by tomorrow's study, but nobody will dispute the status of that publication as scientific. A photograph of an ordinary crime victim would be appropriate for a magazine essay on crime, but would be regarded as totally out of place as part of an academic lecture on the crime rate. And a clip from a film about policing would be acceptable only as a sort of dessert shown at the end of a traditionally formatted, audiovisually grey lecture – and only in large introductory classes, and only as a rare entertaining bit.

In this way, mass media images and stories about crime and policing, in so far as they are mentioned, are immediately assigned to the lowest rung on the scale of knowledge. My students love nothing better than to pour scorn on the racist theories of crime found in our local tabloid, and I find it difficult to resist the temptation to join in self-serving sarcasm. Even when they are not directly mentioned in the classroom or in texts, popular accounts and visually appealing images of crime exist as the populist Other that constantly confirms our own sense that we speak the real truth about crime and about law and order.

Commercial communications about crime and danger do of course need to be critically challenged, since they often make implicit factual claims that are simply wrong. But in dismissing popular representations, the feelings and experiences voiced by ordinary people in non-commercial communications about crime are also often dismissed. If students speak up and share their personal experiences of victimization, or of being policed, the lecturer will likely quickly reinterpret those experiences as either typical or atypical 'examples' of larger truths, thereby letting the class know that the real truth about law and order is to be found in aggregate data, not in the meaning of personal experiences.

Are young beautiful women statistically likely to be given poisoned apples? Social science's failure to address popular knowledges

Let me give a final example of the marginalization of non-academic communications about danger and crime, drawn from my teaching experience. For some years now I have asked students in my 'Representing Crime' course to collect a kind of story about crime and risk that circulates either orally or through email, namely, the urban legend. We then analyse the scenarios and characters and set-piece narratives that recur over and over and that purport to give information about some new source of danger that is, typically, either unknown to or dismissed by official authorities. What we have found is that, like the stories about UFOs insightfully analysed by Jodi Dean in her book *Aliens in America: Conspiracy Cultures from Outerspace to Cyberspace* (Dean, 1998), urban legends about weird crimes committed in unexpected venues succeed in circulating and being repeated even when they are not believed. Most of my students confessed to forwarding at least some of the emails coming from anonymous sources and titled something like 'Warning to girls,' even if they did not believe that the story had happened or thought that the event might have happened once but was highly unlikely to recur.

The populist, low-tech, low-budget, unofficial format of the urban legend circulating either by word of mouth or through email transmits certain kinds of messages about danger and safety. Crime statistics do not circulate in this form. But there are feelings and facts about urban dangers that cannot be put on a graph. What are some of these? Some stories circulate simply by virtue of being completely bizarre; but there are many that are stock stories, as it were. These appeal to a populist scepticism about governments and about large corporations – like the UFO stories, which are usually accompanied by a statement about NASA or the FBI not wanting to admit what is really going on.

Appealing to the same populist fears of a conspiracy among the powerful exhibited in the UFO stories, one email urban legend that was very prevalent a couple of years ago, among University of Toronto students at any rate, told us that Kentucky Fried Chicken did not use real chickens, but only animals genetically modified to the point of having no legs or heads, being composed solely of pure white-meat breasts. This story manages to combine a new fear – anxiety about genetically modified food – with a much older populist mistrust of big corporations.

Other relatively new fears are addressed in stories about waking up 'in a bathtub full of ice', as one legend put it, having been unwittingly deprived of a kidney or other valuable organ, often in Mexico or some other Third World locale. The privatization of healthcare is here addressed without an explicitly political analysis, simply by invoking the fearful image of rich but desperate patients buying new organs on a world market.

There are also large numbers of stories about the internet itself as a source of danger. Among these, my favourite subgenre consists of variations on the theme of 'Bill Gates is the antichrist, if you need proof just translate the names of Microsoft programs into ASCII code and see how often 666 occurs.' This of course redeploys old Christian stories about devils and the end of the world, as well as allowing a non-political outlet for the distrust of monopolistic big corporations that most ordinary people feel.

A wealth of information about people's fears about technology, about corporations, about the failures or excesses of modern medicine, and about the fragility of official knowledge itself could be obtained by carefully following the production and dissemination of these stories. And the least interesting question one could ask would be 'Is it true?' or 'Is it likely to happen?' The interest lies elsewhere. Literary scholars have shown that fairy tales with no identifiable author that circulate either orally or in lowbrow formats (such as children's books) have served important cultural and psychological functions for centuries now. One cannot confront or displace the modern fairy tales about Bill Gates or KFC by waving a sheaf of scholarly studies. Urban legends and scientific studies are simply not on the same plane, either psychologically or from the point of view of knowledge (as a recent study has shown [Donovan, 2004]; see also Best and Horiuchi, 1985).

Predictably, an enterprising well-educated person, possibly a criminology student, has taken it upon him/herself to counter this most lowly of populist discourse by analysing urban legends one by one, so as to tell the world which ones are 'true' and which ones are 'false' (see www.snopes.com) – as if proving that the Snow White poisoned apple story is highly unlikely to occur in real life in any way helps us to understand the social and psychological meaning of legends.

Generally we (academics, intellectuals) ignore these popular knowledges, especially if they circulate outside of newspapers. And when we do not ignore them, we limit our work to proving that these knowledges are not factually true. Joel Best and Gerald Horiuchi showed, in regard to the popular North American fear of Hallowe'en poisoned treats being given to unwary children, that only two documented instances of Hallowe'en treat poisoning could be found, and that these involved family members, not strangers (Best and Horiuchi, 1985). They found, however, that even after a US newspaper editors' agreement not to publish rumours of Hallowe'en poisonings, parents' fears about unwrapped candy, apples and home-made treats continued unabated. Stories about psycho killers putting razor blades in apples circulated purely by word of mouth, without the support of the commercial media, but contrary to what one would expect in a highly technological society, the legend did not die. Decades after the original panic, the whole of North America is still subjected to an informal and yet very strict rule that only commercially sold, wrapped candy be given out at the door when children go out for their annual trick-or-treating.

A criminologist trying to prove empirically that razor blades in apples are not a significant crime risk because of statistical rarity would be barking up the wrong tree. The cultural myth of girls poisoned by apples is simply too deeply rooted in our collective psyche to be displaced by a few facts. Versions of the Snow White story, on film and in children's books, continue to perpetuate the fear about children being given poisoned treats. The psychic and cultural resonance of the razor blade in the apple urban legend needs to be taken seriously and analysed in its mythical and psychological dimensions, since the feelings and anxieties mobilized and invoked by such stories have a life of their own. One can and should inform oneself about the actual distribution of risks; but this will not make feelings deeply rooted in collective stories and images go away.

'Blackletter law' as a format for the Enlightenment knowledge project

The social science academy is not the only site in which high-culture assumptions about the intrinsic value of certain kinds of communication formats play such a key role in excluding certain phenomena from view or sharply limiting the 'legitimate' academic questions that can be asked about them. In legal contexts too, the belief in what is tellingly still called 'blackletter' law includes a fundamental, rarely questioned assumption that the legal format – black letters on white paper, little formatting, no headlines, no pictures, no colour, no first-person remarks, no graphics of any kind, even graphs or charts – is the royal road to truth and justice. We shall see this in detail in Chapter 9, which explores the judicial assumption that crime-scene pictures have an inherent ability to inflame the passions of a jury to the point of risking the conviction of the innocent.

'Gruesome' photos are always considered to be potentially prejudicial to the accused, even when they are allowed in because their 'probative' value is said by the judge to outweigh the potential prejudice. That gruesome pictures fuel the flames of passion and thus undermine rational justice is not a conclusion justified or backed up with social-psychology studies of jurors. It is an assumption. The fear that the ordinary people serving on juries will have their passions 'inflamed' by photos of mangled or injured bodies – especially colour photographs – is an instance of a much larger assumption: that ordinary people (but not lawyers or judges) are more easily moved by passion than reason, by feelings than facts. This highlights the importance of understanding the historical roots of what I here call 'the knowledge project of the Enlightenment', including its built-in preference for rationalist formats.

The term 'rationalism' may be misleading, in so far as it has been used to designate a particular school of philosophy. But it is difficult to think of another term to describe the usually unspoken preference – shared by the academy and the courts – for grey, technical, impersonal, neutrally worded, 'blackletter' communication formats. As feminist scholars have long pointed out, any time that grey, unemotional formats and contents are being praised, one should immediately search for a wider prejudice against feelings, emotions and the body – a preference that is simultaneously a prejudice against the 'vulgar' masses who are thought to be insufficiently enlightened and hence always at risk of derailing the Enlightenment project.

Even in our own pluralistic era, certain deep-rooted eurocentric, masculinist and elitist cultural assumptions, which the term 'rationalism' describes, cannot be set aside or ignored. In universities, students have certain expectations of what a university course is, as do department heads and deans. But, as Kant said in his 'What is Enlightenment?' essay, even though public servants like university teachers can only go so far in practising autonomy and creativity, more can be done to continually question the built-in values and format choices of the institutions within which we work. This book will have achieved its aim if it helps to challenge us to continually question our assumptions about what counts as a proper communication format for facts about or analyses of safety, danger, order and crime.

Beyond crime

Much good work has been done in the past 30 years or so in analysing the content of newspapers and newscasts, and also of fictional representations of crime, criminals and criminality. In the 1970s Stuart Hall and his collaborators at the Birmingham Centre for Cultural Studies produced the highly influential, innovative work *Policing the Crisis* (Hall et al., 1978), which taught a generation or more of university students how to critically scrutinize media reports about crime for their political assumptions and their political effects (see also Ericson, 1995). Another key element in that first, pioneering group of works was Stanley Cohen's *Folk Devils and Moral Panics* (Cohen, 1972). A larger and more systematic study of television news, which covered not only crime but also all manner of social conflicts, was carried out in Glasgow by scholars who invented (before desktop computers) techniques for systematically studying both content and format (Glasgow University Media Group, 1976, 1980). In Toronto, Richard Ericson and his collaborators carried out an in-depth study that was remarkable for getting inside television studios and newspaper editing rooms and documenting how the news about crime is literally put together (Ericson et al., 1987, 1989, 1991).

More recently, some insightful works by both film scholars and criminologists have surveyed television and film portrayals of crime and criminal justice (e.g. Leitch, 2002; Sparks, 1992, 1996). This literature has shown that ordinary people do not watch television or read the newspaper out of a rational desire to be well informed about social issues or about current events, as John Ellis (2000) and other writers on television have long pointed out. Instead, they engage with and consume the products that the mass media generate as a result of often unarticulated motives and desires; and consuming these products has a number of different, sometimes contradictory and not always predictable effects.

In one influential account, Jack Katz has argued that we read stories about unlikely or unusual crimes not for information purposes but because they provide us with a kind of daily moral workout (Katz, 1995). Reading the crime pages, we can experience anger at evildoers, extreme fear, horror, anxiety, a sense of the community pulling together in crisis, and deep parental love, all at the same time. And experiencing these emotions is something that people seem to need to do – vicariously if possible.

Vicariously experiencing deep emotions, such as hate and extreme fear, is a need that people felt long before the mass media existed. The ancient Athenians loved to go to the theatre and see tragedies featuring highly unusual criminal events (incest, parricide, etc.). As a society, we rarely go to the theatre, and if we do we cannot expect others in our community to have seen and to know all the same plays. We also do not, on the whole, attend church regularly. Thus, most of us no longer have the opportunity to collectively experience fear, joy and love simultaneously, through the recounting of familiar tales that is afforded by old-fashioned religion. Katz's argument about crime news providing an opportunity for a collective daily moral workout – one that, like physical workouts, needs to be repeated daily or at least weekly – sheds light on processes documented by many other media scholars.

However, most of the scholars who have undertaken the sort of analyses of the emotional impact of images of crime that have made this book possible (scholars such as Stanley Cohen, Alison Young, Richard Sparks and Ian Loader) are criminologists by trade. This means that they tend to focus on images of crime (and sometimes of the policing of crime). Breaking out of the boundaries of criminology (including the 'crime and the media' subdiscipline), I argue in this book that it is important not to confine our analytical gaze simply to 'crime', or even to 'crime and law'. The urban legend exercise that I do every year with my undergraduates, described above, is a case in point here. Many of the dangers imagined and represented in urban legends are not feared because they are crimes. Indeed, 'fear of crime' needs to be understood in a larger frame. Fear of crime is a mostly negative emotion that is part of a larger and less negative psychic process, namely, people's strong, passionate desire for safety and order.

If people find it difficult to stop worrying about the presence of razor blades in Hallowe'en apples, even when they know that this is more of an urban legend than an empirically important form of crime, this is likely because of the sheer strength of the desire for neighbourliness and community, the deep longing for transparent and trustworthy everyday relations with those who live near us. When we examine representations of urban dangers and fears, we may find that people, practices and objects well outside of the legal system may play important roles in the complex cultural and emotional processes that certainly feature 'crime' – including the fear of crime and the policing of crime – but which ultimately have to do with the definition, contestation and reproduction of the basic features of the social order.

This book, therefore, is concerned with representations of order – which include representations of that particular form of disorder which is crime. Its scope is thus much less narrow than that of most literature on crime and the media.

Beyond images

One of the limitations of the 'crime and the media' literature is that it somewhat artificially isolates representations that are commercially and technologically mediated – newspaper stories, films, etc. – from representations that occur in real time, in real life. In the course on representations of law and order that I teach, we begin with media analysis, but we quickly progress to analysing the official statues that are visible outside government buildings in the immediate neighbourhood. This communicates the message that this is not a media studies course but rather a course teaching students how to analyse representations in general, not just pictorial or printed representations.

Walking down the main street of our city and seeing a statue commemorating the heroes of World War I; participating in a demonstration about police racism; and being confronted with a series of people and objects representing the nation-state – or the European megastate – when going through Customs at an international airport, are all everyday examples of representations of law and order that are 'live', as it were, rather than captured on print or electronic media. Undoubtedly, experiences with 'live' enactments of law and order shape our consciousness, perhaps as much as the mass media do, but very few serious studies of such 'live' representations exist. Just to give one example, the singing of the national anthem performed every morning at my children's school is a cultural practice whose effect has not to my knowledge been studied, but which surely counts as a possible research site for studying the social semiotics of law and order.

This book, then, encourages the critical study not only of 'media images of crime' but of representations of any kind, live or on the media, that feature either crime or crime's nemesis, the forces of law and order – all the forces of order, not excluding inanimate objects like statues, uniforms and flags. To the extent that it addresses 'live' representations, it goes outside the purview of media studies. It also goes beyond the limits of criminology by placing law breaking and law enforcement in the broader context of order production and maintenance.

Chapter overview

The second chapter presents an overview of a number of key concepts in 'semiotics' (the science of signs) and cultural studies. Terms such as 'sign', 'signified', 'metaphor' and 'myth' are defined and explained. Some of these terms are repeatedly used throughout the book to analyse specific representations, whereas other terms are used less often, for reasons related to the particular choice of subject matter.

After the definitions of some basic technical terms, the second chapter proceeds to develop some strategies for using the tools of semiotics specifically to understand and appreciate the way in which certain theories of what law and order is and how it is best maintained come to be upheld by representations that are often not explicit arguments but rather visual signs. Whereas literary scholars analyse meanings for their own sake, sociologists and anthropologists are more interested in the social and political effects of signs and their combinations: this is what 'social semiotics' covers. Chapter 2 also introduces readers to a fundamental principle of media studies, namely, that it is as important to analyse the format of a representation as the content. Formats send out their own messages, as the famous Canadian media theorist Marshall McLuhan said in 1964 ('the medium is the message'; see McLuhan 1964).

The third chapter adds a third element to the usual media studies dichotomy of content and format: context. Since the analyses developed here are not literary, that is, are concerned more with the cultural and social roots and effects of representations than with the inner dynamics of texts, some time is spent showing how one can analyse the social effects of representations, emphasizing that the context within which a representation is 'consumed' also shapes meaning in important ways. In later chapters, representations are often analysed by recourse to this three-part template (content, format, context).

Chapter 4, 'Science and the semiotics of deviance' traces, in broad outline, the history of the criminal justice system's own efforts to represent criminality. It pays particular attention to changes in the technical means used to 'capture' live criminals in a two-dimensional medium, i.e. on paper or on photographic film. This necessarily partial history reveals that in the English-speaking world there have been two main ways of attempting to represent and 'capture' either individual criminals or the essence of criminality. One general approach seeks to identify deviant, degenerate and criminal human types. But for the purposes of investigating particular crimes – rather than crime and deviance in general – what has always mattered has been the old murder-mystery question, 'Who done it?' Knowledge of types is not very useful when it is necessary to identify one particular person as the perpetrator and to do so beyond a reasonable doubt. Thus, the criminal justice system, while always interested in keeping up with scientific knowledges of human types, has been more centrally concerned to experiment with what we will call the *forensic gaze*, a way of seeing that is centrally concerned with linking clues to individual criminals. The history of fingerprinting features large in this account, since until the recent advent of DNA testing, fingerprinting was the gold standard for identifying specific criminals and, even more importantly, to certify that the police's identification was indeed correct in ways that satisfied criminal courts.

From the representations generated by the criminal justice system itself we move, in Chapter 5, to the world of fiction. Focusing once more on the work of detection – only one of many parts of the criminal justice system, but one that has generated more than its fair share of memorable representations – we examine representations beginning with Edgar Allan Poe's Auguste Dupin, usually considered as the first private eye, and going on to Arthur Conan Doyle's Sherlock Holmes and Agatha Christie's Hercule Poirot. This chapter deals primarily with detective novels and other forensically oriented literary representations.

Chapter 6 takes us into a largely American world of film and television. We first visit the private eyes and insurance investigators featured in the 1940s black-and-white Hollywood productions known as 'film noir'; and, leaping over a few decades, we go on to analyse some current popular US television shows featuring police work, namely *Law & Order*, *COPS* and *CSI* (Crime Scene Investigation). The chapter ends with a consideration of the Steven Spielberg futuristic film *Minority Report*, which features a special police unit – the 'Pre-Crime Unit' – which is the fulfilment of that longstanding utopian dream of modern policing, namely, detecting and punishing crime even before it happens.

It is argued throughout the book that each representation of badness/crime implies or even creates a particular kind of authority, a specific knowledge, even if this is not directly mentioned. In Chapter 7 we undertake a case study in the dialectic of authoritative knowledges and forms of deviance: an extended consideration of the 'psycho killer', a figure that Hollywood would revise and recycle numerous times in the decades after Hitchcock's classic 1960 film. The focus here is not so much on the criminal but on the tight relationship between the specific kind of criminal memorably portrayed by Anthony Perkins and the (unnamed) psychiatrist who after a short examination reveals the whole truth about Perkins's twisted personality to an astounded and respectful audience of victims and police officers. We see that representations of crime and danger also work to constitute certain authority figures – the psychiatrist, in Hitchcock's case. The chapter argues that the absence of authoritative psychiatrists in later 'psycho killer' films may be a symptom of the general breakdown of professional authority that many theorists have identified with the break-up of the welfare state.

Having discussed representations of individual criminals, of criminal types, and of authorities who claim to know crime and/or criminals – private eyes, police detectives, psychiatrists – we move away from persons and go on in Chapter 8 to discuss spaces. Like people, urban spaces usually appear to us as either safe or unsafe, as either good or bad. And when we make instant judgements about where we will go or not go, we are not usually aware of the fact that we are processing a large amount of data consisting mainly of visual clues (broken windows, litter, graffiti, persons, trees, etc.), and then generating a Gestalt-type judgement about the character of the space. The strategic deployment and re-arrangement of visual cues connoting safety is precisely what the 'Crime Prevention Through Environmental Design' (CPTED) movement has highlighted. I argue here that this and related crime-prevention efforts involve not just a transformation of the look of urban spaces but also a profound transformation of the citizen's gaze. Once educated about crime risks and about the signs of disorder and danger, we come to see our everyday world with new, risk-driven eyes.

The chapter also shows that the 'broken windows' hypothesis about the need to crack down on minor disorders such as litter, drinking on the street and broken windows, which has become so popular among police chiefs and municipal politicians around the English-speaking world and beyond, is not just a crime-control campaign. It is also a campaign to re-educate the citizen's gaze, to make us see differently, to change the way in which we represent the world to ourselves as we walk down the street.

The final chapter (Chapter 9) considers that images of crime do not just 'represent' crime, but can also occupy an important role within the criminal justice system as 'evidence', that is, as objects in their own right. Many books analyse how lawyers and judges and trials are represented in films and on television; but no social science analyses exist of the circulation and the fate, in the context of criminal trials, of visual images that have the legal status of evidence. Some of the American and Canadian case law governing the admissibility of what American law classifies as 'gruesome pictures' is canvassed here to show that legal actors produce all sorts of interesting theories about the meaning, significance and power of the image as they engage in legal battles about the admissibility of this or that piece of evidence.

I chose the 'gruesome pictures' topic as the concluding chapter as a result of an event that occurred in my own city of Toronto in the autumn of 2003. A judge ruled that a jury could be shown a black-and-white drawing of a mangled girl's body, but not the original colour photograph as the latter might have a prejudicial effect on the jury. It seemed that the whole history of Western philosophy's efforts to insist on blackletter rational texts rather than visually striking images was at work in that courtroom. Furthermore, the 'gruesome pictures' cases demonstrate that the analysis of the meaning, significance and effects of different types of representations is by no means an academic enterprise. Judges, police officers, prosecutors, jury members, crime reporters and citizens who watch the crime news on television are all involved, every day, in theorizing the relations between signs and their meanings, on the one hand, and 'real life' events on the other. Having some tools with which to critically analyse the formation and circulation of meanings is thus useful not only for scholars and students but for all citizens. Representations, and people's theories about what representations do or don't do, constitute a fundamental dimension of the everyday life of citizens.

Chapter 2
Social Semiotics: the Basics

'Semiotics' is defined as the scientific study of signs and their meaning(s). An offshoot of linguistics, semiotics was developed from the 1920s onwards by a series of linguists and other scholars, such as Charles Peirce in the US and Ferdinand de Saussure in Europe. For several decades, semiotics was an abstruse pursuit, combining linguistics and formal logic, used by scholars to trace and analyse abstract, non-historical relations among words and other signs. This was an important innovation because for a very long time the study of language had been dominated by the historicist approach of philology, the approach popularized by such well-known educational tools as the *Oxford English Dictionary* (OED). Developed at the late-Victorian height of the prestige of philology, the OED devoted great institutional resources to tracing the history of words and locating significant historical shifts in usage. Semiotics, and later structuralist linguistics, opened up new, non-historical ways of scientifically studying languages and meanings.

In the 1960s, certain intellectuals, mainly in France, who were beginning to pay serious attention to popular culture, advertising and mass media, found it useful to borrow some tools from the hitherto little-known world of semiotics. From there it was adapted for various uses by theorists of film, and also by scholars working in the then brand new fields of 'communications' and 'media studies'. The whole field of cultural studies, which grew so quickly from the 1970s onwards, was to a large extent made possible by semiotics. (The other main influence on cultural studies, in the UK at any rate, was an unconventional form of psychoanalysis.) Since the 1970s some knowledge of semiotics has been necessary for anyone who wants to study cultural products, whether highbrow ones like alternative films or lowbrow ones like advertising.

It is somewhat artificial to separate 'social' semiotics from ordinary semiotics, since the study of meaning is never without some reference, however implicit, to social relations. But I borrow the term 'social semiotics' here from two innovative Australian scholars (Hodge and Kress, 1988) whose detailed analyses of ordinary conversations and everyday signs – e.g. billboards – encouraged scholars in the social sciences to think in terms of signs and meanings but without leaving sociology for literature. It was found that semiotic tools can be very useful to explore questions about the social, cultural and political effects and meanings of various representations.

'Social', here as elsewhere, does not have a precise meaning. But it can serve to draw some rough lines distinguishing the kind of analyses found in this book, which focus on social and political meanings and consequences, from other ways of using semiotic tools. Analyses that are focused on the psyche of the consumer of cultural products like film are beyond the scope of this book, as are studies, mainly by literary scholars, that are concerned only with the internal workings of texts. Scholars taking up the challenge of 'social semiotics' have been mainly concerned with tracing the ways in which specific signs and representations either support or challenge prevailing societal relations of power and knowledge.

Let us then introduce a few key semiotic terms that are widely used as tools to analyse the production and consumption of social meanings. These are a small sample of the rather numerous set of more or less technical terms used in film studies, media studies and similar enterprises – psychoanalytic terminology, in particular, is omitted here. But, in my experience of teaching social science students to analyse representations of law and order, they suffice to generate analyses that are interesting, informative and widely accessible.

Signs and semiotic systems

Signs are, within semiotics, the units of meaning; conversely, semiotic systems are composed of signs. Let us take each of these two terms in turn, beginning with 'semiotic system'.

Semiotic system

A particular language – English, say – is among other things a semiotic system, that is, a more or less coherent, self-sufficient system of meaning. In the case of what linguists call a natural language, it may seem obvious that English words are all part of the English language whereas French words are obviously the relevant units – signs – making up a competing semiotic system. Thus, drawing a boundary separating 'English' from 'French', a boundary that would keep all the 'English' words or signs on one side, facing a parallel array of French signs or words, appears to be a straightforward task.

But in real life semiotic systems do not come neatly wrapped in separate packages. Numerous English words are actually part of the French language, whether the Académie française admits them into the official dictionary or not. Similarly, words like 'croissant', 'coup d'état', and 'savoir faire' are found in most English dictionaries, alongside 'filet mignon' and a host of other terms from gastronomy, fashion, perfume making and diplomacy.

Semiotic systems, then – including 'natural' languages, but also extending to other systems of meanings – are not self-contained and insular. In contrast to the neat formal diagrams drawn by early semioticians, living semiotic systems flow into one another, overlap and interact in creative ways. Sometimes signs are directly borrowed from another system, a move that after a time has the effect of making that foreign word or sign native – 'croissant' is indeed now an English word, as is 'latte'.

At other times, the meaning of a sign is reinforced by being duplicated, as it were, with a sign from a different system. This is what we see when a graphic that is part of the system of traffic signs is supplemented by English words like 'Give Way' or 'Parking prohibited'. The red point-down triangle is a sign of warning (the same form and colour are used for other warning signs), and the word 'Yield', drawn from the English language rather than from the international system of traffic signs, specifies what exactly the warning is about.

Similarly, when the door on a public bathroom has both an icon indicating the female gender and a word that communicates the same meaning with a different sign, say, the English word 'Ladies', we are faced with an overlap between two semiotic systems, one graphic and one linguistic. In this case no additional information is conveyed by the addition of the two signs. Thus, the relation between the two signs is thus one of reinforcement, not specification. Television is particularly noted for using several semiotic systems at once to reinforce one another, as if the average viewer were so inattentive and distracted that the same message has to be simultaneously shouted out in images, text and graphics. This phenomenon, known as *redundancy*, differentiates television from radio. Radio can at most use two systems to convey the same message – words and music – but television can use three or four.

In addition, television can carry several sets of independent messages simultaneously. This is evident in the case of the running bands of text that communicate the breaking news or the latest stock market quotes while other messages are being communicated, at the same time, in the main part of the screen. Thus, we see that radio has both less redundancy than television and a lesser ability to be sending out totally different messages at the same time. One cannot split a soundtrack the way one can split a TV screen.

The point here is not to delve into the details of how the technical features of certain media impose certain limits – and enable certain possibilities – for the communication of meanings. For present purposes I only want to draw on existing research comparing radio and television to underline the key point of this section, namely, that semiotic systems are neither independent from one another nor self-contained, nor mutually exclusive. One can analytically draw a line around a particular semiotic system (e.g. the famous study of the semiotics of fashion advertising and fashion magazines done by the literary theorist Roland Barthes [Barthes, 1967]). But in everyday life, semiotic systems are often present in fragmented form only. In turn, the fragments of systems appear often as the components of a hybrid which combines a variety of semiotic systems – with these hybrids being usually unstable over time and space. The system of wordless international traffic signs is in this respect unusually stable, unusually self-contained, and unusually free of connotation and emotion. This is no doubt because it is one of the few semiotic systems to have emerged as a result of conscious international planning, rather than emerging more organically.

This may be a good place to pause to issue a sort of warning for those beginning to practise semiotic analysis, namely, the need to keep in mind that a semiotic analysis, however insightful, is never a total analysis. Some of the negative things that are often said about cultural studies by more positivistically oriented social scientists are simply based on bias and professional rivalry. However, some of the complaints about 'research-free sociology' have a grain of truth, in that some enthusiastic practitioners of semiotics presented their analyses as if they explained the totality of a particular social situation or phenomenon. This, in my view, is to jump from the frying pan of rationalistic positivism into the frying pan of cultural reductionism. Cultural meanings are everywhere in everyday life, and anyone claiming to understand social relations needs to know how to use some of the simpler tools of social semiotics. But the cultural meaning of representations is not wholly contained within semiotic systems. Structural power relations act to shape the ground upon which signs circulate and communicate meaning. Sometimes these underlying power relations are visible in particular signs, but sometimes they are not visible, in which case historical and sociological studies are invaluable supplements to purely semiotic analyses.

The final point about semiotic systems is that the boundaries of each system are rarely objectively fixed. For example, students interested in understanding the symbolic power of police forces might well take the various uniforms and other clothes used by a single police force as the relevant semiotic system. This would involve contrasting the black, heavily armed persona of the riot squad officer, which draws on military semiotics, with the blue uniform with shiny buttons that links ordinary police to non-armed government workers like gas inspectors and train conductors. The plain-clothes suit of the detective is yet another sign that forms part of the system of fashion of a particular police force.

Much could be done by analysing a police force's fashion system semiotically. However, it would be equally valid to take as one's system a larger grouping of signs, including not only clothes but also other signs – say, vehicles, horses and dogs – all of which have deep cultural resonance as signs of power, speed, masculinity and efficiency. (Dogs also have connotations of loyalty, intelligence and devotion.) Different definitions of a semiotic system's boundaries serve different analytical purposes. There is no magic number of signs that is required to form a semiotic system; the boundaries of the system under analysis have to be specified by the researcher. If one wanted to compare and contrast military semiotics to police semiotics, it would be useful to include in one's study not only uniforms and other clothes but also vehicles and animals; but an analysis limited to clothing would still be informative.

Signs

If the boundaries of semiotic systems are not fixed, but are in some degree drawn by observers for particular purposes, how do we know that what we are analysing is indeed a system, and not just a bunch of signs? A semiotic system can be said to be a system, however open-ended and subject to redefinition, because the meaning of signs is constituted precisely through the relations that signs have with one another – the relations that make up the system. This was the great insight of semiotics pioneer Ferdinand de Saussure: that meaning is not inherent in words or other signs, but is created in the process through which signs differentiate themselves from one another.

To refer to the police uniform example above: we only know that a certain police uniform conveys a military meaning (rather than a community-relations meaning) because we already know both what military uniforms generally look like and what non-military uniforms (such as those worn by Post Office employees) look like. And by comparing the police uniform we see before us to the large storehouse of representations of uniforms that we all have in our heads (from movies as well as from our own life), we can very quickly, without even being aware of the process, arrive at the conclusion that what we are seeing is a sign or set of signs telling us that this unit in the police is willing and able to act as if they were an army occupying dangerous foreign territory.

In turn, the somewhat military style of current police uniforms reinforces and amplifies the meanings of related signs. Let's take helicopters, which like everything else are signs as well as useful devices. Steven Herbert's study of the Los Angeles Police Department shows that when helicopters begin to be used for ordinary urban crime control rather than just for highway patrol work and rescue operations, the connotations of the social relations of military occupation – connotations that would be familiar to Americans from watching films and news footage – shape both the citizens' experience of being policed and the attitude of the officers who do the policing (Herbert, 1997). One does not need to have seen the powerful helicopter scene in *Apocalypse Now* to know, in one's bones, that observing a neighbourhood from a helicopter creates certain attitudes and dispositions in people that are not produced by the activity of walking the beat.

More generally, we can see that the creation of meaning requires more or less system-wide relations of contrast and comparison. What one vehicle or uniform means is totally dependent on its differences from other competing signs and its associations with similar signs.

The original semioticians made this point by noting that linguistic signs – words – do not have intrinsic meanings, contrary to the impression created by the existence of dictionaries. A dictionary might tell us that 'cat' is a domestic mammal with fur: but we all know what a cat is by about age 3, long before we know what a mammal is. Children learn the meaning of 'cat' by repeatedly comparing and contrasting the sign 'cat' with other signs that are part of the same semiotic system. Parents and kindergarten teachers do not encourage children to look in the dictionary or to memorize a definitional sentence but rather to compare 'cat' to 'dog' (either as pictures in a book or in real life), and to then contrast 'cat' and 'dog' with 'cow', 'tiger' and so on. The meaning of 'cat' emerges through these repeated contrasts and comparisons. *The meaning of 'cat', in other words, is relational – as is the meaning of every other sign.* The child learns, for example, that this live animal (a Siamese) is indeed a cat, just like Muffy at home, even though Muffy is a different colour and shape, whereas this other being (a small brown dog) is 'dog', not 'cat', even though it is the same size and colour as Muffy. And once they know that, they know the functional meaning of 'cat'.

Relations linking signs

Metonymy (displacement) and metaphor

A pair of technical terms that will be used in subsequent chapters arises from the fact that relations among everyday-life signs are seldom coldly logical and rational. In everyday life, the desires, feelings and emotions of both producers and consumers of the communication are not kept at bay, as they are in academic communications. One way of understanding the ubiquity of non-rational communications is to recall Freud's findings, in his analyses of patients' words and non-linguistic signs, that chains of meaning often do not work according to formal logic. For example, someone may well come to attach certain feelings to sign X simply because that sign (say, a mirror) happened to be beside some other sign (say, an adult engaged in sexual molestation). The child who was molested in a room that happened to have a mirror may well grow up to have inexplicable feelings about mirrors. Indeed, the emotion produced by the trauma may be *displaced* onto mirrors, such that the adult would experience anxiety or fear only when in the presence of mirrors, not when in the presence of leering adult males or some other more logically connected sign. To trace this causal chain back to its source involves discarding formal logic and appreciating what Freud called 'primary processes', among which the simple, non-logical relation of '*metonymy*', which can be roughly taken as the semiotic equivalent of Freud's displacement, is an important one.

Metonymy or displacement is not exclusive to traumatic or other psychological events. Advertising campaigns often work on the principle that if a particular sign that is not logically connected to a product is placed beside it repeatedly, the audience will experience a displacement. The Nike swoosh has no logical connection to 'speed'; the association between the two is produced in the mind of the public through repetition. Repeatedly placing an already known sign of speed (say, the photo of a famous runner) beside a sign (the logo) that has no intrinsic meaning, has the long-term effect of changing the meaning of the logo. It started out as an abstract graphic but through the repetition of a metonymical representation, it has become a powerful, transnationally understood symbol of speed and grace.

If metonymy can be visualized as a horizontal connection between signs that are not logically related, but only placed together, *metaphor* can be visualized, by contrast, as a vertical relationship between a sign that one can plainly see and another sign that is not actually visible. When Homer used the famous phrase, 'the wine-dark sea', wine was not present in the story, but its semiotic riches were being drawn upon to specify a particular event, a particular look that the sea sometimes has. Similarly, the English poet Alfred Noyes's line: 'the moon was a ghostly galleon, tossed upon cloudy seas' features a sign one can see – the moon – being given an extra dose of meaning by the metaphorical reference to another sign (indeed, a whole other semiotic system, that of ships sailing on the ocean). The metaphorical invocation of a different, powerful set of signs relating to oceans, travel and adventure, performed in the course of describing the night sky, has the effect of specifying the sort of moon that was visible in the sky on the night in question, thereby specifying the mood.

Metaphorical relations are found not only in literature. The Volkswagen 'beetle' is a well-known instance of a non-literary metaphor, as is the claim that Canada Dry is the 'champagne of ginger ale'. In the realm of urban crime, a well-worn set of metaphors establishes a vertical relationship between actually visible signs of urban danger and decay, on the one hand, and (invisible) tropical jungles on the other. The phrase 'the urban jungle' is one of those metaphors that has almost lost its metaphorical force through constant use – it is a dead metaphor. Nevertheless it continues to do a certain kind of social and political work. Using the phrase clearly racializes the working-class areas of a city and implicitly compares the 'native' inhabitants of these areas to wild beasts and/or to dangerous 'savages'. The person using the phrase 'it's a jungle out there' may not be intending to generate racist meanings: but the effects are contained in the metaphor, and are to a large extent independent of the intentions of the speaker.

Signifier and signified

A sign, semioticians tell us, is composed of two elements: the signifier and the signified. In the case of the entity that readers know as 'cat', which in semiotic terms is a *signified*, one possible *signifier* is the English word 'cat'. Another equally valid signifier is the sort of children's book picture that would be universally read as 'cat'; and yet another valid signifier for the same signified is the French word '*chat*'. (This, by the way, is not strictly correct: proper semioticians distinguish between the signified and the referent, and would call the mammal with fur the referent, not the signified. The signified would be the concept 'cat'. But for present purposes it seems overly complicated to use three terms where two will do; as it will become apparent in the course of the book, there is no need for our purposes to distinguish too sharply between the concept and the object.)

The Union Jack, to give another example, is a signifier – a signifier specifying and in a sense forcing into visibility a certain political entity that cannot directly be seen. Red and orange and green traffic lights are also signifiers within a different semiotic system.

A signifier can represent two or more different signifieds at the same time. An image of Tony Blair's face, for example, signifies an individual with a particular biography, but it also signifies the Labour Party. A police officer's badge has a similar dual meaning. It conveys both information about the particular person and the usually more important information that the person in question has the authority to question you. Someone planning to launch a complaint will ask to see the badge for purposes of identifying an individual officer, but more often than not the badge represents police authority in general, not an individual. In other words, the badge is a signifier for at least two signifieds.

These examples begin to illustrate the very important point that signification is not generally a one-step process. Signification tends to rely on and work through networks or chains. In these chains – which can link the invisible to the visible, as with metaphors, or the specific object in front of one's face to a series of similar and contrasting images contained in the brain's all-purpose archive – one and the same element can be seen to be playing different roles, depending on the direction from which we are approaching the semiotic system. In other words, a signified can in turn be used as, or read as, a signifier denoting another, higher-order entity. When the British fictional detective Inspector Morse shows his badge to someone reluctant to open the door, the badge both names the individual at the door and represents the whole network of criminal justice institutions. The witness's reluctance to open the door is more likely to be rooted in his or her experiences of and theories about criminal justice in general than in any opinion regarding Mr Morse personally.

The chain of meaning that we are here considering as starting with the simple sign of the officer's badge does not have any set endpoint. In general, the chain or network along which meaning flows and is constantly made and re-made is of indeterminate length. Only the analyst's time, patience and/or interest puts an end to the regression. Just as one tenant's ceiling is another tenant's floor, so too in a chain of signification a signified can act simultaneously as the signifier for a new chain.

This brings us to the final technical term introduced in this chapter: myth.

Barthes on myth

The great French cultural critic and semiotic theorist Roland Barthes, whose work changed the course of interdisciplinary studies of culture from the 1960s onward, proposed a particular way of using the term 'myth' in a popular book entitled *Mythologies*, which appeared in French in 1957 (English edition 1972). The book marked a revolution in semiotics, since it was the first time that a serious literary theorist had taken popular culture and studied it with the same tools previously reserved for highbrow literary texts. The book consists of a series of one- or two-page vignettes analysing the semiotics of ordinary products and representations: laundry detergent; steak (analysed as the emblem of Frenchness); tourist photography; the face of Greta Garbo; and so on.

A theoretical appendix to the work developed: first, the distinction between 'signifier' and 'signified' that has already been outlined above. The second part of the appendix developed an approach for understanding how a certain signifier – the face of a famous actress, for example – can signify both something specific (a particular woman) and a whole range of much more generalized meanings, mythical meanings to be precise. Regarding the actress's face, Barthes's point was that the meaning of the signifier – as seen on a movie screen, on a poster, or in a magazine photo – is hardly exhausted when one has identified the particular woman signified by it. Someone filing pictures in a photo archive is only interested in the first-order signification. They want to be able to retrieve a picture of actress X for purposes of future stories. But from the point of view of the sociology and the anthropology of culture, the interesting meanings are the second-order meanings that one can begin to discern as one turns the first-order signified (Greta Garbo) into a signifier. In other words, when switching levels from first-order to second-order meaning, we no longer ask 'Who is this lady?' but rather 'What is the cultural meaning of Greta Garbo?'

Let us cite what may be the most famous text in social semiotics, namely, Barthes's own account of the chains of meaning contained in a magazine photograph. To understand Barthes's text, however, we need to know something about the context, namely, that when Barthes wrote this passage, France had gone through years of agonizing debate about its role in the colonies, in Algeria in particular, and that a strong anti-imperialist movement existed not only in the French colonies but in France itself.

And here is now another example: I am at the barber's, and a copy of *Paris-Match* is offered to me. On the cover, a young Negro in a French uniform is saluting, with his eyes uplifted, probably fixed on a fold of the tricolour. All this is the [first-order] *meaning* of the picture. But, whether naively or not, I see very well what it signifies to me: that France is a great Empire, that all her sons, without any colour discrimination, faithfully serve under her flag, and that there is no better answer to the detractors of an alleged colonialism than the zeal shown by this Negro in serving his so-called oppressors. I am therefore again faced with a greater semiological system: there is a signifier, itself already formed within a previous sytem (*a black soldier is giving the French salute*); there is a signified (it is here a purposeful mixture of Frenchness and militariness); finally, there is the presence of the signified through the signifier . . .

We now know that the signifier can be looked at, in myth, from two points of view: as the final term of the linguistic system, or as the first term of the mythical system. (Barthes, 1972, p 116)

To say that a representation conveys mythical as well as purely informational meaning is not to say, I hasten to add, that the representation is somehow false, posed, biased or inaccurate. It may well be that the picture Barthes is discussing was highly contrived, that *Paris-Match* magazine specifically set out to find a good-looking black soldier to make a point, etc. But the point is that even if the picture were not posed in the least, but was simply a candid shot of something that actually happened, it can still convey a mythical meaning (as well as, at the first level of meaning, tell us where private X was at a particular time).

A myth, in other words, is not a lie or a misrepresentation. It is not the opposite of 'truth'. In fact, myths are often conveyed by representations that are not manipulated, tampered with, or posed. There are few myths more powerful than the generic 'happy childhood' that is the common denominator of most baby photos, for instance. And yet the parents taking the pictures are hardly engaging in a conspiracy to disseminate the patriarchal ideology of the nuclear family when they proudly show their relatives pictures of little Jane. The point is that mythical meanings get communicated, sometimes very purposefully but at other times unwittingly or even accidentally, through certain representations whose meanings are not within the control of the person taking the photo or writing the words. To take the baby-photo case again, the proud parent sending a photo to distant relatives is certainly engaged in mythical communication, and any social semiotician would have to talk eventually about 'the myth of The Family': but to point that out is hardly to understand either the psychology of parenting or the particular dynamics of that family. As mentioned above, semiotics is useful, but it is not a total method.

Political myths are fairly easy to spot. It does not take a degree in semiotics to know that there are good reasons why television channels around the world would repeatedly transmit photos showing the statue of a recently toppled tyrant being toppled by the people. And it is equally clear that television audiences are not interested in the first-level meaning. In the famous 1989 picture of the young man trying to stop a Chinese army tank in Tiananmen Square, for example, people who were not present don't care who the young man was or what sort of tank was being used. International audiences read the picture directly for its myth-ical meaning. A group of ordinary people tearing down a larger-than-life statue of a tyrant with their bare hands clearly conveys an age-old political myth about democracy and justice that resonates transculturally, as does the picture of the young man putting his body in front of the tank. The myth, like many others in our culture, is found in the Bible, under the story of David and Goliath. Countless Hollywood films do nothing more creative than put David in new clothes or give the fighters more modern weapons; once a myth is well established in the culture, it bears being re-told repeatedly.

Two points can be made here about myths – drawing still on Barthes's work, but also on subsequent writing.

Few myths, many signs

The first point concerns the fact that there are, relatively speaking, few myths and a vast number of signs. This is clear in the case of the David and Goliath story that underlies vast numbers of adventure books and films. This is not merely an effect of the poverty of human imagination. If stories or images are to work as myths, they have to be constantly repeated in different versions. And scholars of trad-itional folk tales have shown that people enjoy seeing and hearing myths being re-enacted and re-told. The pleasure may lie in the familiarity of the myth; we all enjoy a good story that borrows traditional myths, even if we do not agree with the moral of the story. For example, feminists have long criticized mythical por-trayals of 'fallen women', but those critiques have done nothing to take away the appeal of stories about harlots with a heart of gold that reiterate in our own day the same basic story told in the Gospel account of Mary Magdalene.

Myths that are common within a culture can thus be found (when we look for second-order meanings) in many different signs. The myth about the people finally waking up to justice and toppling the tyrant with their bare hands, a myth which comes to the forefront whenever societies go through revolutionary change, is regularly told over and over again across a number of sites. Even the people involved often draw upon earlier versions of the myth in question. The French Revolutionaries dressed in Roman togas, whereas the Tiananmen Square Chinese students constructed miniature replicas of New York's Statue of Liberty. Even if people don't know semiotic theory, they generally understand how to com-municate mythical meanings, how to link up their particular problems and their particular signs to larger, more generalized, appealing cultural narratives.

It is not only political myths that are constantly communicated through a variety of signs across a wide variety of signifiers. That police officers are not just crime solvers but trustworthy, all-purpose authority figures, for example, is a common myth – common in liberal democratic societies at any rate. This may well be communicated to the same person (say a schoolchild) over the course of a single day through a number of different signs. One sign could be an actual officer who visits the school to give a talk about the evils of illicit drugs; another sign could be a television show for kids that happens to include as a minor character a friendly uniformed cop; another sign could be a letter from the school authorities sent home via the child that reassures parents that precautions have been taken, including calling the police, in regard to some new threat to children's safety; yet another sign signifying the same myth could be the mother's words of wisdom: 'you can always go to a police officer if you run into any trouble on the street'.

Reflecting on the wide variety of ways in which the same mythical story or symbol is conveyed to us, both in the home and in the public realm, leads to the conclusion that myths gain their power not through logical argument but through sheer repetition. And yet, the repetition often escapes notice, since myths are few and repetitive, but the medium and the particular signifier are always changing. What is called creativity, in Hollywood and in the world of advertising, consists of coming up with innovative signs for the same old myths. Our immediate semiotic universe is much richer on the surface than at the level of myth.

Myth vs. history

The second point about the mythical dimension of signs is that when a sign or a whole narrative is turned into a myth, history is mysteriously drained out of it. Barthes makes this point in the case of the black soldier. The soldier's face and uniform signify, as he says, a combination of Frenchness and militariness, but they markedly fail to communicate any information about France's particular history of colonial ventures in Africa. History is precisely what is excluded from the mythical. As signs that are, unlike most signs, designed specifically to work as myths, national flags could be said to signify the non-historical dimension of national life.

In the commercial realm, chocolate and diamonds have for many decades now come to signify love and luxury. The professionals of myth (the advertising agencies) have to work hard to make it seem as though diamonds are, by nature, the best signifiers of commitment and marriage, and that chocolate is, by nature, the best recognition that we all work too hard and need a little indulgence as a token of love for ourselves or for others. It is not only the history of the product that is deleted from this chain of signification, but also the history of marketing itself, the story of how De Beers and Cadbury came up with ways of successfully linking their commodities to existing cultural myths.

If we return to the example of signs about police that would be available to the average schoolchild, the police (specifically, the uniformed, ordinary cop-on-the-beat police) appear as naturally representing authority, trustworthiness, and protection from evil strangers. That communities managed to maintain safety for many centuries before the invention of police forces is a historical fact that is positively excluded by the set of child-oriented signs about police listed above. The warm fuzzy feelings that many people get when seeing or even thinking about the old-fashioned officer on the beat naturalize certain modern relations of policing, turning a contingent cultural product (in the UK, the 'bobby' with his distinctive, old-fashioned uniform) into a natural and transhistorical signifier of urban order and safety. The cultural icon of 'the bobby' that is so ubiquitous in English culture dehistoricizes both policing and England, as Ian Loader has shown:

... memories of the English bobby offer material for the formation and sustenance of self and collective identity – an identity that often helps to constitute people's sense of ontological security ... This is made up in part of a wistful nostalgia for an inclusive, conformist, monochrome age blessed with such virtues as obedience, obligation, and constraint; one that is contrasted unfavourably with a more socially diverse, contested, and precarious present. But it is also, more specifically, a police-centred subjectivity that holds uniformed authority – and particularly, the organically situated, pastoral presence of *public* policing in everyday life – to be central to the production and reproduction of ordered social life. (Loader and Mulcahy, 2003, p 95)

It is interesting in this context that, while uniforms in other institutions and in other countries have changed a great deal in recent years, in England one still sees uniformed officers who are dressed very much as they were dressed 50 years ago – as if the very meaning of 'England' would be put at risk if more functional uniforms were introduced.

A three-part template for semiotic analysis: content, format, context

Signs, and more broadly, representations (which can be a group of signs), obviously have a *content*. If we ask someone 'What was in the morning's newspaper?', we will likely get a summary of content. Content analysis looks at who is featured and who is not featured, what kinds of crimes get coverage and what events do not get covered, who is quoted and who is not quoted. Content analysis thus provides much useful information. In Toronto newspapers, for example, content analyses done by different people have all found that the vast majority of black faces appear in the sports section, with entertainment pages coming second. In addition, some black faces appear in crime news. But black faces are almost wholly absent from the business section. This information is clearly useful.

However, content analysis is limited. First of all, in this advertising-savvy age, 'ideational content' is sometimes not the most important thing about a communication. Advertising, in particular, often reduces information about products to an absolute minimum – a logo that has been repeatedly linked to a certain feeling or desire through repetitive metonymy, for instance. In the case of logos and symbols, content analysis is very limited; one needs to proceed to analyse connotations and myths.

In addition, the same content is often communicated very differently in different media. Two news stories, one from a tabloid and one from a 'quality' newspaper, might well have the same content (two people were shot to death last night on the street, say). But how the story is told, how it's illustrated, where it's placed in the paper, and what size of typeface is used for the headlines, will all alter the message being communicated.

Variables such as location, tone and language, illustration, and typographical features are all part of the *format* of a representation. Formats convey their own message, as already mentioned in the first chapter. A printed scholarly article, for instance, will immediately look more authoritative than the exact same article when it was in handwritten form.

Format is partly a function of the medium. For example, websites are usually composed of different virtual 'pages' that can be scanned in any order one desires, simply by clicking on one hyperlinked word rather than another. This format, which is unavailable in newspapers, encourages one to encounter only a limited number of the available signs, as driven by personal interest. For example, I can get on a university's website and get the fax number of someone I want to reach without going through webpages giving students information about courses. A student wanting information about courses would browse through the same website very differently.

A printed university calendar, by contrast, has its pages bound in a particular order. One does not have to read every page in order, of course, but one has to leaf through a considerable number of pages before arriving at the spot with the desired information. And the calendar, like other book-like representations, will have a hierarchical organization. Certain kinds of information will be at the beginning and will come across as more important.

But format varies not only with the medium (the web vs. a printed book-like format) but also within each medium. Television drama series with weekly episodes have certain standard formats, but each series has to also differentiate itself from its competitors, and format is as important to this work of constituting a specific market as content. The long-running American television series Law & Order, for example, began with an idea about format, not content. The idea that the original producer had was to have an hour-long show that could be sold either as a whole or as two halves. Some television stations, he thought, might only show the first half, which features a police investigation. The prosecution process, which always takes up the second half of the hour, might not be as popular, he thought. So the two half-hour format was integral to the development of the successful product Law & Order, even though television channels did not in fact choose to run only the police half.

In this case, the format limits and shapes the content to a large extent: since there are only two programme halves, the criminal justice process has to be shown as if it had only two parts. Hence the theory of criminal justice contained in the sentence that opens every show: 'In the criminal justice system the people are represented by two equal but separate groups, the police who investigate crimes and the District Attorneys [prosecutors] who prosecute them . . .'

The relation between format and content is not unidirectional, however. It is difficult to include content that does not easily reflect and fit within the format; but the format of Law & Order is itself dependent on the content of criminal justice systems in the English tradition. In common-law countries, investigation starts with the police. By contrast, in civil-law countries, such as France, judges themselves often undertake investigations and then call police and prosecutors. The format of the programme is thus somewhat dependent on the particularities of the common-law criminal justice process. Content and format, therefore, interact with each other.

The third and final dimension of the template that will be used in this book concerns *context*. In the Barthes example of the African soldier in French uniform, the relevant context was the French occupation of Algeria; that context, which was not spelled out in the representation itself, gave the picture much of its meaning. Context is sometimes described within the representation itself, to the extent that it becomes content. For example, a *Law & Order* episode made explicit reference to the September 11 attacks on New York, in such a way as to suggest that the work of policing had to change to respond to the new terrorist threats. But the September 11 events and their consequences would still be important as context even if they were not mentioned by any of the characters, that is, if they were present merely as context, not content.

Having set out the basic features of the template, the next chapter will develop in more detail each of the three elements of the template and will show with examples how this may be used to analyse the social semiotics of representations of law and order.

Chapter 3
Representations and their Social Effects:
a Template

This chapter lays out a template that can be used to investigate and analyse the social effects of representations. Those readers who are anxious to 'get on with it' can jump from here to the second section, a few pages down, where I begin to lay out the three components of the template – content, format and context. But for those with a somewhat greater supply of patience, it may be worthwhile to detour briefly through a few issues that arise when one begins to prepare the toolbox needed for the work of analysing representations – issues that take us into the heart of the most basic questions about what it is to do social science.

As outlined in the first chapter, sociologists who define themselves as scientists and who use quantitative methods usually ignore the whole world of feeling, myth, symbolism and signification. Sometimes, however, they turn their attention to how people feel about issues such as crime – and attempt to use the same tools developed for analysing such entities as large-scale opinion surveys for the analysis of newspaper stories or other representations. The severe limitations of such studies should become clear as this chapter unfolds. For now though it will suffice to point out that while it is eminently sensible to poll the public, say about their fears of terrorism, and then compare these fears to the actual documented probability of such attacks in that part of the world, it is of very little use to compare the content of either fictional programmes or news reports regarding dangers and crimes to the 'reality' of victimization. The reason is that while it is useful to demonstrate that the public is misinformed about the probabilities of certain dangers, it is hardly news to tell us that neither newspapers nor television reflect 'reality' accurately. Even the 'reality-TV' shows do not claim to represent reality in the way that a random sample represents a larger population. If such claims were to be made, it is highly doubtful that any significant section of the viewing public would be persuaded that just because a programme is using non-professional actors and shows some footage from a hidden video camera, what is eventually shown on the screen is actually 'representative'. People appearing on television, whether they are professional actors or not, do not behave the same way as they do in their everyday life – any more than the photographs in family albums, however 'candid', actually represent a well-balanced random sample of family experiences.

The positivistically inclined academics who feign surprise at discovering that the media eschew statistical representation as a selection criterion could well be criticized for spending a great deal of time and money seeking to prove something that is already quite obvious to the lay person. However, criticism could equally be levelled at many academics at the opposite end of the qualitative–quantitative, theory vs. empirical research divide, who also often engage in less than constructive research practices. Practitioners of cultural studies rarely bother with a discussion of the scientific dimensions of their work, and often make sweeping dismissive generalizations not only about positivism but even about empirical research as such. But while positivistic research methods are of little use in the kind of analysis of the social effects of representations that this book seeks to promote, nevertheless, it is necessary to be vigilant about the occupational risks of cultural studies – which include arbitrariness in choice of case studies; a tendency to generalize from very peculiar samples; and a certain slippage between object-ively documentable social meanings, on the one hand, and fanciful interpretations on the other. To put it very simply: it is very useful, in work using social semiotics and related tools, to be inspired by the spirit of science, even though the letter of the scientific method is rarely directly applicable.

The template offered here (which is my own synthesis of a great deal of existing work, only some of which is referenced) is not exactly a 'method' in the social science sense of the term. There cannot be a universally useful method for the analysis of representations of law and order that can be reduced to a few pro-cedural requirements because the issues that are central to scientific discussions about methodology – validity, reliability, replicability, ability to predict future events – while not wholly irrelevant, are rarely directly useful for the purposes of qualitative analyses of what are often unique sets of signs.

It would be foolish, however, to counterpose social science methodology to qualitative cultural analysis in an either-or manner. There may not be any defini-tive way of determining just how many police films one needs to watch before making generalizations about how officers or crime victims are portrayed by Hol-lywood. However, a researcher who aims to offer solid analyses of a whole genre needs to pay attention both to sample size and to the possibility that there is an oversampling of one director or one subtype of police film. (Of course, for the purposes of semiotic analysis there is no automatic privileging of representative-ness: analysing Hitchcock films is just as worthwhile a pursuit as analysing a broader range of films, as long as one does not misdescribe one's sample or one's findings.) But uttering a personal opinion about a particular representation is clearly different from producing a solid analysis of either one specific representa-tion or one set of them, even if the exact line between personal opinion and informed analysis cannot be drawn in advance, abstractly.

Students who have had the experience of taking courses taught by positivistic social scientists and then other courses taught by cultural studies people and postmodern theorists, and whose lives are thus marked by the 'two cultures' problem that plagues many university sociology departments, may have difficulty understanding that if one leaves the terrain of positivist social science, one does not necessarily fall into the swamp of mere subjective opinion. It is thus important here to note that we all have opinions about cultural products – we like certain films, hate certain architectural forms – but that the *social* effects of representa-tions are not a matter of opinion.

To refer back to the Roland Barthes example mentioned in the previous chapter (the magazine photo of a black soldier saluting the French flag), there is nothing subjective or opinionated about Barthes's conclusion that the second-order, myth-ical meaning of that sign is that all sons of the French Republic regardless of colour are honoured to serve under her flag, and that the claim that France is imperialist and racist is therefore not true. Given the political-social context within which that magazine was produced and consumed, the meaning of that sign is pretty much set. In a different context it might mean something else, since the meaning of representations is always to some extent context-dependent (as we shall see below): but in the given context, there is nothing subjective or opinionated about Barthes's analysis. People can of course be creative with signs – in that sense, meanings are not fixed. A fashion designer may decide to send a beautiful model out on the catwalk wearing a firefighter's hat, just for effect, or design jockey shorts featuring the Union Jack. But the resulting signs will have particular social meanings precisely because the social meaning of such components as the fire helmet or the flag is set in advance. Social meanings, in other words, are objective not subjective.

In my experience, social science students trying to learn the skills set out in this book usually go through a phase, about two or three weeks into the course, in which they experience a serious intellectual crisis. My students have usually not yet been trained to do their own research studies, but they have been taught the basics of the scientific method, and they are generally quite capable of tearing apart a journalist's account and even a sociological study on the basis of its poor methodology. They worry a lot about sample size, for example. (They also generally lack background in cultural studies, unlike many of their British counterparts.) When asked to use the social semiotics tools that they have learned in the first few weeks, they often avoid semiotics and fall back into the habits of social science, asking questions such as 'How representative is that crime anyway?' When queried about why they're shifting the terrain of the investigation, they generally answer that they don't want to simply produce a subjective opinion.

In this, my students are in rather exalted company. Much of the research generated by criminologists and media studies experts on representations of law and order consists simply of asking 'Is it accurate?' – a question that assumes, contrary to the available evidence, that getting accurate information about crime and justice is the reason why people watch the TV news or read newspaper stories about police endeavours. The issue of accuracy becomes even more irrelevant in the context of fictional representations, such as Hollywood films or television dramas.

Representativeness, then, is not a virtue that most representations of law and order aspire to achieve. Unlike films, news programmes do aspire to accuracy; but they are as selective about what is presented as fictional representations. Selectivity is precisely what news is all about. The selection and filtering process is not simply a part of newsmaking: it actually constitutes the news as such. A major British study of television news carried out in the late 1970s found that what they call 'the code' – roughly, the criteria for separating the newsworthy wheat from the cutting-room floor chaff – has several distinct steps:

> The code works at all levels: in the notion of 'the story' itself, in the selection of stories, in the way material is gathered and prepared for transmission, in the dominant style of language used, in the permitted and limited range of visual presentation, in the overall duration of bulletins, in the duration of items within bulletins, in the real technological limitations placed on the presentation, in the finances of the news services, and above all, in the underpinning processes of professionalisation which turn men and women into television journalists. (Glasgow University Media Group [GUMG], 1976, pp 10–11)

There can be many questions about how journalists and editors and newspaper owners select and present the news, of course, and those are the questions asked in the large-scale Glasgow study just cited and in similar works (Ericson et al., 1987, 1989, 1991). But studies that tell us, for example, that 26 per cent of the *Chicago Tribune*'s crime coverage consists of murders, whereas the actual proportion of murders as a percentage of all reported crimes is only 0.2 per cent (Gruber, cited in Ericson et al., 1987, p 45), only gives media studies a bad name.

Another way of making the same point in a more general or theoretical manner is to point out that signs can be considered as 'data' for some purposes – but only up to a point. One can count how many men in uniform appear every night on a particular television network, and in that work, each representation of a uniform is a datum: but for an analysis of the social meanings of uniforms, we need tools beyond counting.

Learning to analyse the cultural-social meaning of representations of law and order, then, necessarily involves challenging deep-rooted assumptions about the process of gathering knowledge about 'social' life and generating reliable analyses. The binary opposition between the 'hard facts' of positivist social science and the 'interpretations' of humanities scholars falls to the ground – or at least, shakes a bit – if one engages in intellectual work that cannot draw on conventional social science methodological tools, but which nevertheless subjects itself to questions about the thoroughness of the research and the rigour of the analysis.

Let us now proceed to describe a 'template' that can be used to organize one's analysis of representations, including representations with a mythical, second-order social meaning. The social meaning of representations, it will be shown, is constituted at three levels: content, format and context.

Content analysis

Representations or signs obviously have a content. If we ask someone, 'What was in this morning's newspaper?', we will likely get a summary of the content, or more accurately, the bits of content that the particular reader managed to absorb and remember. She may tell us: 'There was an earthquake in Iran, an anti-war rally in Washington, and some new photos of the surface of Mars'. (This is what the early social-semiotic scholar MAK Halliday called 'ideational content'.)

When web designers hire a low-paid journalist to generate 'content' for their pages, they are acknowledging that fancy formatting and clever icons cannot exist on their own. Content can be reduced to a minimum, for example in advertisements that are long on implication and symbolism and very short on information about the object being marketed. Our current economy tends to privilege the medium, not the message, since the emphasis is on finding more ways to reach more people, not on gathering new information or producing more original movie scripts. But, as failed internet entrepreneurs and bankrupt owners of cable stations have discovered, content, however downgraded, is still necessary.

While conveying information, 'content' is not reducible to information. The

story about the earthquake in Iran will undoubtedly include some facts and figures. Readers expect that sort of thing, not so much because they care to know or
are likely to remember, but simply because the story would not count as an item of
'news' if it failed to include at least a few facts and figures. But the story will
inevitably be told from a particular perspective, with a certain slant.

What journalists call 'the angle' is as much of a necessary marker of 'news' as
the inclusion of a few – not too many – facts and figures. The angle is partly a
matter of a particular reporter deciding to highlight something about the event
that he/she believes is being neglected by competitors (and in the present 500-
channel universe, competition among journalists is a much greater factor in news
production than it used to be). But reporters work for a particular outlet, and
variability among reporters is limited by that outlet's place in the market. Thus, a
paper for the Muslim community will describe the hypothetical Iran earthquake
tragedy from the inside, as it were. If operating in a country like the UK, the US or
Canada, such a culturally specific medium will seek, in the local community in
which the paper is sold, people with connections to the affected area, and will
regard them as what journalists call 'sources'. A mainstream American or British
paper, by contrast, may have no personal stories from particular people (though
they will usually have a wire-service photo of a victim, whose biography is never
deemed of much interest), and may devote more column inches to what Western
NGOs and governments are doing to help than to the suffering of the people
involved.

But apart from these issues of audience and market, stories about catastrophes
also inevitably engage the really big questions of social science: the story, as
developed by particular journalists, will also have to 'take sides' in the age-old
debate about nature vs. culture. Why? Because it will either focus on the inevit-
ability and unpredictability of earthquakes as natural phenomena, hence taking
the standpoint of 'nature', or else it will stress that the tragedy is not 'natural' but
man-made, since if a strict building code had been in force, very few people
would have been killed in destroyed buildings. And it is clear even from this one
example that the choice of emphasis (nature vs. human action) has clear, objective
political effects. It is thus impossible to separate 'information' from 'perspective',
at any of the multiple levels of social, cultural and political relations that make
up 'the news'.

'Content' though is rarely reducible to purely factual information, since stories
and other representations are always told by a specific author (and a corporation
is an author, for our purposes) for a specific audience, in a particular market
context, and are thus embedded in particular political and cultural relations. This
is why the first wave of studies of media representations of law and order in the
1970s – which focused almost exclusively on crime and criminality – produced an
interesting body of work, despite limiting itself by and large to what came to be
known as '*content analysis*'. Content analysis consisted partly of noting who was
featured and who was not featured, and what kinds of crimes and criminals were
newsworthy or not.

Content analysis begins by counting; but it also involves examining exactly how
certain people or events were described. Many of the early media/crime studies

were small-scale, count-and-tabulate jobs, but the more important and influential studies paid attention to the 'how' of representations right from the beginning. For example, the large-scale, very empirically reliable study of television news carried out at Glasgow University by a group of eight media researchers cited earlier in this chapter showed that news coverage of a strike by garbage collection workers focused on the danger to the public posed by rats and other potential health hazards, rather than emphasizing the issues that were important to the striking workers (GUMG, 1976). This meant that the broadcasts generally took the perspective of the taxpayer/public/citizen and not that of the workers. This was the objective social effect of the way the strike was portrayed but, as noted cultural analyst Richard Hoggart stated in his preface to the volume (Hoggart in GUMG, 1976, p xii), the perspective was probably not due to a political conspiracy in the newsroom, but was, instead, a side effect or result of the television journalist's constant search for good footage. Rats prowling around garbage cans being eminently memorable footage, and issues like pension and employment rights being notoriously difficult to turn into good footage with striking visuals (GUMG, 1980, Chapter 9), it may be that in this case the social-political effects were accidentally caused by a politically neutral, professional imperative.

This example demonstrates the perils of trying to impute motives to makers of representations, and by the same token highlights the benefits of the approach developed here, an approach that focuses strictly on the social *effects* of representations rather than either the actual or the imputed goals and ideas of journalists and media owners. Relatedly, the approach developed here is also cautious about concluding that documenting either actual or imagined economic or political benefits will reveal the truth about particular representations. While in the 1970s scholars found it very difficult to resist theories that saw the media as nothing more than an ideological tool of the ruling class, a number of developments, ranging from the end of the Cold War and the decline of Marxism to the popularity of Foucauldian and other work that highlights governance effects rather than ideology, have made it increasingly possible to do analyses that are critical but avoid conspiracy theory. This does not mean that this book or similar approaches to social semiotics are necessarily apolitical. It simply means that the old question about ideology – the question of 'who benefits?' – is bracketed for much of the time. It is no doubt true that many mass media representations of law and order directly or indirectly benefit the ruling class and, in general, the powers that be: but if one only asks 'who benefits?', then all representations that do not critique the status quo will end up being lumped together under the banner of dominant ideology. That popular culture and mainstream news have political effects has been well known since the early days of cultural studies. But this generalization will not help us to understand the particular effects of particular representations. Furthermore, as the later wave of cultural studies research showed, it tends to erase the contradictions and instabilities that are found in most complex representations.

What is thus accomplished by the deliberate setting aside of questions about political and economic interests? What we gain is an ability to document and analyse the fine texture of representations by understanding the differences – in content, in format and in context – that make, say, the BBC 10 pm news different from the Sunday tabloids, and the work of a great filmmaker from what is shown on commercial television. The early critical work done in the 1970s tended to homogenize 'the establishment', and to focus almost exclusively on the question of ultimate, 'in the last instance' economic and political gains and losses. But although that kind of persistent single-mindedness did reveal how deeply capitalism and other established interests are embedded even in apparently political neutral representations, every product of both high culture and popular culture ended up being merged together into a monolith often called 'the culture of control' (Hall et al., 1978). Analytical tools from post-structuralist theory, film studies, social semiotics, postcolonial studies and elsewhere have in more recent years afforded us opportunities to continue asking about political effects, but also to look, first, at contradictions within 'dominant' cultural products, and second, at differences among representations.

It may be useful here to look back and spend a few minutes on what was arguably the most influential of all of the crime-media studies of the 1970s, namely, the work on the social invention of 'mugging' carried out by Stuart Hall and his colleagues and published under the evocative title *Policing the Crisis* in 1978. While Hall's work did not include an ethnography of news media production, nevertheless, partly due to the political timeliness of the focus on race and crime, and partly because of Hall's stature as a British public intellectual, *Policing the Crisis* remains the work that would be near the top of most people's lists of 'influential social science works of the 1970s'.

In this work, Hall and four other colleagues at the Birmingham Centre for Cultural Studies, a group that pioneered cultural studies in ways that would have an impact around the world, decided to study in depth the newspaper coverage of a mini-moral panic that emerged as the British public came to be concerned about a new (to Britain) phenomenon: 'mugging'.

'Mugging' was (and is) an American term for what is arguably as old and as English as Robin Hood, namely robbery in public places, often with violence and/ or with weapons. In the early 1970s, at a time when British cities had not yet experienced race riots or highly publicized police–black conflict, labelling a particular, supposedly new form of crime as 'American' achieved a particular effect: stirring up Britons' fears that their cities might fall into the kind of economic and racial chaos that marked certain US cities in the late 1960s. 'Mugging', as a sign, had as its first-level meaning a kind of crime – a personal crime committed in public, against strangers, usually with weapons, often in groups. But 'mugging' also had a very powerful second-order meaning, a mythical meaning, which according to Hall and his colleagues ended up becoming more important than the first, more concrete meaning. 'Mugging' – which newspaper story after story insisted on linking with 'blackness', 'refusal to work', 'inner city decay' and an abandonment of English courtesy for American violence – became more important as a symbol of general social decay than as the name for a particular experience. Mugging functioned as 'an index of the disintegration of the social order, as a sign that the "British way of life" is coming apart at the seams' (Hall et al., 1978, p vii).

Some of the participants in the discourse about mugging and the decline of English ways of life felt comfortable directly attacking black youth; others took a more indirect route, blaming 'American' examples, without directly mentioning African-Americans. Thus, Birmingham MP Jill Knight was quoted, a few months into the panic, as saying the following:

> In my view it is absolutely essential to stop this rising tide of mugging in our cities. I have seen what happens in America where muggings are rife. It is absolutely horrifying to know that in all the big American cities, coast to coast, there are areas where people dare not go after dark. (quoted in Hall et al., 1978, p 26)

The possibility that white people in US cities might stay away from black areas because they hold racist fears, and the further possibility that crime might increase in those neighbourhoods as people from other parts of the city stop frequenting them, are both excluded before the speech even starts. 'American cities' – which most British people had only seen on television shows and Hollywood films – function here as a background myth giving meaning to the more temporary, more topical myth of 'mugging'.

The Birmingham group's analysis of 'mugging', which was innovative in part because it broke with the British left's longstanding focus on class issues by paying real attention to race, was deservedly famous. Today it continues to be a set text in numerous courses on crime issues and on media studies. It may seem churlish to discuss flaws, given its originality and its importance. But mentioning its limitations – limitations that are not errors on the part of the authors but are rather symptoms of the general intellectual climate – can help us to understand how the kind of analysis promoted in this book differs from these earlier media-and-crime studies.

First, the Birmingham study studied content alone, and newspaper content alone at that, paying virtually no attention to issues of format. Content differences among different newspapers are studied, but not format differences; nor is there analysis of more general formatting features that distinguish papers from radio and television. The authors read hundreds of newspaper stories and noted what they said, who they cited, who was featured, and which facts were mentioned, situating all of this, very thoroughly, in a particular political context. But by paying almost no attention to newspapers themselves as a site of study – the researchers do not seem to have attempted to interview journalists or visit newsrooms, for example – they fell into assuming that 'the media' were simply conduits for (ideologically biased) views and facts. Insisting that the media do not create moral panics or engage in active definition of the issues, they labelled the media as 'secondary' authorities, subordinate to the 'primary' authorities – which were in turn homogenized as the establishment or the 'culture of control'.

Second, the Birmingham study did not consider differences among different reading publics. Later studies, borrowing from 'reader response' literary studies, would be much more careful to allow for alternative readings – for instance, that a black reader of a mainstream paper might experience the story about the latest mugging as yet another opportunity to get angry at overpolicing – instead of documenting only the responses that mainstream readers could reasonably be assumed to have. Many of the later generation of studies were much influenced by feminist film critics, who showed that women spectators watching mainstream masculinist movies may well end up with an unintended non-mainstream message by identifying with the tough hero. In the wake of these feminist film studies, other cultural studies scholars began to pay more attention to the gap between the supposed reader – the typical member of that publication's market – and the actual, individual reader, who may well read the same text for different reasons and with different effects. (To give an illustrative anecdote I could cite the example of my father, who, having become a communist later in life, faithfully read the business pages of the newspapers in order to fuel his anger at capitalism.)

Third, and closely related to the second point, the Birmingham study and other media studies of that time tended to regard the tricky business of persuasion as a matter of simple indoctrination. In the 1980s, the phrase 'the culture of control', with its Marxist implications of a single powerful ruling class, began to go out of style; instead, sociology departments witnessed an explosion of talk about 'fragmented subjectivity'. This was no mere linguistic fad. Intellectuals who no longer wanted to simply separate the (good) Marxist sheep from the (mistaken, deluded) ideologically indoctrinated goats needed new tools to understand how, for example, British trade union members could vote for Margaret Thatcher. Calling such a person 'a puppet of the bourgeoisie' was just not appropriate any more. Post-structuralist theory, influenced by Jacques Lacan and later by Jacques Derrida and Michel Foucault, suddenly became useful, because such theory began by rejecting the Marxist (and humanist) notion of a single subject with a single, unified consciousness in favour of a model of consciousness stressing contradictions, fragmentation and inventive recycling.

Stuart Hall himself contributed much to this kind of post-Marxist analysis of political subjectivity. The debates among the left-wing intellectuals of Hall's generation about the popularity of Thatcherism among the working classes – and about other populist phenomena previously neglected or dismissed by Marxism – used tools that had not been available in the early 1970s. A good example of this kind of new, more or less post-Marxist work was Rosalind Coward's analysis of popular feminine culture, *Female Desire* (Coward, 1984), which tried to understand how women might find pleasure in products of mass culture, without thereby becoming the sort of 'puppets of patriarchy' that earlier, 1970s feminism saw under every bed. Trying to understand the persistence of English working-class fascination with the royal family, Coward highlighted the parallels – the formal and substantive parallels – between the perpetual saga of the royals, on the one hand, and the structure of soap opera family life on the other:

> Royal soap is based on the same narrative structures as 'Dallas' [a very popular American evening soap of the time]. It offers all the pleasures of a good family melodrama. Like 'Dallas', it is the long-running story of an extremely wealthy and powerful family. The two soap operas share the same preoccupations: the unity of the family; family wealth; dynastic considerations like inheritance and fertility; sexual promiscuity; family duty; and alliances with outsiders/ rivals/ lower orders. The fact that 'The Royals' is loosely based on reality only adds to its fascination. (Coward, 1984, p 163)

Hall himself went on to develop a complex analysis of right-wing populism that regarded political subjectivity as fundamentally fragmented and contradictory, at the same time that other cultural studies scholars were also beginning to develop tools to study popular culture in a non-condescending manner. Going well beyond the analysis presented in *Policing the Crisis*, which had stuck to Marxism in describing young black men as a 'fraction' of the working class, Hall's later work argued that working-class support for Thatcher should not be dismissed simply as a case of false consciousness. Hall stated that Thatcherism and other successful political movements should not be reduced to a single set of interests or a single ideological content, since their success hinged precisely on the fact that they held a number of different resources that could and were used creatively – in unconsciously creative assemblages – by all sorts of people from all classes.

> For example, the whole discourse of Thatcherism combines ideological elements into a discursive chain in such a way that the logic or unity of the discourse depends on the subject addressed assuming a number of specific subject positions ... these imaginary positions ... trigger off and connote one another in a chain of linked interpellations that constitute the Imaginary ... [T]he liberty-loving citizen is also the worried parent, the respectable housewife, the careful manager of the household budget, the solid English citizen 'proud to be British'. The discourses of Thatcherism are constantly in this way formulating new subjectivities for the positions they are constructing. (Hall, 1988, p 49)

In this way, a working-class black mother may well end up assuming a number of positions – and hence a number of cultural and political habits and reactions – that would appear to contradict her 'basic' 'material' interests. Because she worries about schoolyard violence, she may well end up supporting 'safe schools' campaigns promoted by conservative groups: but it matters, both to her and to the analyst, that she has come to support that campaign via a different route than the upper-class Tory gentleman who also supports it. The connections linking the different political projects being less than visible even to their participants, 'Thatcherism', Hall argued, succeeded not because it appealed directly to a unified public who was then rationally persuaded to adopt a general programme, but because 'it' managed to link a number of quite disparate needs, desires, interests and values into a politically solid chain. This is what it means to say that 'political subjectivity is fragmented'. The particular chain of positions, desires and values that was 'Thatcherism' eventually fell apart, as is the fate of all such political projects; but many of the links built by Thatcherite engineers of the human soul proved to be long-lived.

Indeed, current analyses of Tony Blair's New Labour policies on criminal law and policy – and on related issues, such as alcohol regulation – reveal that many of the old links in the Thatcherite chain were simply reused. Semiotics teaches us that the old Thatcherite fear of crime discourse would not have exactly the same meaning, and thus the same social effects, when it is recycled and joined to other semiotic elements of different provenance (e.g. 'community'), as is arguably being done by New Labour's social and criminal policy innovators. Current criminal justice policy research, on the whole, bears out this prediction.

Hall did not pursue the analysis of the recycling and recoupling of different signs and semiotic systems in the area of crime, but others who did generally accepted the new idea that political subjectivity is inherently fragmented. Similarly, feminists such as the above-cited Coward, writing in the mid- and late 1980s, tried to avoid the older, simplistic separation of popular culture products into 'sexist' vs. 'feminist'.

This brings us to the final point regarding content analysis. Although numerous studies of crime news, television shows and Hollywood films concluded that the media and popular culture in general simply mirror and glorify law-and-order views, newer studies are beginning to show that a representation's content does not necessarily have a single political or social message; indeed, ambiguity – especially in films, which are aesthetically more complex products – is often central, even in ideologically mainstream Hollywood productions. Along these lines, Leitch's thorough study of police films concluded that police forces are typically shown on film as either corrupt or incompetent; but, to complicate the political story, just as often, the hero of the story is also a cop who heroically devotes himself to crime fighting and to justice despite the constraints of the institution (Leitch, 2002). The rather trite plot of the hero who pursues justice despite his organization's indifference, incompetence or corruption – a plot found in lawyer books and films of the John Grisham variety as well as in older police narratives – remains perpetually fascinating because it allows for a contradictory message about the forces of law, a message in which the 'bad' side of policing is attributed to the organization while the 'heroic' side is attributed to the individual hero.

Similarly, as Nicole Hahn Rafter points out (Rafter, 2000), prison films, while not glorifying crime, usually feature prisoners (that is, criminals) as the sympathetic heroes of the story. And escapes from prison, interestingly, are generally glorified. Along the same lines, wardens and guards are usually presented as either cruel or indifferent. The potentially radical message about punishment is, however, usually blunted by showing most prisoners – but not the hero – as criminals who deserve to be in prison. The hero, unlike the others, was wrongfully convicted or otherwise subjected to unjust punishment. By not directly challenging the idea that prison is the right place for most criminals, and yet leaving lots of room for viewers to identify with criminals, particularly if they make a heroic escape from a corrupt or violence-filled institution, Hollywood can have its law-and-order cake and eat it too, and so can the audience.

Another genre whose persistent appeal can also be shown to rely at least in part to the fact that its social and political effects are deeply contradictory is the classic English murder mystery: Agatha Christie's novels, for example. Christie's books in no way challenge the status quo or send out radical social messages. Nevertheless, the murderer is almost always a member of the ruling classes (the locked-room plots she favours are devices to exclude, from the start, the possibility that a down-and-out psycho killer or a professional criminal might have done it); and the murder almost always takes place in an upper-class setting, not a slum. Even more remarkable is the fact that murderers are not always brought to justice. While the reader is always reassured that Hercule Poirot or Miss Marple will indeed find the truth, murderers often conveniently commit suicide or otherwise escape formal punishment. *Murder on the Orient Express*, one of Christie's most popular novels (turned into a star-studded feature film), has Poirot tell a deliberate lie to the police, so as to enable the murderer – in this case a collective of revenge-seeking indirect victims – to get away with it. While the upper-class 'period' ambience of Christie's stories may lull the reader/viewer into a complacency about the English class structure, law and order is not unambiguously promoted in most of the works, if only because the desire and the ability to commit murder are shown to lie within the hearts of the most respectable upper-class ladies and rural vicars.

In later chapters we shall examine the production of contradictory messages about law and order in more detail. Here, however, the point is to highlight the fact that the content of mass-produced as well as highbrow representations of law and order is often ambiguous and/or contradictory. This may be clearer in the case of aesthetically complex representations, such as feature films made by sophisticated directors, producers and actors: but ambiguity and contradiction can also be seen in relatively simple cultural products. Content analysis is thus not simply a matter of finding the hidden ideology.

Content analysis was an important tool for carrying out, in the realm of media and representation generally, the kind of critical social research that flourished in the 1970s and 1980s and which is still informative today. But in the years since the pioneer studies of media content were published in the late 1970s, it has become clear that content analysis is limited, just like any other single tool.

Format analysis

The line between format and content cannot be drawn too sharply, but, roughly, one can distinguish between *what* a representation tells us – the content – and *how* the representation is structured and presented – the format. In most cases that are relevant to our purposes here, the format of representations is meant to be relatively invisible and unobtrusive. For that reason, it is easiest to analyse format by comparing and contrasting, since format choices become visible when we examine other possibilities (in the same way that the meaning of signs, generally speaking, emerges clearly through contrast). To analyse the format of a particular newspaper section or a particular television show, then, the best way to proceed is to draw a chart on which the representation in question is compared both to representations that directly compete with it – e.g. in the case of a news story in the paper, other accounts in other printed media – and to representations of the same issue or event found in other media.

Let's say that the representation of interest is the long-running American television programme *Law & Order*. First, it should be mentioned that for the purposes of format analysis, it makes sense to look at a programme as a whole, format being generally consistent from one show to another, whereas at the level of content it may be more useful to take each show as a separate unit of analysis. Looking at the programme as a whole, then (and limiting the scope of these comments to the original programme, excluding recent spin-offs such as *Law & Order: Criminal Intent*), the programme clearly has certain distinctive presentational or format features. These include a certain theme music, some consistent opening graphics, a consistent opening shot that shows certain familiar characters, and certain typical ways of separating out the segments that make up the show. In regard to the latter – one of most invisible aspects of formatting – it is worth noting that while a newscast will separate but also link segments either with 'hookers' (very brief trailers of the news item to come after the commercial break, say) or with a standard phrase that indicates a change of speaker, such as 'And now for our Washington correspondent . . .', fictional shows have other, usually unobtrusive and non-verbal, ways of simultaneously putting an end to a segment while maintaining the audience's interest in what is yet to come. In *Law & Order*, a typical 'end of segment' shot has the camera linger on a face for longer than usual. As the camera's movement slows down, the audience gets the message that a break is imminent – whether that break contains commercials, or whether it is only a change from one venue/institutional setting to another. There is also a recurring noise/music, sounding something like 'clang clang', that occurs at the beginning of each segment, and is usually accompanied by a title at the bottom of the screen that give the place, date and time of the scene about to unfold.

Analysing format in this manner, paying attention to pacing, graphics, music and devices used to separate segments and provide continuity, will allow us to draw some conclusions about the specific programme, as compared to competing programmes in the same *genre*. This is the first level of format differences – the level at which producers, camera operators, graphic artists and directors work to create a 'signature' for their show that will serve mainly to distinguish their product from other products in the same general category, that is, genre. No viewer with any television experience would confuse *Law & Order* with the news or with a daytime soap. However, given that there are a lot of police shows on prime-time television, it is necessary to provide some formal markers that allow audiences to discern very quickly the programme's distinction, that is, what makes it different from other dramas and even other dramas featuring police and/or lawyers. These formal markers, including the opening graphics and music, send out messages that are replicated in the content. Let us give an example, limiting our attention to the opening graphic sequence, here considered as a single sign.

The *Law & Order* standard opening sequence features a two-colour graphic showing only two words, with the 'and' being reduced to a '&'. The word 'law' is blue and the word 'order' is red; the background is black. Blue and red are of course the two key colours in the American flag; blue and yellow would not work as well to signify the combination of 'law and order'. But what is curious about the colours is that while one would expect 'order' to indicate the police, and to be dressed accordingly in blue, in fact it is the word 'law' that is dressed in blue. The colour scheme thus tells us that 'law' is blue. Given the longstanding identification of the police with blue uniforms, 'the thin blue line' and so forth, the colour choice makes law appear as police-like or police-driven. And if law is shown as police-like, the police officers we are about to see are simultaneously elevated, put on a legal pedestal, by their subliminal association with 'law'. This message is reinforced at the level of content: unlike most other television cops, the detectives on *Law & Order* are a singularly devoted group who are never careless with the evidence and who never take bribes or act out of political or personal feelings.

The identification of the police officers with the rule of law is re-enacted by the show's trademark format: the police story always comes first and is followed by the prosecution's stories, just as the colour blue comes first in the graphic. Of course, any crime show set in a common-law jurisdiction has to first have the police investigating (by contrast with inquisitorial jurisdictions, in which complaints may be brought directly to prosecutors and/or judges, who then call in the police). But the fact that the police are seen during the first half of each show is a formal feature that once more identifies police with 'law' as such.

If one wanted to identify the police with order maintenance, leaving law to prosecutors and other lawyers – which would be more legally correct – this would pose marketing problems, since one could not use the handy familiar phrase 'law and order' to itself re-enact the show's structure. 'Order and law' just doesn't sound right to English-speaking people. But in forcing the show's structure and the opening graphics into the format already given by the phrase 'law and order', the producers are – purposively or not, it does not matter – sending a strong message to audiences about the police being 'the law' itself.

But back to the graphic. How 'law' ends up being blue, and with what effects, is fairly clear. But what is accomplished by colouring 'order' red is less clear. The main function of the red colour seems to be to evoke the colours of the flag. Corroboration for this interpretation is found in the fact that the producers have put a large American flag on the show's webpage, despite the fact that the characters deal with garden-variety local crime rather than with war, terrorism or state security. Other than accomplishing a more or less literal waving of the US flag, it is difficult to see any other particular political or cultural effect achieved by the choice of red.

But what should be noted about the use of red is that 10 or 20 years ago, the colour red, in the United States, had strong communist connotations (as in 'the red peril'). Producers might have been wary of using the colour red for the word 'order' – a word which is certainly not monopolized by democratic legal systems. In today's world, however, the US is generally thought to be threatened by Arab/ Muslim terrorists, not reds. Perhaps on its own, 'red' might still have, for older viewers at any rate, radical associations, but when presented together with blue (and white, since there is a white outline around the words), it is just part of the flag. But let us move on to the soundtrack.

As we are seeing the graphic, we hear a solemn voice-of-god voice-over that tells us: 'In the criminal justice system, the people are represented by two separate but equally important groups: the police, who investigate crime, and the District Attorneys who prosecute the offenders. These are their stories.' Now, the voice-over, as a form, is not a normal feature of television drama; in drama (unlike in documentaries) every statement comes from a particular speaker, and *who* says something is as important as *what* is said. Indeed, in drama (particularly in soap operas, but other dramas too), the fact that character X knows fact A or B is usually crucial to the plot, since who has what information is more important in many plots than the information itself. The use of voice-over in the drama's opening sequence is hence an unusual choice whose effect is to suggest that the statement being made by the narrator with the baritone voice comes from a god-like position above the fray, and – unlike all the other statements made to the police and the prosecutors by various witnesses and suspects – it is not subject to questioning, denial or confirmation. The statement that these two institutions are the crucial ones in criminal justice is simply the Truth – it is not anyone's statement.

In regard to the voice-over's content, which cannot be totally separated from the format, it should be pointed out that in American criminal law, it is only the prosecution that represents 'the people'. Unlike in Britain and Canada, countries in which the formal position of prosecutor is still attributed to the monarch (so that each criminal case is designated as '*R. versus Joe Bloggs*', where R stands for the monarch), in US law it is the people who prosecute, not the sovereign: a criminal case is called, say, 'the people of the State of California versus O J Simpson'. The voice-over, however, tells us that the people are represented by two groups, the second one being the police. This is very inventive, legally, not to say incorrect. Stating that the people are represented by two groups – and two equally important groups, at that – has several social effects.

One effect of the opening narrator's statement is that it constructs the viewers (who are clearly meant to identify immediately and wholeheartedly with 'the people' in the statement, in keeping with other American political rhetoric, e.g. 'We the people . . .'), as already participating in the work of policing. That the people are mystically embodied in local police officers is not only legally incorrect but also factually problematic. This becomes clear if one reflects on possible alternative messages about policing and the criminal law that could be used as opening words for (other) television crime shows. For example: 'In the United States the people are policed by the FBI as well as local and state police.' This statement is much more correct, factually and legally, than the theory propounded by the voice-over – but it would not work as an opening statement for a programme that invariably presents police and prosecutors as the characters with which the audience identifies. That the people are policed is a statement that would fit with paranoid films with George Orwell-type plots, but in the current, post September 11 political climate, programmes focusing on state persecution of ordinary people would be unlikely to make it to prime time. We therefore see that the political implications of the voice-over – explicated and reinforced by the binary structure and colour scheme of the graphic, in which ordinary people are absent except in so far as they can see themselves 'represented' by the forces of law and order – are much more far-reaching than might at first appear.

The use of a voice-over with the graphic is thus, in this case, not merely a case of redundancy, as is the case when, in a commercial, we hear the same words that are written on the screen. The graphic, without the voice-over, would be more ambiguous, more open to contestation. 'Order', in particular, is a highly ambiguous word, invoked by democrats and by dictators, by teachers and prison guards, by parents and theologians. As it is, however, the combination of graphic and voice makes two substantive claims. First, we are told that law = police and order = prosecution (a claim that, made as explicit as I am making it here, would be questioned by at least some viewers, particularly lawyers and criminologists). Second, we are told that police + prosecution = the people. The latter claim would appear as debatable if made explicitly: Americans are in other contexts told that 'the people' is first and foremost represented by elected legislators. But the claim that the police and the prosecution (and nobody else) represent the people recedes into invisibility when made through the combination of formatting and (minimal) spoken and written content.

The fact that the judiciary is not presented as an integral part of the system in the opening sequence is not likely to be noticed by the viewer, since the two-part graphic already suggests, without this being explicitly argued, that there are only two institutions that make up 'law and order', and this is reinforced by the voice-over. The judiciary do of course regularly appear: but, in keeping with the binary theory of democratic criminal justice presented in the opening trademark sequence, the judges appear merely as cogs in the system, not as human beings with whom viewers can identify. Their deliberations, their struggles with their superiors and with other institutions, are deemed simply as not of interest. Neither are the deliberations of juries deemed of any interest. The erasure of judges is interesting in the context of current American television, since the judge is everything in the popular daytime *Judge Judy* programme (which features actual people with apparently real conflicts) and in its imitators.

One might conclude, after watching *Judge Judy* one day and *Law & Order* on another day, that the American people are deemed too stupid to understand that there are at least three major players in the criminal justice system. Other institutions – e.g. prisons, courtrooms – are often shown on *Law & Order*, but they are usually only venues for conversations featuring one or the other of the two key institutions, i.e. police and prosecutors.

And in the meantime, the institution that most significantly represents 'the people', that is, the legislature, is simply excluded from consideration.

Treating the opening sequence of *Law & Order* as a combination of two signs – a graphic and a voice-over – and analysing this combination of signs in the context of the half-and-half format of the programme, we see that what looks like an unremarkable choice of format itself conveys a strong message. In the course of a few seconds we are taught a whole theory of what justice looks like in a society in which the people are supposed to be the ultimate source of law and authority: a society in which, despite the existence of capital punishment and other legal features considered as barbaric elsewhere in the world, all's well because the cops not only represent the people but are identified with law itself. The theory of representation and law/order presented in the opening sequence also functions as a way to differentiate a product within a market: unlike other dramatic shows about policing, this show's distinction is precisely that it features both the prosecution and the police, and indeed often focuses on the conflicts generated by the two institutions' differing priorities and abilities.

We thus see how content and format go together. The show's distinctive content – presenting the interaction between police and prosecution as central, rather than focusing merely on police procedure or, alternatively, on lawyers and their courtroom dramatics – is replicated in the opening graphic sequences. But the graphic/

voice-over combination, as a format choice, also does some work of its own. In general, formatting choices differentiate *products* that compete for the same market, or in other words, differentiate products within the same *genre*. At the same time, however, formatting differentiates one genre from another. This is the second dimension of format analysis.

In the context of television, a reliable device for formally indicating a particular genre is the use of close-ups of faces. Soap operas, as a genre, are full of extremely close shots of faces. A drama might zoom in to give us a close-up view of the detective's face on occasion, but normally the camera is further away, so that we see the whole room or at least a good part of it. And dramas rarely stay completely indoors, whereas soap operas often do. This in turn is linked to conventions about lighting and make-up. Soaps take place in indoor spaces and are usually shot in lighting that does not change whether it is day or night, a format choice that emphasizes timelessness and lack of geographic specificity. The opposite effect – highlighting temporal and geographical co-ordinates – will be what one observes in historical dramas.

Cinematography conventions about camera work, lighting, focus length, background music and so forth are invisible most of the time. They are generally only noticed when a particular product uses the 'wrong' conventions to get attention or invents a new one. But viewers know them, even without knowing that they know them. Ordinary people who watch a lot of television are walking encyclopedias of esoteric knowledge about technique and format. Upon switching channels, most people will be able to state accurately what genre of show is being shown on that particular channel even before any words are heard. You can try this at home: spend five minutes changing channels quickly and see how many seconds it takes you before you can identify the genre of the particular product. This exercise will also reveal the importance of format, since in most cases it will not be the content of the script that tells you the genre – it will be such signifiers as tone of voice, focal length, dress, demeanour and location of persons shown, music or other sound, and cinematography.

Thus, particular products distinguish themselves through explicit format choices from others in the same genre, while yet other formal features distinguish genres from one another. Format analysis does not stop here, however. Noting the genre within which a representation falls (comedy, drama, daytime soap, news, sports, business reports, in the case of television) is not sufficient. Each major media outlet usually contains a variety of genres, depending on the time of day and of the week. But media outlets (e.g. a television channel or a newspaper) are usually differentiated from one another socio-economically. This is particularly evident in the case of newspapers and magazines, although it is also visible on television. In the UK most quality newspapers like *The Times* now publish 'compact' editions. In this respect, the traditional visual distinction between popular formats ('tabloids') and quality formats ('broadsheets') has been eroded. In North America, however, the smaller page format of the tabloids is correctly read as a sign of popular content.

The final point in the discussion of format analysis is that the universe of producers of popular representations is divided not only by genre, and by the split between quality and popular outlets, but also among different *media*. Each medium has certain formal technical features that are relatively constant across outlets within the same medium (although they change slowly over time). For example: newspapers, as a group, are composed of stories with headlines (unlike radio or television news, which only have headlines some of the time) and, importantly, these headlines can be scanned in any order the reader chooses. This allows for longer and somewhat more specialized items. It is easier for a news-paper to carry an opinion column, for example, than for a television channel. On television, explicitly marked opinion items have to be kept to a minimum, since viewers are very likely to change channels if they see something they don't like. Newspaper readers, by contrast, can easily turn to their favourite columnist and avoid the ones they don't like. Newspaper owners and editors know that their readership does not, in general, read the whole newspaper. Ericson's study of newspaper crime news puts this as follows:

> A newspaper can build its readership by appealing to an aggregate of minorities, each of whom will select and read only particular sections and items from the total volume available in the newspaper. Television must do the selecting of items for its audience and hold its attention through the newscast. (Ericson et al., 1991, p 37)

This technical difference between television and print helps to explain why tele-vision tends to be bland and homogeneous; in most countries, there are far fewer ideological and content differences between television channels than there are among competing newspapers.

Another formal distinction, this time between radio and television, is the fact that with radio the sound has to carry the whole weight of signification; thus, the pacing can only be altered with sound signs (the spoken word or bits of music). This has a tendency to encourage shorter items. When a long item is presented, for example an interview, the interviewer constantly interrupts the speaker, thus gen erating very short bursts of speech. Talk shows often solicit ordinary people's speech through telephone calls or via studio audience participation, but no one person is allowed very much time: callers are always interrupted so that no listener has to listen for too long (more than a few seconds) to anyone who might be annoying them. The listener might hate the caller who is now on, and might be tempted to turn the radio off; but he/she knows that this caller will fairly quickly be cut off and replaced by another caller who may more closely reflect the listen-er's own views. This hope sustains the show's market share.

On television, by contrast, a relatively lengthy item can be livened up and fragmented either by varying the visuals while the sound remains steady (e.g. as maps or film footage are shown while a foreign correspondent is droning on uninterrupted), or, less often, by varying the sound while the same image con-tinues to be shown. Television's technical or formal ability to change visuals while the same voice is speaking is a very important factor to consider if analysing how different kinds of social actors are presented. The Glasgow University study of British television, for example, found that lesser social actors (e.g. labour union leaders) were likely to see their speeches cut down to a very short clip, which was then presented only as audio, with the visuals showing something else; only the channel's own correspondents and very high-status speakers (the Prime Minister and very few others) had the opportunity to speak at length to the audience and to be seen the whole time they were speaking (GUGM, 1980, p 269).

A complete analysis of the format of a representation, then, will have four levels or dimensions.

(a) Format choices that individualize the story or the programme in relation to other stories or programmes;
(b) Format choices that differentiate genres from one another (e.g. drama, comedy, news);
(c) Large socio-economic divides ('quality' vs. 'popular');
(d) Formal/technical differences among media (television, radio, newspapers, internet).

Format and objectivity

Research on media and journalism has shown that it is pointless to ask: 'Does objectivity exist?' It is simply not useful to think of objectivity as if one could physically measure the distance between an account and 'the real world' and award prizes to those journalists who reduce that gap to a minimum. First of all, the news is an important *part* of the world, not a mere representation of it. Second, as research in photography has shown, presenting an accurate depiction does not mean that one is not biased or that the audience will not get a partisan political message, or a strong social message about what needs to be done about X or Y. A picture of a refugee camp or a war zone, just to refer to one type of image, is never just a descriptive statement. It is an image that mobilizes the viewers, appealing to existing ethical habits and conventions (Ellis, 2000). Written descriptions too are seldom merely descriptive. Language is always doing something, to the world and to the audience, as the pragmatist philosophers discovered a century ago.

Nevertheless, even if one has given up on the highly outdated idea that words and images can be judged in terms of how objectively they depict reality, the fact is that accounts, and in particular accounts that purport to be news, can usefully be said to be more or less fair and more or less accurate. If one thinks of objectivity not as correspondence between words and things but rather in this more sociological manner – as more a matter of fairness to all human actors and interests involved – how can one go about studying its production? How is it that some newscasters, some channels, some newspapers, appear to audiences generally as more authoritative and objective than others?

Objectivity can usefully be treated as an *effect* – an effect created by certain writing practices, certain lighting and make-up practices, sound-editing practices, etc. There is of course a substantive, content-based dimension to the production of objectivity through journalistic practice, having to do with avoiding preconceived ideas, seeking out a variety of sources of information, and the other standard techniques and values taught in journalism schools. But here we are mainly concerned with the format issues. In so far as objectivity exists, as an effect of certain practices if not as some kind of 'real' relation between the world and a text, objectivity is as much a matter of format as a matter of content. What kinds of format suggest objectivity?

Defining justice may be impossible, yet one can make a good start on this elusive inquiry by documenting what most people consider to be situations of clear injustice. So too, perhaps it is easier to tackle the issue of objectivity by beginning negatively, that is, by looking around for examples of formats that suggest a lack of objectivity. There is little if any doubt, for example, that extremely large headlines with exclamation marks in the realm of print, suggest what is called 'sensationalism' and a lack of objectivity. On television and on radio, certain channels and programmes pride themselves on being vehicles for extreme opinion, and this choice, this positioning as a market segment, is communicated through format even before audiences have a chance to absorb any content: shrill, loud, emotional voices are de rigueur in such programmes. The shrill tone – usually emitted by a speaker with a regional and/or working-class accent – acquires its specific meaning (namely, extreme opinion and populist affiliations) by contrast with the measured, sober, neutral tone of voice characteristic of newsreaders on national television channels.

It is interesting to reflect on the assumptions about the relation between emotions and truth that underlie the fairly obvious fact that emotionality, in headlines or in speech, acts as a sure mark of lack of objectivity. When a BBC announcer tries to keep the emotion out of his/her voice to tell us that X number of people were just massacred somewhere in the world, a statement is being communicated to the audience through the voice tone alone. The message communicated by the tone of voice is that truth, fairness and accuracy in reporting means taking one's emotions out of the equation.

This point about BBC tone of voice may seem unexceptional. But when one thinks about the European/Western tendency to believe that events like massacres are more likely to happen in the Third World than in Europe because those 'Others' are more passionate about their culture, their ethnicity and their religion than 'we' are, it becomes apparent that the message communicated implicitly by the format (tone of voice, in this instance) parallels and reinforces a substantive belief. This substantive belief about the uncivilized Others, in this day and age, is unlikely to be explicitly given, but is quite likely to be indirectly communicated by how Third World political events are portrayed.

Thus, the unemotional newscaster on the highbrow channel, who tries hard to use the same unemotional tone throughout the newscast, is unwittingly reproducing the same ethnocentrism and history of colonialism that is generally implicated in the historical background of most 'ethnic' massacres. That some events do really cry out for an emotional response is not a possibility that a highbrow, 'quality' news outlet can let itself contemplate. A newscaster working for a quality outlet would be as unlikely to cry about a massacre as to shout for joy when reporting a victory by his favourite football team. This would be discussed as 'professionalism' among journalists; but, whatever the journalist's motives for maintaining a poker face and an unemotional tone of voice, the effects – in the context of certain events – is to reinforce a certain ethnocentric construction of the 'quality' journalist as reasonable, dispassionate, race-less and race-blind. This stance is an essential precondition of the self-image and the market share of 'quality' media. And if unemotional tones function as an indicator of objectivity on radio and television, the print equivalent of that peculiar, unchanging voice is a marked, unrelenting greyness. The *New York Times*, which has not seen fit to increase the size of its headlines in many decades even as other newspapers did, and which almost never uses colour in the news (as opposed to the supplements) is a wonderful example of objective-looking formatting. We may consume various items (e.g. newspapers) without reflecting on or even being aware of their formats, but the messages communicated by the formats are easily apparent if one simply buys several newspapers oriented to very different markets and examines them for format, putting aside content.

A final point about the creation of objectivity as an effect is that journalists, particularly print journalists, are taught to seek comments from two sources – the 'two sides' of a story – whenever possible. Ericson's massive study showed that most news reports had no sides at all, since they were short items that did not cite anyone directly, but, in somewhat longer items that did cite sources, the vast majority cited two and no more than two sources (Ericson, 1991, pp 169–171). Ericson comments that this is rather artificial, since many events don't clearly suggest two opposing 'sides'; many social and political conflicts have three or four distinct sides, for instance. But the two-sources rule does more than simply reflect the political habits and customs of liberal democratic societies, societies long used to the idea that there is a Right and a Left in the legislature, and that two parties are all one needs for a democracy, even if more parties are allowed.

The two-source rule, I would suggest, not only replicates the political and architectural arrangements that characterize liberal democracies, but also itself enacts a dearly held myth about politics, and indeed about social conflict in general. This is the (liberal) myth that truth is somewhere in the middle, that 'extreme' opinions are wrong by virtue of being far from the geometric centre, and that the person who occupies the middle ground and seeks to moderate or mediate is automatically more sensible and more objective than anyone who occupies what is regarded as an 'extreme'.

Television talk shows are good places to observe what I like to call the 'Loony A, Loony B' technique for propagating the liberal myth that 'the truth is in the middle'. The moderator, by virtue of being physically in the middle, already appears to the audience as more reasonable and more reliable than the contestants or participants. In addition, the moderator usually has no strong views on the subject of the debate, perhaps because he/she has rarely spent the time and energy on the issue that the participants have spent. The moderator is also trained to speak in a not-too-professional, relatively informal but nevertheless even-tempered tone of voice. Thus, by virtue of tone of voice, physical location on the stage, and absence of strongly held views, the moderator appears as the voice of reason, the one with whom the audience will identify. The two opposing participants, by contrast, will appear as immoderate even before they open their mouths.

The journalistic rule about presenting both sides, a rule that encourages readers to think that the truth must be 'in the middle', is thus not only a rule but is itself a sign whose mythical, second-order meaning is something like this: strong passions are to be distrusted; truth and reason are dispassionate; and truth is likely to be found in the 'middle' ground. This middle ground ('middle' here being a very useful word because it refers both to physical space and to ideology) is not constituted through solid research or careful argument – I do not know of any talk show that opens with a voice-over explicitly explaining that the physical location of the moderator is meant to symbolically represent middle-of-the-roadness as a political virtue. The objectivity effect is achieved simply by putting two opposing positions at either end of a table or a stage. This apparently simple action automatically creates a 'middle' and characterizes that middle ground as the space of reasonableness, fairness and objectivity.

A case study of format: television maps and graphics

> 'Wars become maps, the economy becomes graphs, crimes become diagrams ...'
> (Ellis, 2000, p 101)

A large-scale study of British television news (GUMG, 1980) revealed that in the late 1970s graphics took up about 10–11 per cent of the news time, with maps taking up an additional 11–12 per cent of the total news time. At that time, graphics and maps were almost always static, with minimal animation being used. Since then, however, advances in computer-aided design have made it possible to create and use all sorts of visually lively, full-colour graphics and maps that move, change shape, and generally hold the audience's interest better than 'talking heads'. Given the prominence of maps and graphics on today's television screens, it makes sense to briefly consider how the apparently unremarkable choice to use a particular format – a graphic or a map – establishes and reinforces certain social relationships. First we shall briefly discuss the use of maps in newscasts, and then turn our attention to an American television show, CSI, that has transformed the way in which crime is seen (literally) by an innovative use of graphic representations of bodily injuries.

Maps

Maps are particularly useful in the context of news because they appear as inherently objective and authoritative. Someone chose to draw the map, leaving some things in and excluding other things. And while maps in newspapers are usually presented on their own, on television choices have to be made about how to present the map. Thus someone chooses whether to present a map on a screen behind a speaker, which is a merely illustrative position, or, alternatively, occupying the whole screen – a position by which the map replaces the speaker and thus appears as 'speaking for itself'. Perhaps most importantly, someone made the initial formatting decision to show a place – a foreign country, typically – as a map. This already implicates the news programme in question in certain relations of power – colonial and/or military relations, more specifically.

People who live in Iraq don't need a map to get from Basra to Baghdad; either they know how to get there already, or they can ask for directions that use local knowledges (e.g. 'You can take a bus from the bus terminal that's in front of the hospital'). But ever since the great European age of 'discovery', military forces have used maps as tools of conquest, war and occupation. While maps can of course be used for many different purposes by many different people (e.g. one can use an Ordnance Survey map to go on a nature hike, rather than to invade a country), nevertheless, there are technical or format features built into maps that facilitate certain kinds of power moves. A map gives a top-down, bird's-eye view, which is not the perspective of the people who live there. To get around in our own familiar environments, we use prominent landmarks and street names and familiar objects as signposts – and we know that if we venture into unfamiliar neighbourhoods we can always ask for directions, something that occupying forces have difficulty doing, for reasons that are more than linguistic. When a war is going on in a place that is foreign to the audience, then showing the place as a map is not just a means of conveying information. It also signifies a particular political relationship between 'us' and 'them'.

Maps are used for domestic events if the precise location of an event is particularly important, for example to show which neighbourhoods are affected by the derailment of a train carrying chemicals. In this case too the use of a map indicates that the newscast is adopting the perspective of the authorities – the fire, police and health authorities that are trying to contain the problem and protect the population. While the authorities in this latter case would not be 'occupying' in the military sense, nevertheless they are seizing control of the territory too, albeit for benevolent purposes. Hence, this is not a counter-example of the general thesis about maps and power over territory.

The political effect of the map format is often compounded, when wars are involved, by the common television news practice of having a military officer, or a civilian expert on military issues, appear beside or in front of the map and proceed to literally seize control of the territory shown. This can be done in the old-fashioned way, by taking a pointer or a set of coloured push pins and literally inscribing military actions upon the map – something that has the effect of erasing not only the blood that may well be flowing, but even the people, their homes, their crops and so on. Or it can be done through modern technology, by having a computer technician change the elements of the map (e.g. highlighting one place or one road, or changing the colour of the element that is being referred to) as the talking head explains 'what is going on'. Because the map format carries with it military and colonial connotations, we will not be at all surprised if the spoken explanations that constitute the soundtrack accompanying the map visuals are exactly that, i.e., military.

A map, therefore, is not simply a neutral representation of far-off territory. As Foucault might have said, a map literally seizes territory. A television newscast that is heavy on the maps and light on pictures of the people being attacked, surrounded, bombed or cut off from their food supply will tend to reinforce a military perspective, quite apart from whatever the soundtrack and the other visuals tell us. Maps are never shown as having authors but, as a genre, they have a certain political perspective.

Graphics as the visual voice-of-god

Graphics have been used for a long time to visually represent abstract entities, such as a currency that is rising or falling, the movement in the stock market, weather predictions and so on. The Glasgow study of the late 1970s found that certain entities were more likely to be routinely represented by simple, easily understood graphics – namely, those of concern to business, such as stock market trends and inflation changes (GUMG, 1980, pp 300–305). Economic facts of primary interest to employees and families, by contrast, might be mentioned orally by a correspondent or newscaster, but they were far less likely to be turned into easy-to-remember, simple graphics.

This observation was made a long time ago, but it seems to still apply today. On Canadian television newscasts, stock market changes are always given in the daily news, and they are packaged in highly professional, standardized graphics that are shown at a set time during the broadcast. Tellingly, the American stock exchanges are given pride of place. Information about unemployment and wage rates, however, is only given very occasionally, when major quarterly economic reports are issued or at some other particularly newsworthy point in time. The only other economic fact that is sufficiently privileged to warrant a daily update by using a standard, easy-to-read graphic is the value of the Canadian dollar – which is always, without exception, shown by comparison to the US dollar.

The two simple graphics used every day manage to convey quickly two key economic/political messages. The stock market graphic tells us something about the domination of business/investor interests within the Canadian economy (the interests of investors are shown as having universal appeal and deserving daily updates, but not the interests of employees). Second, the daily comparison of the value of the Canadian dollar against the US dollar tells us something about the structural domination of the Canadian economy by the American economy. And all of this is done with two simple graphics, without a single grammatically complete sentence.

Concerning representations of crime, a recent trend on American television – and one that is creeping into Canadian-made television shows – is the innovative use of graphics to see inside the body, the body of the victim to be exact. *CSI* (Crime Scene Investigation), the most watched show on North American television, pioneered a technique whereby technologically mediated visualizations of injuries and dismemberments were presented not just as accompaniments to a forensic technician's words but as speaking for themselves. As discussed in more detail in Chapter 6, the technique in question is as follows: a technician is first of all shown peering into a machine, say an X-ray machine, a microscope or an MRI machine. The perspective is quickly changed, so that the picture that is appearing on or through the machine now fills up the whole television screen. If there was a voice during the first shot, this disappears as we move into this second shot. Then, the image – usually highlighted with very artificial-looking colours, in the manner used for brain scans – is animated with movement. The movement is supposed to replicate how the injury in question was created. Thus, the bone, say, whose X-ray image appears filling the screen, is shown as literally fracturing – even though the machine, of course, can only show the final result, never the process. Often the technologically mediated picture of the broken bone will subtly merge into or fade into a picture of a real leg or arm.

This is an interesting innovation because it achieves what forensic sciences have always pursued as their utopian dream: namely, to literally show the truth of a crime as a set of physical, bodily events (Cole, 2001; Valverde, 2003, ch. 3). The criminal events actually took place in a non-photographed past, of course; but, on *CSI*, the chain of events is magically shown as taking place again, in the lab, before our very eyes. And there is no voice, either from the technician or from a voice-of-god voice-over. The picture speaks alone. We can thus see, for ourselves, without being told, what sort of weapon had to be used for such a fracture to occur. And so, without any need for detectives, or indeed without any need for the spoken word, the truth of the crime is revealed.

How this televisual technique changes audience's perceptions of the work of policing will be discussed in Chapter 6. Here, however, it suffices to point out that what looks like a merely technical innovation in graphics facilitated by computer-aided-design software is by no means merely technical. What we are being told is this: we (we the audience, we 'the people' with a stake in the criminal justice system) don't want any long-winded psychological explanations of what was felt by this or that person; we just want 'the facts', namely, the physical, bodily facts. The truth is in the physical details; the truth is directly visible. Interpretation is unnecessary. Guilt is not a legal or moral relationship of one human being to a set of (social) events; guilt is directly inscribed on skeletons and bodily tissues, and can be read off directly by anyone who looks. No knowledge of criminal law or procedure is necessary when you have a (technologically mediated) picture of the real moment of crime – identified on this show with the moment of physical injury.

The fact that the rise of forensically focused television programmes and books coincides with the new popularity of shows about crooked lawyers and corrupt law firms suggests that there may be some general cultural process by which words – and law is all words – are no longer trusted, whereas images of bits of bodies, however technologically mediated and highlighted with odd-looking fluids, are regarded as trustworthy witnesses and interpreters.

Analysing the use of graphics is thus one fruitful line of inquiry for those interested in seeing what the format of representations tells us. And since it is a general established principle of social semiotics that formats tend to reinforce the content of representations, we can always use changes in content (e.g. the sudden popularity of forensic technicians and forensic anthropologists in representations, and the simultaneous discrediting or erasure of formerly authoritative figures such as psychologists and lawyers) as a clue to begin investigating the effects (including the criminological effects) of trends in formatting.

Context analysis

It may bear repeating that the three dimensions of social semiotic analysis presented in this chapter – content, format and context – are not to be taken as three totally separate realms or realities. At some point, format choices – e.g. deciding to use a graphic or a map – carry a certain message, and thus become part of the 'content' of the representation. The same cautionary note needs to be repeated in regard to context. Let's go back to the American flag being waved on the website of the television show *Law & Order*, for example. Is the flag content? Or is it an indication of the political, post-September 11 context? A sign can be both content and context, and this is a good example. In 2003, the shows started to include little American flags on miniature poles sitting on the desks of the detectives. Those shows, mainly shot during 2002, had as their political and their immediate physical context New York City post-September 11, when flags sprouted from any and all locations. The flags on the desks and the flag on the website echoed one another. Together, they had the effect of taking the show a little further away from local issues, such as the current re-election chances of the District Attorney, and correspondingly closer to the national events that were only occasionally mentioned on the shows but which were represented by the (new) desk flags.

But if the context also creeps into the content, nevertheless, it is still possible to draw a schematic chart in which content and format analysis are followed by an analysis of the context. Context analysis, in turn, has two dimensions or parts: (a) the context of production and (b) the context of reception or consumption.

The context of production includes factors that are visible in the representation itself (e.g. the new desk flags of the *Law & Order* detectives), but it also includes many factors that would only become visible to a diligent researcher. Data to be included in an analysis of the context of production would consist of such facts as the ownership of the media outlet producing the representation; the biographies of director, writers and actors; the decisions taken by the producer/editor; the customary practices about the use of actors; the generally available repertoire or menu of formats which media outlets in that market draw from, and so forth.

These contingencies and these decisions involved in the production of a representation are always in a dynamic interaction with the context of *consumption*. A Hollywood studio with a particular history and a particular set of conventions about the use of actors and the discretion afforded to directors is always engaged in producing a product that is aimed at a particular audience. It may, of course, then migrate to other audiences as well, or it may fail miserably with that first intended audience; but the point is that a huge part of the production process involves thinking about what the intended customer wants. The intended audience, whose desires are no doubt objectified for the producers through surveys and various techniques of market research, is thus a factor in the production itself.

Despite sophisticated market research, research shows that audiences can on occasion play a relatively autonomous part in the semiotic process at the final stage, the point of consumption. A book intended for children and teens may become a bestseller among adults (as happened to the Harry Potter series). A newspaper addressed to an upper-middle-class business audience may become a working-class favourite because of its superior football coverage (or more likely, the opposite). And, as mentioned earlier, films made from a male point of view and intended for male audiences may become popular with women, with curious effects on the construction of femininity.

In conclusion, there is no particular set of questions, no abstract method, that can be automatically applied to representations so as to reveal their social meaning. However, a template that organizes the inquiry into three main steps – content, format and context – can be of much help, if one keeps in mind that each of the three main vectors of meaning works not independently but in (unpredictable) interaction with the other two vectors.

Introduction: the mutual constitution of cops and robbers

One of the key contentions of this book is that representations dealing with issues of crime, law and order always convey messages about the authorities to whom we are supposed to entrust our safety. More specifically, in both news media and in fictional accounts, messages about authorities and solutions will emerge at the same time, and from the same signs, as messages that tell us who the bad guys are. Each account of a killer's doings will always tell us something, however implicitly, about the kind of expertise and authority that is required to find and deal with killers.

The main focus of this chapter will be how authorities – criminologists, police photographers, biochemists, etc. – have over the past century and a half or so developed techniques for rendering criminality detectable and visible. These techniques involve finding ways to literally picture intangible legal and moral relations – not only the fact that X committed the crime but also more legalistic constructs, such as intent. And we will then see that each technique for visualizing criminality and/or criminals also constructs authority in a particular way. To anticipate the final section of this chapter, DNA evidence visualizes criminal identity as a set of genetic markers that – unlike the skull shapes perused by 'criminal anthropologists' in the late nineteenth century – are not visible to the naked eye, and are not meaningful except in the context of the larger semiotic system that gives the traces of genes their meaning, a system composed of biological theories about humanity's genetic diversity. The white and black streaks that, magnified hundreds of times, are shown to juries in murder trials only make sense in the context of a certain scientific paradigm: thus, the images serve to empower biologists and molecular genetics specialists, whether or not they are present in the courtroom. By contrast, when prosecutors use everyday moral terminology to describe the accused as 'evil' or as 'heartless', scientific expertise is set aside in favour of 'common knowledge'. Thus, the partial history of representations of criminality sketched out here is also, simultaneously, a partial history of changing representations of authorities on crime.

This chapter covers the history of key real-life techniques for identifying and keeping track of criminals. The survey of real-life, detective-centred, police-driven techniques for visualizing deviance and crime will be followed by a chapter that analyses a small sample of the vast array of English-language fictional representations of detective and forensic work.

It should be noted that the division between Chapter 4 and Chapter 5 is somewhat artificial. As forensic science textbooks are fond of pointing out, real-life policing sometimes lags behind its fictional counterpart. The famous Arthur Conan Doyle stories featuring Sherlock Holmes, for example, featured forensic techniques not yet practised in any police department. Hollywood films have also sometimes anticipated real-life policing inventions, not only in the case of films set in the future but also in the case of supposedly realistic films. The 1949 gangster movie *White Heat*, to give an example, shows law enforcement officers (from the US Treasury department, not the police) using a cumbersome but effective radio-based form of global positioning technology to follow, at a safe distance, the progress of the gangsters' vehicle. Nothing of the kind was available to ordinary law enforcement officials at that time. Nevertheless, despite the artificiality involved in dividing fact from fiction, it will be easier for the reader if we separate out the story of real-life, largely state-produced representational techniques used for identifying and keeping track of criminals from the history of fictional representations.

The chapter begins in the mid-nineteenth century. The choice of chronological starting point is justified because this was the time of the birth of criminology and of the development of detective expertise within police departments. (Municipal police forces as we know them are conventionally traced back to Robert Peel's 1820s reforms, but early police forces in the UK and in North America had virtually no detection capacity.) And as we shall see, modern police methods were very much products of their time. The methods we have come to take for granted as neutral tools of good detective work, from collecting clues left at the scene of the crime to the fingerprinting of known criminals, were not the product of ahistorical human inventiveness. They were very much rooted in their context – the context of an explosion of biological, psychological and cultural expert knowledges about human evolution, human diversity and human deviance.

The quest to identify and classify human types

The middle years of the nineteenth century are often regarded as 'the Age of Darwin'. The educated public living at that time witnessed the beginning of the still ongoing quest to identify scientific laws explaining the physiological development of humans – with humans regarded, for the first time, mainly as animals. Less well known is the fact that this period also witnessed the birth of anthropology, namely, the attempt to use scientific methods to document and classify existing human societies, especially 'primitive' or 'exotic' societies. While for Darwin's purposes it made sense to speak of the human species as a whole – with even the whole human species getting very short shrift in Darwin's own writings, although commentators focused on the implications of evolution for humanity's self-understanding – the anthropological science that emerged in the second half of the nineteenth century focused almost exclusively on differentiation. Anthropological accounts of human differentiation stressed physical features construed as markers of 'racial' difference. Social commentators writing about the urban underclasses at home did not necessarily use racialized language (although sometimes they did, especially to describe poor Irish communities), but they too emphasized graduated differences and assumed that types of humans fell naturally into a hierarchical arrangement. Henry Mayhew's explorations of the world of London street sellers, for example, elaborated a complex taxonomy that began by dividing the human species into 'settled' and 'nomadic' races, and then proceeded to articulate fine distinctions among various kinds of London nomads. Later, prison managers and prison doctors used the same approach to construct taxonomies of different kinds of offenders, sometimes succeeding in isolating particular groups (alcoholics, the intellectually challenged, etc.) in specially built institutions. The Victorian passion for classification owed a great deal to methods and approaches to knowledge developed decades earlier by those practising 'natural history', the predecessor of modern biology.

One of the key features of mid- and late-nineteenth century discourses on humanity, human difference and human types is that the line between 'nature' and 'culture' was not very sharply drawn. It is difficult for us today to understand why physiognomy (the study and classification of faces) and phrenology (the study of skull shapes) had such tremendous scientific prestige. We ridicule scientists who insisted on linking skull capacity with intelligence and pour scorn on Dickens-era fiction writers. We think that giving long-lost aristocratic heirs blonde hair, taller than average stature, and markedly symmetrical facial features is a simplistic plot device; however, Victorian readers would have felt misled by the author if the long-lost, blue-blooded heir had turned out to be short, dark and crooked-nosed. In Victorian social semiotics, social identity and moral character were thought to be – with some exceptions – directly readable on the surface of the body.

In our own time, science is still regarded as providing some knowledge about the link between physiology and morality. But while we give credence to stories about how people with neurological abnormalities or a fragile X chromosome are predisposed to deviant behaviour, we no longer believe that the face, or the head, or the body as a whole, is the mirror of the soul. We have become accustomed to thinking about illness or abnormalities at a more minute level, as if we had an electron microscope or a brain-scan machine at our disposal. Psychology textbooks today, for example, are abundantly illustrated with diagrams of neurons and receptors of brain proteins, and with some artificially coloured images obtained from brain scans. Human bodies and human faces, however, are notable by their absence. When thinking about the 'truth' of human identity, we tend to think in terms of highly mediated images that render the 'inside' of the body visible, usually by magnifying tiny bits that would not be visible even if they were on the outside – think of the fetal ultrasound sonograms that illustrate not only medical textbooks but even family photo albums, or the diagrams of how certain proteins lock or unlock certain brain receptors that one finds in popular science accounts of mental illness and addiction. The outside of the body is no longer very meaningful to us: it therefore takes some imaginative effort to put ourselves in the place of the skull-measuring criminological anthropologist.

Perhaps more importantly, we do not believe that acquired character traits are inherited. Despite the efforts made by certain Darwinians to remind people that mutations are random, large numbers of people in the second half of the nineteenth century, and into the twentieth, believed Lamarck's theory of evolution. As against the random mutation Mendelian theory that eventually prevailed, Lamarck posited that just as giraffes who stretched their neck a lot would have offspring with slightly longer necks, so too men who became alcoholics or murderers would pass their defective physiology and their moral traits on to their children. The Lamarckian take on evolution, in which children paid a biological price for the sins and vices of their parents, hard-wired culture and morality to biological evolution in ways that are no longer current.

The process of inheriting acquired characteristics was not always seen as direct, however. Many writers spoke of 'degenerate tendencies' or 'a degenerate constitution' as that which is inherited. And degeneration could take many forms. Thus, if an alcoholic father had four children and none of them grew up to be an alcoholic but one or two showed some other deficiency typical of working-class urban life (low intelligence, for example, or criminality), the theory was confirmed, not disproven. Educational texts on sexual hygiene and on temperance, for example, often featured line drawings tracing the process of 'degeneration' quite literally on the bodies and faces of parents and their offspring. An alcoholic father – shown with typically 'degenerate' facial features, of course – would be shown siring a new generation suffering from epilepsy, feeble mindedness (low intelligence) and other conditions, with all of the conditions being portrayed in the illustrations as directly visible to the naked eye.

For their part, writers about cultural subjects also tended to erase certain lines that we now feel are very important. They mixed with great abandon comments about the physiology of certain ethnic groups and discussions about culture. It was common among scientists and among laymen such as journalists and politicians to state, as a fact, that blacks should not emigrate to the United States or Canada because the climate was simply too cold for them, or to assume that the reason why Latin countries had less developed economies was that hotter weather made people, individually and collectively, lazy. In general, human progress was seen as simultaneously biological and cultural, while the opposite of progress – degeneration – was also a hybrid category. Drunkenness and a sloping forehead could thus be cited one after the other, without a break, as two indicators of potential criminality, without having to clarify whether the indicators, or for that matter criminality itself, was mainly natural or mainly cultural or some clearly defined combination of both.

Another very important feature of the way knowledge of deviance was generally organized, in the period that saw the emergence of the sciences of crime and criminality, was that the individual was regarded as little other than the product of or an instance of a group – often a race, but also groups like 'the feeble-minded' or 'inverts' (homosexuals). Contemporary genetics has habituated us to thinking about physiological events probabilistically, so that ordinary people tell their friends, 'I have a 50 per cent chance of developing type 2 breast cancer before age 60'. By contrast, in the 1880s, although probability was well established in such areas as life insurance, the human sciences did not generally use statistical formats to visualize danger and deviance. The connections between individual and group were constructed using different modes of reasoning and different techniques for visualizing information.

One way of connecting individuals to groups, for example, was that provided by 'recapitulation theory'. This influential view claimed that the development of an individual human being from baby to adult mirrored and 'recapitulated' – that is, re-enacted – the development of the whole human species. And each 'race', in turn, had not only a specific geographical distribution but also a fixed place, or rather time, in the evolutionary diagram of the human species. A toddler in London, therefore, was regarded as similar to an adolescent in a very 'primitive' culture, while a full-grown adult of African descent was in turn thought to behave just like a European adolescent because both were essentially at the same stage of development.

Presupposing the truth of this way of comparing human types across time and space led many otherwise innovative thinkers to make what now look like ridiculous statements. In the 1890s, Émile Durkheim, for example, put forward as scientific fact the claim that differences between the sexes increase with evolution, such that the 'higher' the society, the more different women are from men – just as one finds more differences between adult men and women than one does between male and female babies. Socialization was not considered at all, as he wrote:

> Prehistoric bones show that the difference between the strength of man and of woman was relatively much smaller than it is today ... If one admits that the development of the individual reproduces in its course that of the species, one may conjecture that the same homogeneity was found at the beginning of human evolution, and see in the female form the aboriginal image of what was the one and only type from which the masculine variety slowly detached itself. (Durkheim, [1893] 1964, p 57)

Durkheim then quotes an expert on skulls who supposedly proved that men's propensity to have greater skull capacity than women 'grows proportionally with civilization ... The difference which exists, for example, between the average cranium of the Parisian men of the present day and that of Parisian women is almost double that observed between male and male of ancient Egypt' (Durkheim, [1893] 1964, pp 57–8). This then leads to a justification of the gender division of labour in nineteenth-century France.

This chain of reasoning is a semiotic one: for Durkheim as for his contemporaries, perceived sex differences in cranium capacity are read as signs telling us that nature intends women to act differently from men, engage in different kinds of work, and so forth, just as racialized signs of physical difference are interpreted as simultaneously cultural and natural.

The sets of signs collected by anthropologists and others and interpreted by theorists like Durkheim were of course always embodied in particular bodies, in the skull of Mr X or Ms Y; but the individuality of the body being 'read' was not important. The type was the real object of science, not the person. And what seems peculiar, from our own perspective, is that the human types elaborated by anthropologists and by journalistic writers fascinated with urban social deviants were regarded not as abstractions or ideal types but as really existing. Socially oriented journalists would travel through the slums and claim to be describing not a specific person but the perfect Jewish type. They would also amuse themselves by breaking down a category such as 'thief' or 'prostitute' into subtypes regarded as ontologically separate from each other. The scientist Francis Galton generated composite photographs not only of 'the criminal type' but also of such subtypes as 'the hotel thief', 'the forger' and 'the pickpocket'.

For their part, anthropologists – not yet fully differentiated from travel writers –

brought back information about exotic peoples in which the measurements of one particular person's body figured as fully and adequately representing a 'tribe'. The stories that emerged toward the end of the twentieth century about metropolitan museums owning and displaying the stolen skeletons or body parts of particular African or aboriginal individuals would not have seemed at all scandalous (to white people at any rate) a century earlier. For the 'explorers' who brought Mr Y or Ms X's embalmed body or skeleton from the wilds to the metropole, and for the 'civilized' multitudes who saw them exhibited, there was no breach of ethics or even of good taste: the skeleton or body part was seen not as the remains of an individual but merely as a signifier of a 'race' or tribe.

This semiotics of racialized bodies may appear as a hopelessly old-fashioned racist approach, but it should be pointed out that even today, it is common to see newspaper photographs of disasters in the Third World with captions that do not identify the individual Africans or Asians in the image. The grieving mother does not have a name, as she would have if she were a Londoner or a New Yorker: the photo of her body is merely a signifier of an African famine, an Asian monsoon, or some other disaster in far-off locales. Occasionally, victims of large-scale disasters in metropolitan white cities will also be portrayed in this generic manner, but journalistic ethics demand that journalists obtain the name and age of photographic subjects and their permission to publish the image – ethical demands which are rarely observed in the case of 'exotic' locales.

This background information on Victorian knowledges of human diversity and social deviance is necessary in order to understand properly one of the first scientific projects to identify and describe criminals and other deviant human types: Francis Galton's invention of the composite photograph, in the 1880s. Firmly believing that what was most important about particular humans was the type or group to which they belonged, the late Victorian English polymath Galton thought that if one could devise a technique for literally eliminating from the picture idiosyncratic features, while highlighting those features common to the group, then one would be able to really see human types – literally see them.

His solution to the problem of rendering groups visible (and thus making the group or tribe more real than the individual, as in the museum skeleton example above) relied on the then new technique of portrait photography. It occurred to Galton that by taking, say, 12 criminals or 12 Jews and exposing each image only for a fraction of the total time, one would obtain an image which, because individual features would be rendered very blurry unless they were also present in the other hapless subjects, would truly represent 'the type'.

It is important to note that Galton was no crank. He was a leading scientist of his day, a close relation of the great Darwin and a pioneer of statistics. And it was precisely as a statistician that he took care to emphasize that the composite photograph was not a statistical average. The composite photograph was a truly accurate, unmanipulated, concrete representation of the human type of which the actual photographic subjects were but mere examples. Unlike statistics giving the average height or weight of a certain population, the type portrayed in the composite photograph was not a numerical entity created by abstracting from the concrete features of particular bodies; it was what Galton called a 'real generaliza-

The late Victorian polymath scientist Francis Galton, who invented the composite photograph as a technique to render 'types' directly visible, was particularly proud of his 'Jewish composite' (Galton Papers, University College Library, Special Collections).

tion'. The composite portrait was as good a picture of the group as the individual portrait was of the individual.

In addition, the composite portrait of the type had a feature not found in individual portraits. The composite photograph gave information about the features generally found in the group, but it also contained information about how much group members differed from the norm, or more accurately, from the type. Since taking 12 exposures of physiologically similar individuals generates a sharper image than a photograph produced through multiple exposures of people who look very different, the amount of blurriness at the edges contains important information about the type. It provides a visual, non-numerical representation of that statistical term of art, standard deviation. Allan Sekula's account of the links between early photography and early criminology contains a long quote from Galton himself which explains this:

Composite pictures are much more than averages; they are rather the equivalent of those large statistical tables whose totals . . . entered on the bottom line, are the averages. They are real generalizations, because they include the whole of the material under consideration. The blur of their outlines, which is never great in truly generic composites, except in unimportant details, measures the tendency of individuals to deviate from the central type. (Galton quoted in Sekula, 1984, pp 49–50)

As Sekula notes, Galton, the founder of the scientific study and manipulation of human breeding (eugenics), was particularly pleased with his Jewish type. Needless to say, Galton cannot be directly blamed for the deeds of Nazi science, but it is not unfair to suggest that Galton did provide technical and intellectual tools – and some substantive ideas about hierarchical human differentiation – which helped to make Nazi science and other later eugenics projects possible.

No information is provided in Galton's writings about the particular individuals who were photographed because they looked like Jews. By contrast, we do have some information about the individuals whose identities were merged to create the composite portrait of the generic criminal, since for some reason Galton chose many individuals – like Canada's Louis Riel or France's Louise Michel – who were convicted of notorious political crimes. For these famous individuals, both specific deeds and racial and family background are a matter of public record. And a surprising number of the featured criminals are French, Italian or otherwise darker than the average Englishman.

That many of the criminals chosen for the procedure also happened to be members of ethnic groups with olive skins and wiry hair is of course something that we see today as immediately discrediting Galton's efforts. It is important to understand, however, that in his own day signs of criminality and signs of 'southern' or aboriginal ethnicities overlapped or merged to a very large extent in both popular and scientific discourses.

As mentioned earlier, in Galton's day – the 1880s and 1890s – there was some debate about whether acquired characteristics were inherited (as the Lamarckians thought) or whether parental behaviour made no difference to the offspring's biological capital. But there was much less discussion about an issue that became a hot debate in the mid-twentieth century, namely, whether deviance and/or crime should be regarded as mainly biological or mainly cultural. 'Traits' – that crucial concept of the human sciences around 1900 – included elements and signs we would call biological, together with signs that we would call cultural, without necessarily even making a distinction between the two. The homosexual, for example, was thought to be physiologically recognizable as well as culturally and psychologically distinct. And the same went for Galton's favourite types, the Jew and the criminal.

In the early twentieth century targets shifted. The 'feeble-minded', in particular, became the key target of North American, and to a lesser extent British, eugenic strategies to prevent the 'unfit' types from reproducing – strategies developed from around 1900 to the 1930s. In Germany the disabled and intellectually challenged were targeted as well, but efforts concentrated on racial types, not only Jews but also Slavs and gypsies. But whatever the specific target, science and political projects using science continued to think in terms of hybrid physiological-cultural types as the key unit of scientific knowledge about humans.

It was only the horrifying revelations about Nazi uses of eugenic science that came to light after 1945 that put in question the whole project to govern humanity through 'types'. The reaction against Nazi science discredited not only eugenics (the project to scientifically breed human groups so as to favour 'the fit') but, more broadly, the whole long tradition of regarding types as the key units of the human sciences. Individual rights and individual differences became more important. This seismic shift in thinking underlay the rise of such legal mechanisms as the UN Declaration of Human Rights of 1948, legal/political texts that would have a great impact on popular perceptions of human sameness and difference.

Galton's project to identify and visualize human types was not completely abandoned, however. Thinking in types continued alongside the new, more legalistic focus on individuality. However, the human types that began to emerge in the human sciences of the 1940s and 1950s were no longer visualized as bodies. Indeed, they were strangely disembodied, consisting mainly of psychological 'personality' traits. The stereotyped photographs and cartoon-like diagrams of criminals and degenerates that were popular from the 1880s to the 1930s disappeared from educational and journalistic texts. The new deviant Euro-American types of the 1950s (the alcoholic personality; the maladjusted child; the neurotic mother; the criminal sexual psychopath) were not biologically different from normal people. They looked 'normal' on the outside – which meant that psychological science was required to spot them and track them.

Somewhat later, the biologization of non-Europeans also began to lose popularity. The biological/cultural discourses on 'Oriental' degeneracy and 'the Yellow Peril', which spread through the US and Canada in the period from the 1880s to the 1940s, were not explicitly criticized and rejected after 1945, but they tended to slowly fade from view. In general, typologies of human groups today tend to use cultural rather than biologistic idioms. It is no longer polite to talk about 'shifty-eyed foreigners' to refer to Asians, although it is quite permissible to make generalizations about the Japanese being deferential to authority.

It is thus more accurate to say that Galton's project to isolate, classify and theorize human types was transformed than to imagine that with the rise of human rights thinking it was abandoned. From the 1940s onward, projects to identify, visualize and manage deviant groups would rely very heavily on psychological tools and terms. For example, the homosexual became in the 1950s a purely psychological category. Precisely because homosexuality was no longer thought to be directly visible on the body, various security organizations across the so-called 'free world' instituted campaigns to detect, harass and fire homosexuals, mainly from public services and the armed forces. These campaigns had to rely on informers, covert surveillance and gossip, since homosexuality was now a purely psychological and hence not visually identifiable category.

Many of these campaigns are only now beginning to be documented by historians. For example, many people in the UK do not know that the great mathematician Alan Turing, who played a key role in the breaking of the German Enigma code during World War II and who is credited with inventing the modern computer, was arrested for 'gross indecency' after casually revealing to a police officer investigating a break-in at Turing's home that he sometimes had sex with men. Turing was given the choice of going to prison or being chemically castrated. He chose the latter option, with terrible consequences for his physical as well as his mental health, and eventually committed suicide. This was no isolated incident: in the armed forces, the civil service and the diplomatic service, homosexuals were hounded, dismissed without cause, or charged with misconduct. If homosexuals were routinely suspected of being disloyal to their country or even spies, this may have been not only because lack of family ties were thought to weaken citizens' ties to their State, but also because (like spies) homosexuals were middle-class white men of ordinary appearance. Special semiotic exercises involving gossip, undercover surveillance, psychological tests and rumours were required to identify them.

Similarly, alcoholism, which had long been considered a hybrid moral-physical disease with dire biological consequences for offspring, was in the immediate postwar period reconceptualized as a purely psychological disorder. It was so heavily psychologized that respected specialist journals insisted that pregnant women's drinking had no effect at all on their offspring; it was only deficient (overbearing) mothers and absent fathers that caused alcoholism among young white men. Thus, instead of a total person with a distinct and deviant physiology, there now emerged the alcoholic 'personality'.

The post-World War II psychological knowledges generally used purely textual (and some numerical) representations of deviance and criminality. But in one field more visually striking techniques of representation were routinely used: this was urban sociology. Studies of urban ghettoes and other urban spaces of deviance fit well with the new emphasis on psychology and culture, since from the very beginnings of English-speaking sociology (and even before, in Victorian novels about urban poverty), certain spaces of the city had been considered to give rise to criminogenic or otherwise deviant cultures. Cultures of poverty and criminality could be studied with tools borrowed from social psychology and with visualization tools (e.g. mapping techniques) borrowed from urban studies.

Urban spaces of poverty had been mapped before, particularly in the first wave of what could be called 'slum travel writing', in the 1890s. However, the 1950s and 1960s saw urban planners and sociologists map and describe 'ghettoes' and 'blighted areas' with new gusto. That certain street layouts and certain types of housing were inherently criminogenic became the new postwar gospel. This was furthered in practice by the massive destruction of so-called 'blighted' areas and the construction of hygienic, uniform, planned public housing estates which, for the first time in the history of European urban forms, intentionally did not have streets. (In many cities in the UK and North America, many of these streetless housing estates are currently being replaced by conventional housing fronting on to ordinary-looking streets, in part because the new urbanism sees urban streets as more aesthetic and much safer than streetless estates.)

Despite this enthusiasm for architectural solutions, the culturalist/urbanist interest in developing urban-planning solutions to the culture of poverty that was popular in the 1950s and 1960s did not displace psychiatry and psychology.

Psychological categories and explanations coexisted without much conflict with culturalist discourses, in part due to a certain division of labour whereby the 'psy' experts were given responsibility for carceral institutions – mental hospitals, prisons – whereas the study of working-class and ethnic neighbourhoods was the domain of urban sociologists and other experts on cultural types. Urban planners and sociologists devised a number of ways of visualizing 'good' and 'bad' neighbourhoods and cities, mostly based on the pre-computer black-on-white line diagrams first disseminated in University of Chicago sociology texts on urban issues.

Psychology and psychiatry in this time period, by contrast, were remarkably non-visual. The pictures of bodies that had illustrated the texts of the criminal anthropologists of the 1890s and the eugenicists of the 1910s were now gone, having been discredited as a mode of visualizing deviance. With brain imaging not yet invented, the psyche of the criminal in the 1970s was largely a matter for expert speech, not for pictures. Charts organizing symptoms and diagnoses into neat boxes with plain writing inside them were the typical 'illustration' found in expert texts on deviance and criminality. Writing on urban crime and poverty, by contrast, was not totally grey, but the most common illustration consisted of hand-drawn, black-and-white diagrams, either the highly abstract ones favoured by the Chicago School or the more specific neighbourhood design diagrams drawn by urban planners and pioneers of 'crime prevention through environmental design' (CPTED).

This account of some of the key shifts in the ways knowledge about crime and deviance was formatted and given visual form is not complete, of course. But it suffices for our purposes, since it covers a diversity of formats and ways of seeing. It is now time to get to the question that is likely of most interest to the reader, namely: What has happened in the very recent past to the longstanding quest to identify, describe and visualize deviant and criminal types?

This is not an easy question to answer: the very fact that we are still living in the period under analysis means that we don't yet know which knowledge formats and representational habits will emerge as dominant in the near future. But, without making grand and incautious claims about tomorrow's fashions, it is possible to discuss briefly two ways of visualizing deviant social/moral conduct that are very popular today across numerous nation-states.

A much-used approach to representing human difference relies on recently invented techniques to graphically represent processes going on inside human bodies. For most of the twentieth century, X-rays were about the only technique to make the inside of the body literally visible; but X-rays can only capture hard solid materials, and only if they aren't moving. Nowadays technological inventions allow physicians and scientists to see soft tissue and liquids and to capture processes rather than just things. Scans of various kinds, especially brain scans, are used frequently to diagnose particular conditions. But what is important for present purposes is that scans are also used by behavioural scientists interested not in a particular patient's suffering but in scientific knowledge of types. Conditions such as schizophrenia and depression, and even fuzzy entities such as 'addiction', are now thought to have a distinctive pattern of neuronal activity that can be captured, almost in real time, by using scanning equipment and various

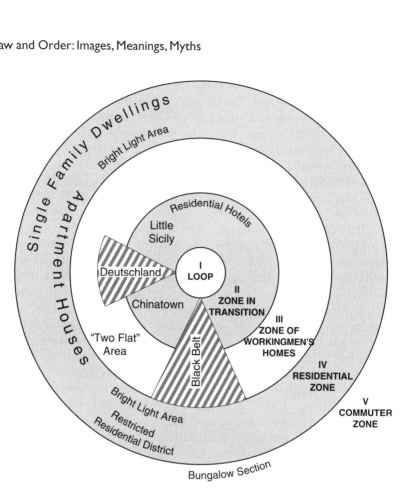

One version of the Chicago School semi-abstract diagram of the generic city (in Mike Davis, *Ecology of Fear*, New York, Vintage Books, 1998; Davis states this is the most famous diagram in the history of sociology.)

techniques to enhance the visibility of neuronal and protein activity. The brightly coloured images generated in this manner are then used (without any information about the particular person whose brain it is) to graphically represent certain types. American anti-drug agencies, for example, feature images of 'the brain on Ecstasy' on their websites, images often formatted so that teachers and other educators can quickly make PowerPoint presentations out of them. Looking at an image that has certain red, blue and yellow shapes, and comparing it to an image placed next to it and labelled 'the normal brain' (as if one could actually capture the clinical artefact 'the normal brain' in a picture), the viewer can see for him/ herself that drugs do indeed appear to 'fry your brain', as the American television commercial has it. What exactly the coloured shapes stand for is not made clear; neither are audiences informed of the fact that ordinary people who don't use drugs and who don't have brain abnormalities don't all have identical-looking brain scan images.

The normal brain that is presented so as to highlight the message that taking drugs changes the brain structure, or perhaps the function (such key scientific differences are not relevant for popular purposes) is not what Galton called a 'real generalization'. The production and labelling of the image rely on the more primitive technique of choosing an image generated from a specific individual and simply labelling it as representing a whole, rather large, group. In that sense the normal brain featured by the US National Institute for Drug Abuse (NIDA) is just like the aboriginal skeletons that used to be displayed in museums – an image of someone's actual body that is not seen as representing a person, but rather as a perfectly accurate signifier of a type.

The second currently popular format for visually representing deviance and criminality is far less pictorial. Biomedical science today is highly visual, but bureaucratic organizations are still living in the age of largely black-and-white and mainly textual formats. In bureaucratic representations of deviance (such as those used by the probation and parole service, or among school psychologists dealing with 'children at risk'), a ubiquitous knowledge format is the risk assessment form. Risk information is not always conveyed in the same format, since each kind of expert and each type of institution has somewhat different interests and somewhat different standards for what is important. But the common denominator is an interest in isolating and managing subpopulations differentiated not through a certain physiology or a shared neurosis but rather through a shared risk. 'Women at risk of domestic abuse' is one such type; offenders with a high risk of violent re-offending is another; patients with an elevated risk of heart attacks is another.

Risk classifications are also used to provide services to individuals in a personalized manner; but the point here is that typical risk formats – such as lists of items to be checked off supplemented by a statement such as 'a score of four or higher indicates high risk' – enable the constitution of new human types. New human types (women at risk of breast cancer, boys at risk of dropping out of school, etc.) have been created by a combination of biomedical and bureaucratic knowledges, but they have on occasion been enthusiastically embraced by the ordinary people in question. The internet provides access to numerous support groups not only for those who suffer from certain diseases or conditions (e.g. being HIV positive) but also for those who are merely 'at risk', for example because genetic testing has determined that they carry a gene that may or may not give rise to an actual illness. These groups function somewhat like those for young gay people 'coming out', or for alcoholics in recovery, but the common denominator of the group is being in the same risk category, not necessarily sharing an identity.

The new risk-based human type is visualized and otherwise represented in a variety of ways. Genetic counsellors draw family trees in which relatives affected by a particular condition appear not as persons with a biography but as black squares or circles, a coding practice that depersonalizes the relatives in question not only for the counsellor but also for the patient, who receives a copy of the family tree in question and thus sees his/her family in a new way. More relevant to criminology are the formats used to predict risks of recidivism and to manage probation and parole processes – the quasi-actuarial tables and bureaucratic forms that are the currency of what some have called 'the risk society'.

'Whodunit?' Criminality as a matter of unique identity

As we have seen, scientific truths about human wrongdoing have relied on images of and discourses about human types, since – as Aristotle said long ago – science is concerned with general categories and truths, not with individual events. But while knowledge of types comprises a key element in the work of school psychologists, probation officers, and a host of other public officials, the labours carried out by police to investigate crimes and to collar criminals have limited use in this area. Detection work may well begin with general truths (now often in the form of 'profiles') but general truths about human types never solve actual crimes. Detection requires the identification of individuals, not types. In *Murder on the Orient Express* the Belgian detective, Hercule Poirot, states as a fact that Italians generally stab their victims, while the English are fond of poisoning: but knowledge of nationally specific methods of murder, while perhaps initiating certain lines of inquiry, can never prove beyond reasonable doubt who actually killed the victim in question.

If finding the actual individual who committed the particular crime is a task that requires knowlege beyond the anthropological, sociological and psychological generalizations about types that we have surveyed in the previous section, the work of identifying the individual is rendered particularly difficult, but also particularly rewarding, in the case of repeat offenders. In the late nineteenth century the criminal justice systems of many countries began to distinguish between those who had committed a single crime, however serious, and those 'habitual offenders' and recidivists who made a career out of crime. While anyone might murder once in a fit of passion, habitual offenders were regarded as a distinct, deviant, identity-based group. This group was regarded as requiring different dispositions (such as the indeterminate sentence, an invention of this time period).

Targeting habitual offenders was not easy, however, in the big and anonymous cities of the late nineteenth century. How could one tell if offender X had a record or not, assuming that they did not volunteer this information and assuming that they were not personally known to the arresting officers or other officials? Many police departments in the 1880s and 1890s had voluminous photograph albums of offenders, and the most notorious criminals were often featured in 'rogues' galleries' that could be seen on a daily basis by the police and other state personnel. (In the US one can still see rogues' galleries of the FBI's 'most wanted' on the walls of post offices and public buildings.) But while one might be able to widely distribute many copies of the pictures of a few particularly wanted criminals, for most run-of-the-mill repeat offenders, it was not practical for large police departments to leaf through thousands of photographs of previously convicted people to see if the current suspect was to be found among them.

This information systems difficulty underscores the more general point that, in the criminal justice system as in all bureaucracies, the accuracy of a written or pictorial representation is often beside the point. The real challenge is devising and implementing a filing system that will allow for quick retrieval of the desired information at the right time and with a minimum of expense.

The first person who successfully implemented a solution to the complex problems of generating, sorting, filing and retrieving criminal records was the Paris police employee Alphonse Bertillon. The young Alphonse had grown up in a house full of anthropometric instruments: his father was a scientist whose friends included the leading statisticians and anthropologists of his day. While Bertillon senior focused, as anthropologists did, on human types, the son realized that the methodology of measuring the outside of human bodies could be somewhat modified to suit the purposes of police departments. Since the police's interest lay precisely in individualizing the criminal, Alphonse Bertillon's representational project was in a sense the reverse of Galton's. While Galton sought to use images of individuals to represent the group, Bertillon devised techniques for relegating to the background that which is common to the group and highlighting instead that which is unique to the individual – the non-racial features that allow us to recognize someone walking down the street as Mr X.

It became clear to the pioneers of forensic measurement that the more measurements one took of an individual body, the surer one could be about personal identity. More numerous and more precise measurements than the vague descriptions that most witnesses provide were needed for legal identification. Bertillon hypothesized that even if two people's noses, say, were not only similar but identical, this did not mean that other parts of their bodies would also be identical. Thus, he decided that police departments should take 11 separate physical measurements, and, on top of that, record hair colour and eye colour with great precision. Bertillon decided, for example, that his system would use over 50 eye colours.

In keeping with the view common in his day that people of the same racial group had markedly different, almost unique ear shapes, Bertillon spent a large amount of energy – and a large amount of the space allotted to each criminal on a file card – on the ear. As Simon Cole's authoritative history of criminal identification techniques tells us, Bertillon's cards divided the ear into four areas and provided four possible descriptors for each of these (Cole, 2001). To save money, the description thus generated was not written out in full, but abbreviated using Bertillon's own system. Each ear was thus described by an apparently incomprehensible succession of 16 letters, the order of the letters of course also being standardized.

Interestingly, an early Sherlock Holmes mystery also relies on the notion that human ears are highly distinctive. As Carlo Ginzburg notes in an article linking detective casework to psychoanalytic case studies, Holmes's ability to solve a mystery – concerning a pair of severed ears mailed in a box to an otherwise impeccably respectable lady – lay precisely in the fact that, like Bertillon, and unlike the Metropolitan Police, he was up on the most recent findings of anthropometrics. Here's Ginzburg's quote from the Holmes mystery:

> As a medical man, you are aware, Watson, that there is no part of the body which varies so much as the human ear. Each ear is as a rule quite distinctive and differs from all other ones. In last year's *Anthropological Journal* you will find two short monographs from my pen upon the subject. I had, therefore, examined the ears in the box and had carefully noted their anatomical peculiarities. Imagine my surprise, then, when on looking at Miss Cushing [the lady to whom the ears had been mailed]

I perceived that her ear corresponded exactly with the female ear which I had just inspected. The matter was entirely beyond coincidence. There was the same shortening of the pinna, the same broad curvei of the upper lobe, the same convolution of the inner cartilage . . . (Quoted in Ginzburg, 1987, p 98)

Holmes thus concludes that the lady had to be the sister of the victim, which needless to say turns out to be true.

This notion about the uniqueness of ears lingers in the criminal justice system's unconscious. Unlike passport photographs and driver's licence photographs, mug shots – which were standardized when Bertillon began to insist on using the same lighting and the same focal length for all criminal portraits – still include a profile, and some claim that this is because of the old belief about the value of ears as unique signs of personal identity.

Nevertheless, the vast amount of labour involved in generating criminal record databases on the Bertillon system was soon rendered redundant, as a new theory of human individuality came to the fore. The new idea was that the fingerprint, not the ear, was the one indubitably accurate marker of individuality.

The use of fingerprints as identity documents for legal purposes was pioneered in British India. British imperial authorities, who had taken control of India from the East India Company in the wake of the 1857 rebellion, worried about fraud among their subjects. They feared that people were claiming property and pensions that did not rightly belong to them but to some other, often dead, person. William Herschel, fingerprinting pioneer and grandson of the famous astronomer, wrote that there were alleged pensioners 'whose vitality . . . has been a distracting problem to government in all countries' (cited in Cole, 2001, p 64). The persistent problem of welfare fraud was, the British thought, aggravated by the fact that Indians all looked alike, and that written descriptions such as 'black hair and black eyes', while useful in countries like England, were useless for detecting fraudulent claims among Indians. (Chinese police authorities today, incidentally, do not bother to record eye colour or hair colour, for obvious reasons; instead, they note the way in which the eyelid folds.)

Having been used in India for some time, fingerprinting migrated to Europe and North America and from the realm of welfare fraud into the domain of police records. Its introduction was slow because the system had to compete with the existing Bertillon system. The rivalry between the two systems did not hinge on whether Bertillon's measurements and descriptions were a more accurate marker of individuality than the fingerprint; there was a general consensus that both types of information, under ideal conditions, generated unique representations. The real issue had to do with information storage and retrieval. If pensioners or property owners put their fingerprint on a document, it was easy to check whether claimant X, appearing before the authorities, had the same fingerprint as the one on the document. But in the context of police work, it would not be very helpful to simply collect fingerprint impressions from all convicted or charged offenders, for it would be clearly inefficient to expect the arresting officer to then laboriously go through the whole archive of existing fingerprints and compare each one to that of the current offender.

For police purposes, what was really needed was not a method for generating a unique record, but rather a system for archiving records and indexing them for future use. Our old friend Francis Galton was one of the inventive men who tried to find a way to sort fingerprint patterns into numbered groups so as to generate a filing system. At first he devised a very fine-grained system, something like Bertillonage, with 60 types of fingerprint whorls, but then he decided that there were only three basic types of whorls and that it would be best to treat more minor differences as subtypes.

While Galton and others were experimenting with information technologies to sort, archive and retrieve fingerprint data, the British Home Office established a committee to recommend whether to accept the Bertillon system or fingerprinting for use in Britain. The committee recommended, in 1893, that the Bertillon system be implemented nationally, not so much because the measurements generated more accurate identifications but because it was easier to retrieve records.

In the US, by contrast, fingerprinting became accepted more quickly, in part because a few famous criminal cases from India demonstrated to international police and legal authorities that fingerprints unsuspectingly left behind at the scene of the crime could be successfully used to convict in cases where there were no witnesses and little other evidence. An additional factor that helped the eventual success of fingerprinting was that while the Bertillon-system operators could quickly find and retrieve existing records, taking the 11 measurements and closely observing the ear and other body parts that needed to be described on the form took a lot of time and required certain conditions that were often absent in the field. Thus, even though the Bertillon system had excellent retrieval capabilities, it was more laborious at the point of data entry, to use a computer-age analogy.

Today, the image of the fingerprint is a cliché signifier for policing and criminal justice generally. (Sadly, I have to report that the undergraduate criminology programme in which I teach features a fingerprint image on the cover of the handbook.) But it is more than that: it has become a familiar icon of human individuality as such. It is used by both state and commercial institutions to signify uniqueness and personalization. For example, a large craft show in my own city, the 'One of a Kind' show, uses the fingerprint – the generic fingerprint, which is rather an oxymoron, but let that pass – as its logo. It seems that the highly magnified image of a fingerprint is capable of signifying the importance of identifying and marking individuality not only in criminals but even among Christmas presents.

The success of the fingerprint was not due to inherent scientific superiority. In fact, fingerprinting succeeded in the legal system precisely because, unlike high-status scientific discourse such as the pronouncements of forensic psychiatrists, it was regarded as merely technical, and hence as neutral, untheoretical and uncontroversial. In his book *Suspect Identities*, Cole shows that international networks of fingerprint examiners explicitly defined their work as 'technical' rather than scientific, and that this was the key to their still unchallenged success (Cole, 2001). In addition, whereas criminal trials often featured battles between psychiatrists wielding conflicting theories, the fingerprint examiners made a pact not to contest each other's expert judgements in court so as to protect the honour of their craft. Because there were no counter expert witnesses, juries, lawyers and judges all got used to thinking of fingerprint evidence as uncontestable, not just uncontested – even though fingerprint impressions, especially when taken at the scene of a crime, often require a fair amount of interpretation.

Although the fingerprint is still the visual icon par excellence of the criminal justice system's quest to identify 'who done it', and of individuality as such, in recent years another technology of identification has to a large extent displaced fingerprinting, at least in the context of major murder and rape trials. That technology is of course DNA sampling and typing. It is unlikely that DNA will totally replace the fingerprint; for example, in those countries in which every citizen has an identity document with a fingerprint, it would be cumbersome and expensive to replace the fingerprint under the photograph with an image of the person's DNA profile. But in certain policing situations (as well as in other contexts, e.g. paternity determination), DNA sampling and typing has become the technique of choice.

The way in which DNA can be tapped to reveal 'who done it' has been brought to the fore in some recent cases in which wrongfully convicted prison inmates were set free after DNA tests. Thus DNA has come to be associated with truth in criminal justice, and even with freedom. It is likely that just as many people have been put away behind bars through retroactive DNA testing as have been liberated, but given that wrongful convictions are more newsworthy than ordinary convictions, the general impression, at the second-level or mythical order of signification, is that DNA tests equal truth – and the truth, as they say, shall set you free.

From the perspective of visualization techniques, it is important to note that, unlike the taking of fingerprint impressions, DNA sampling and typing cannot be done by the average cop on the beat or by an ordinary prison official. Scientific expertise is required both to do the test and to interpret the results. Additionally, the idea that DNA is unique to the individual does not rest on everyday observation of one's relatives, but on a scientific theory that most of us have to accept on faith. The vertically arranged smudges, blown up thousands of times, that are presented to judges and juries as 'the DNA evidence', are thus not as directly visual as Bertillon's ear, or even the fingerprint impression. The form that the image takes suggests that technology is necessary for the criminal justice system to produce truth.

The use of DNA tests in the criminal justice system – and in other systems – is thus linked to a new, highly mediated, scientific form of visuality, in which the image we look at bears no resemblance at all to any body or body part. Humans can't see gene sequences. And the images that we do see are not even magnified genes. We thus gaze at images that show what happens when a certain liquid is used to manipulate a microscopic bit of human tissue so as to generate an abstract image. The black-and-white smudges can only be read as a visible trace of crime if one puts one's faith in science and technology. The quest to render individual criminality visible – visible not only to experts but to ordinary jurors and to the public at large – that was pioneered by skull-measuring anthropologists and refined by Bertillon and the fingerprint experts, thus comes to a curious kind of end with the widespread use of DNA tests.

Chapter 5
The Authority of the Detective and the Birth of the Forensic Gaze

Edgar Allan Poe's 1841 short story The *Murders in the Rue Morgue* is widely regarded as the first-ever detective story. The question of who committed the crime drives the plot, as would become standard in the genre of detective fiction/murder mysteries (which would popularly come to be known as 'whodunits'), but the answer to the question takes a highly unusual form. The murderer who savaged two women in their own Paris apartment turns out to be an orang-utan who had escaped from the custody of his world-traveller sailor owner.

The orang-utan as criminal is obviously an unusual plot device; but there are several other plot elements in The *Murders in the Rue Morgue* which are commonly found today in detective thrillers. Three of these will be mentioned in this introductory section: the homoerotic couple, the alienation of the detective from the city's normal life, and the particular mental skills that detection is said to require.

A particularly enduring feature of the detective genre (one that is shared with American road movies) is the use of a male duo. In Poe's story, written well before the popularity of the concept of the homosexual, the bond between the detective, Auguste Dupin, and his sidekick is frankly homoerotic. The two men are shown sharing a household, refusing (or simply uninterested in) family or girlfriends, having a great time together, and wandering about the city at night together enjoying their camaraderie and indulging their curiosity about others. Arthur Conan Doyle did not place Dr Watson fully inside Sherlock Holmes's household, perhaps because by the end of the nineteenth century the spectre of Oscar Wilde made it impossible to present male–male love innocently, but it is clear from the stories that Dr Watson adores Holmes. Late in the series Dr Watson is said to have got married, but the wife is never shown as objecting to Watson's sudden and often lengthy disappearances from the marital home. In current representations there is often greater authorial anxiety to ensure viewers or readers do not imagine the lead characters to be gay: for example, in the Colin Dexter *Dalziel and Pascoe* series, Pascoe is married and his wife plays a role in the stories (and an even greater role in the television series), while Dalziel is often shown having quickie sex with various women, even witnesses.

And yet, the homoeroticism inherent in the very intense bond created by joint detection is never totally suppressed. Dalziel treats everyone including Pascoe with contempt, but despite that Pascoe has much affection for 'the fat man', making him best man at his wedding and godfather (a doting and sentimental godfather) to his daughter. To refer to another well-known British example, in the final episode of the *Inspector Morse* television series, Morse's sergeant, who in previous episodes is repeatedly shown being treated sadistically by Morse, is shown literally weeping over Morse's dead body. Like 'road movies' featuring two close buddies, and war movies in which the main emotional bond is between two male comrades, detective fiction provides a safe place for male viewers/readers to imaginatively inhabit an action-packed world that is also a world without women – but without being directly confronted with the spectre of homosexuality. How female audiences relate to this plot feature is less clear – but, as feminist film critics have repeatedly shown, most mass entertainment is designed for the male viewer, even if women also enjoy the tales.

The two-detective scenario may be important from the point of view of providing a safe outlet for generally repressed emotions but, in both films and novels, it also serves an important formal function. Since describing the thinking processes of the detective in detail would require great chunks of grey prose, in novels, and awkward first-person voice-overs in films, having two detectives rather than one means that more dialogue can be used. Significantly, Poe's original story is narrated by the sidekick, and from his point of view. This works to keep the reader in suspense until the very end, because even when the great Dupin or the great Sherlock has figured out the mystery, the sidekick who tells the story is still in the dark, which means the reader is also in the dark.

It is important that the sidekick in the Poe story, like his better-known successor Dr Watson, is always in awe of the detective. The reader identifies with the narrator, as is normal in the novel genre, and so the detective appears as 'great' without too much authorial effort being required. To have a story told in the first person, but by the secondary character, means that the story has a 'you were there' feeling, something more difficult to accomplish in third-person narration; but at the same time, the reader is put in the role of admiring helper, not that of crime solver. Furthermore, since the somewhat dull sidekick needs to have every step in the deductive process explained to him, the author can very easily take the time to didactically explain to we the readers how the brilliant detective's brain works – while still maintaining a lively format with lots of dialogue and a feeling of immediacy.

Whether they are part of a duo or whether they are loners, fictional male detectives are resolutely single or divorced, often alcoholic, and always leading irregular lives. This is more than a plot device to enable the hunt for killers to go on at all hours without any domestic responsibilities impinging on the detective's time and interrupting the plot, although of course it serves that purpose. A more important effect of this presentation of the detective's private life is what we could call the 'mean streets' effect, following American detective author Raymond Chandler's famous phrase.

The detective story was born in the bourgeois Victorian city, but its focus was and has always been not the Jane Austen-type conventional aspects of bourgeois life (engagements, career choices, marriages, inheritances) but rather the dark underside of urban life. Nevertheless, while spending most if not all their time prowling the 'bad' parts of the city, and always at night, the detective is not himself a member of the underclasses. We the readers/viewers do not see the criminal elements through their own eyes. There is now a small subgenre of crime fiction that tells murder stories from the standpoint of the killer, but such accounts are rare. In detective fiction as in most crime stories, we see evil and crime from the outside, by means of the eyes of the detective – that middle-class and law-abiding citizen whose work consists of investigating the nasty goings-on that are invisible to middle-class people going about their daily routine.

And yet, being almost always single, suffering from insomnia and alcoholism, and lacking most conventional trappings of urban living, the detective is never truly at home in the bourgeois urban world either. Retired fictional detectives are generally shown as longing to get back to 'the job', and are depicted as detached from and sometimes failures at everyday affairs. For example, the protagonist of the 1990s British television hit series *Inspector Morse* tries hard to take up bird watching when confined to his home on health leave, but he just cannot enjoy this ordinary pastime. Similarly, the lawyerly detective Kavanagh QC (played in the television series by John Thaw, already famous for playing Inspector Morse) is shown attempting to emulate his more conventional retired colleague's fly-fishing hobby, but to no avail. His awkwardness with the fishing rod is a powerful sign telling us that he is wholly devoted to his work and cannot adapt his body to ordinary middle-class men's leisure pursuits. And Sherlock Holmes, notoriously, became strangely melancholic and began to do serious drugs when not engaged in a case.

Thus, the second feature of the Poe story highlighted here – the detective's permanent state of alienation from the very bourgeois existence that his work seeks to uphold – is possibly the key element distinguishing detective fiction as a genre. Whether acting as part of a duo or alone, the detective is always a loner and an outsider: he is the go-between between society's two halves. Through reading murder mysteries and police procedurals, generations of quite conventional readers have been able to vicariously experience the 'darkest' corners of their cities – while at the same time not being brought to the point of actually sympathizing or identifying with those who live full-time in the 'mean streets'. In so far as readers see the action from the detective's point of view, we take up his (or less often her) voyeuristic standpoint. We are able to enjoy a good read about a nasty murder because we don't really identify with the denizens of the mean streets. We can experience a horrified pleasure as we go over the gory details of a murder, but without fully experiencing either the fear of victims or the evil thoughts of the murderer. We can enjoy analysing people's words and actions and trying to guess who the murderer might be, learning something about the seamier side of life but remaining firmly ensconced in our own safe armchair.

A third feature of Poe's story, one that would also prove highly influential, concerns the particular sort of brilliance attributed to the detective. Auguste Dupin is shown to be fabulously intelligent, but he is carefully distinguished from mathematicians and other head-in-the-clouds smart guys. The first quarter or so of the story is in fact devoted not to the kind of opening we now have come to expect – the discovery of a dead body – but rather to a long theoretical disquisition on the specificity of the sort of knowledge that makes Dupin suited to a job that at the time did not exist in real life, namely, detection.

Poe calls this very special kind of smart reasoning 'analytical' knowledge. According to Poe's pioneering story, the analytical mind combines strong logical powers with two other things: a quasi-intuitive sixth sense about human frailties and a computer-like vast storehouse of assorted, non-specialized information. Card playing is given as an example of the analytical mind at work. The good player has to be able to read other players' facial expressions – something that mathematicians would be unlikely to do well – as well as quickly perform probabilistic calculations in his head; in addition, he has to be able to remember which cards were played by which players in earlier turns.

The particular combination of deductive skills, intuitive knowledge of the human psyche, and variegated information that constitutes what Poe calls the analytical mind and Arthur Conan Doyle's Dr Watson calls the 'calling' of detection, is explicitly discussed and explained in the first (1887) Sherlock Holmes story, *A Study in Scarlet*. Here Conan Doyle has Dr Watson spend large amounts of time – before any actual mystery has been introduced – trying to understand just what it is that Holmes is good at. Watson's puzzled inquiries serve to explain to a reading public not yet familiar with detective fiction what kind of story they have in their hands.

Watson explains to the reader that while Holmes has a good knowledge of applied biology, he is not a real scientist, since he only understands plant poisons. His archive does not fit the norms governing the knowledge-gathering activities encountered by people like Watson in late Victorian England. Holmes cares nothing for shooting and fishing, he has no family and no estate and, apparently, no desire to acquire any of these accoutrements and habits of the gentlemanly life. But on the other hand, he is not quite the specialist, the then rising technician or professional, the sort of man whose knowledge is acquired through formal education rather than breeding. So if Holmes is neither a gentleman nor a scientist, what exactly is he? After much frustration, Watson – who is a doctor, but an army doctor, not a scientist – resorts to the technique of drawing up a list of Holmes's range of knowledge:

1. Knowledge of literature: Nil.
2. Knowledge of philosophy: Nil.
3. Knowledge of astronomy: Nil.
4. Knowledge of politics: Feeble.
5. Knowledge of botany: Variable. Well up on belladonna, opium, and poisons generally. Knows nothing of practical gardening.
6. Knowledge of geology: Practical, but limited. Tells at a glance different soils from each other . . .
7. Knowledge of chemistry: Profound.
8. Knowledge of anatomy: Accurate, but unsystematic.
9. Knowledge of sensational literature: Immense. He appears to know every detail of every horror perpetrated in this century . . . (Conan Doyle, 2001, p 18)

Watson cannot fit Holmes into his existing classification of occupations and knowledges. This is precisely because Holmes's distinction – his particular kind of capital, so to speak – is his ability simultaneously to use diverse, heterogeneous and mainly applied knowledges of diverse origins, which have nothing in common except the fact that they are useful for detective work.

The reader first meets Holmes as he is performing chemical experiments and coming up with a new original invention – a reagent that will react only with haemoglobin, which will mean that minute bloodstains can be identified with certainty. Nevertheless, Holmes is neither a chemist nor a doctor nor any other kind of scientist: he is a new assemblage of knowledges, and hence the protagonist of a new genre. Quite cleverly, Conan Doyle's mention of 'sensational literature' under point 9 of Watson's list enables him also to specify his (Conan Doyle's) own literary inventiveness and educate the reader in the characteristics of the new genre, the detective story. Point 9 on the list tells us that the stories featuring Holmes will deal with the same events covered in sensational crime stories, but will deal with them differently, from a detached observer's point of view rather than melodramatically, as was the norm in the tremendously popular Victorian genre of 'sensation' literature.

The 'detective', who became a familiar figure in late-nineteenth-century bourgeois households much more through fiction than through newspapers (given that only Scotland Yard and the Paris police had anything like a detective unit as late as the 1860s), was therefore a man of knowledge, but he was not exactly a scientist. Some analysts of the detective genre have so emphasized the role that the Victorian public's fascination with science played in the popularity of the detective story that they have forgotten that the detective is not simply a scientist who runs around the city instead of staying in his laboratory. As Poe clarifies at some length, and as Dr Watson carefully elaborates, the analytical mind is characterized by a peculiar eclecticism that in some ways runs counter to the purer methodologies of scientific work.

Nevertheless, second-hand scientific knowledge, while rarely available to real-life police officers in the nineteenth century, was often crucial to finding out 'who done it' in nineteenth-century fiction, just as it is in today's forensically oriented television shows. Poe's *Murders in the Rue Morgue* is a case in point: the police are shown as baffled by the crime. And one of the things that Dupin brings to the problem of 'who done it' that the police – the real police – could not have utilized in those days is science. (The lack of scientific expertise in real-life police departments is one reason why early fictional detectives, right up until the 1950s, were usually private detectives rather than cops.)

Tracing the steps that Dupin follows, and travelling with him along a path that the police could not have discovered, allows us to see concretely just how 'the detective' emerges as a new type of authority, namely, a very special walking archive of knowledge useful to solve criminal 'cases'. First of all, it is not clear how anyone could have entered the women's Rue Morgue apartment. In an early version of the 'locked room' scenario repeatedly used by Agatha Christie with great success, the doors leading up to the victims' apartment are said to have remained locked, and the windows are described as being too high off the ground and too far from potential handholds to have facilitated entry. But instead of simply giving up, as the police do, the inaccessibility of the murder scene encourages Dupin to search his vast archive of rarely used knowledge to retrieve whatever bit of scientific knowledge – in this case, about the size and the habits of certain large primates – might fit with the observed clues.

If the physical examination of the scene only produces bafflement among the police, the verbal examination of witnesses who heard noises proves equally mysterious, to the flat-footed cops at any rate. (The flat-footed, not-too-bright cop is introduced, here as in countless subsequent detective stories, so as to highlight the brilliance of the protagonist, in a perfect example of the semiotic principle that meaning is created through contrast.) In recounting what the witnesses told police, Poe appeals to the then current fascination with classifying humans into types. But what makes his story good literature is precisely that it also subtly undermines the obsession with types. Paris being a cosmopolitan city, many of the neighbours are said to belong to ethnic groups other than French. In a clever twist on popular stereotypes about nationality, these witnesses all declare that the criminal must have been a member of some other nationality, and one whose language the witness does not understand. An English tailor living nearby, for example, deposes that he is sure that the murderer's voice 'was not the voice of an Englishman. Appeared to be that of a German. Might have been a woman's voice. Does not understand German.' A Spanish undertaker, in turn, was sure that the shrill voice was 'that of an Englishman – is sure of this. Does not understand the English language, but judges by the intonation.' For his part, a nearby Italian pastry chef thought it was the voice of a Russian, but 'never conversed with a native of Russia' (Poe [1841], 1998, pp 56–57).

As the subtle ridiculing of linguistic profiling suggests to Dupin, and through him to the readers – but not to the dull police officers – the criminal in question did not speak any European language. Because Dupin happens to have an encyclopedic – but highly practical – knowledge of evolution and biology, he is able to form the hypothesis that the crime might have been committed by an exotic quasi-human being who might sound Russian to an Italian and English to a Spaniard but definitely not to an Englishman.

In addition to critically scrutinizing the witness statements, Dupin takes stock of the scene of the crime much more empirically than the police. The police had made quick assumptions about burglary being the motive: by contrast, Dupin is shown setting aside all theories and carefully examining every little clue with an open mind (just like a scientist). He collects some odd, non-human hair, for instance, and files it away for future analysis. Then he observes that while the window would not allow a human to go in and out, some other, less evolved but stronger creature might have been able to jump in and out. This then leads to forming the hypothesis that the criminal was a being *resembling* a human being – a being having a voice, but not speaking in any known language; having hair, but not human-looking hair; able to use hands to climb, but with the distance between handholds suggesting non-human measurements.

The hypothesis arrived at by a combination of very close empirical attention to clues and unusually keen deductive powers cannot be confirmed purely by logic, however. Some information about potential quasi-human beings will be required to actually solve the crime. And it so happens that Dupin has that information. First, he has a prior archive of knowledge about zoology, and so can fit the clues to the features of various primates. But he also reads every single item in the newspaper every day (not a typical scientist's occupation). And from reading the paper, he knows that an orang-utan from Southeast Asia, brought to France by a travelling sailor, had escaped from its owner in a Parisian park. Therefore, the orang-utan did it. So the criminal was a colonial subject indeed: a dark, large, dangerous creature. But in a plot twist differentiating the Poe story from other European tales in which colonial subjects and entities play a role, he/it was not the standard 'savage'.

Learning to look for clues: the detective as semiotician

A very notable feature of Poe's story, one that would prove tremendously influential for the genre of detective fiction, is that detection is shown to require not only strong logical deductive powers – 'little grey cells', in the famous phrase of Agatha Christie's Hercule Poirot – but something that mathematicians and most other academics lack: an unusual ability to observe. What makes Dupin special, Poe tells us, is not so much 'the validity of the inference' but 'the quality of the observation. The necessary knowledge is that of *what* to observe' (Poe, 1998, p 46). This is just what is emphasized in the Sherlock Holmes stories. As is well known, the stories regularly show Holmes focusing on details that remain invisible to Dr Watson and to the police. A small stain on someone's tie would likely remain unobserved or, if seen, would appear to Watson and to most of us readers merely as food. But Holmes's archive of data about particular foods and their appearance at various stages of decomposition allows him to read the stain much more specifically, e.g. as indicating that the wearer of the tie is staying at the sort of hotel where a certain kind of breakfast is likely to be served. Along the same lines, specks on someone's shoes would look like generic dirt to others, but they appear to Holmes as clues pointing to a particular location with a particular kind of mud. Typically, in *A Case of Identity*, Holmes explains to Watson that the young lady visiting them for advice must be a typist (he reads subtle lines on her hands and wrists to determine her occupation) and must be short-sighted (her nose has faint lines left by the spectacles she habitually wears).

The close attention to the physical traces left not only by criminal activity but by everyday activity on people's bodies and clothes, on floors, walls, gardens and objects – the key feature of the forensic gaze – is such a familiar perspective today that we tend to take it for granted that every activity leaves traces and that every criminal unwittingly sheds clues, including bits of his/her own body, which can be used to reconstruct what happened (Ginzburg, 1987). The world's details can be read, looking backward as it were, to generate an imaginary replay of the events involved in the crime. This insistence on examining the traces of the criminal's identity left upon the urban landscape and upon bodies, clothes and rooms – a way of seeing that is familiar to us today from fictional police novels and programmes and from crime news – was a new way of seeing when Poe and Conan Doyle pioneered the detective story.

While there is no direct relation between developments in criminal justice and innovations in fiction, it is nevertheless important to note that there are some correspondences. Before the rise of what I call 'the forensic gaze', English criminal justice relied mainly on spoken testimony and to some extent also on papers and documents. Even though questions of identity were certainly important, physical evidence was rarely determinative in criminal trials until the late nineteenth century (Thomas, 1999). Furthermore, the increased sophistication of the adversarial system and the increased length of criminal trials meant that lawyers tended to introduce a greater number of witnesses with a wider range of evidence. Judges, for their part, took a more passive role during most of the trial, though often exercising greater discretion in excluding certain kinds of evidence and limiting the weight of admissible evidence (Allen, 1997). Evidence was not always carefully scrutinized for admissibility and weight (mainly because, in England, there was no court of criminal appeals until 1907); nevertheless, the attention to clues that marks the genre of detective fiction is not unrelated to developments in Victorian-era criminal courts.

The rise of the detective and the tremendous popularity of this figure throughout the twentieth century is therefore part of a larger story about the criminal law. In regard to real-life trials, people today are misled by seeing the protracted fights about every tiny bit of evidence that take place in atypical, well-funded trials (e.g. the OJ Simpson trial and the Michael Jackson trial). Complex battles about clues and their interpretation are notoriously scarce in low-level, workaday trials and even more so in the large number of cases that are plea bargained. But people imagine that sophisticated disputes about forensic details go on every day in their local criminal courts.

The impression created by the media's selective coverage of criminal trials is reinforced by developments in fictional representations. The forensic gaze, as we shall see in the next chapter, can be said to have reached its all-time apotheosis in the American television programme *CSI: Crime Scene Investigation*, in which the physical traces of the crime are always determinative. In *CSI* forensics is no longer a subordinate technical pursuit but has taken over the whole sphere of detection.

Poe's philosophizing about the analytical mind and Dr Watson's lengthy inventory of Holmes's range of knowledge can be regarded as both narrating and performing the birth of the forensic gaze, the gaze now privileged in countless crime television shows. It is important to note that contrary to what one might have expected, it is the self-taught jack of all trades, Holmes, who perfects the forensic gaze; Watson, who is medically trained, is shown as sharing English law's traditional preference for words, stories and documents (Welsh, 1992).

As Ronald Thomas's insightful study of detective fiction notes, Holmes represents a marked turn toward legal objectivism (Thomas, 1999, ch. 5). Holmes would rather spend hours analysing the chemical composition and the watermark of the paper used to write a note than spend a lot of time following up on the note's contents. Neither the spoken words of clients and witnesses nor the texts found in notes and diaries are treated as the best indicators of what really happened. For Holmes, human speech, even in written form, is always potentially deceptive. After all, no witness knows 'what to observe', to repeat Poe's words. Objective clues, by contrast, speak for themselves, often revealing secrets that are not known to any humans (or which are being concealed by criminals). The focus on the material world is a knowledge preference that the forensic gaze shares with the scientific gaze: but while the scientist's scrutiny of the material world is aimed at revealing general truths – about natural types, about the causal relations between generic events, about the laws of motion of the universe – Holmes's scrutiny is solely devoted to uncovering the unique story that led to this particular crime.

The detective's distinction thus lies partly in his semiotic approach to the world, his ability to see not so much general scientific truths (the general truth that arsenic is a poison does not suffice to solve crimes, even if it is important) but rather the unique narratives that can be reconstructed by observing stains, bits of dirt, and objects that are taken for granted by others as mute generic objects. Objects and the traces left by objects are turned into clues – that is, signs. If properly read, the signs make up a highly individual story – a story always reconstructed backward in time. The detective is the one who is able to determine which of the million impressions available to us at any one moment should be treated semiotically, that is, as a sign connected to other signs in a chain. The chain of meaningful material objects, stains, etc., is later turned into a verbal narrative, a feat of semiotic genius which characterizes the detective.

The fact that most Sherlock Holmes stories do not open with the conventional sign of murder – the body – is important. Other detectives already know where to start looking, namely on and around the body; but if there is no body, then it requires some inventiveness to first decide where to look. Holmes is thus shown spending a great deal of time deciding what is and is not a clue – in contrast to the more simplistic forensic gaze depicted in the US show *CSI*, where forensic technicians always have a body or some body parts to start the episode, and quickly stumble on to conveniently placed clues so the plot can get going before the first commercial break. Arthur Conan Doyle's more leisurely pace allows for a more complex approach to the semiotics of crime. As Holmes constantly reminds Watson (with little success), the first task is to observe the whole scene of crime, to look around carefully, treating *everything* as potentially meaningful. And because Holmes doesn't employ a crime-scene photographer, he has to memorize what the scene looked like for possible later use, which is another unique feat. To ordinary people, including nearly all police, who don't know what to observe, only bloodstains and footprints and a few other standard clues appear as meaningful. But to the true detective, clues are never standard; they are potentially everywhere, and it takes a special talent to determine which visual impressions are or are not clues.

To put all of this in the context of European intellectual history, we could say that for detectives, as for the Renaissance astrologers who found correspondences and divine messages on every tree leaf and every snowflake, the whole world is alive with wonderful stories which can only be told by those who have the talent and the patience to treat things as signs. Unfortunately for us moderns, however, what we are likely to see if we exercise the twentieth-century, crime-oriented semiotic imagination is a criminal behind every bush, rather than divinely ordained numerological analogies.

Let us now turn to the third element of the forensic gaze. In Poe's *The Murders in the Rue Morgue*, the combination of biological knowledge, logical powers and a superhuman ability to note and record the presence of myriad objects and substances that might later end up in the realm of semiotically important clues – the combination that is presented as constituting the detective's capital – is said to need one more element, or perhaps more accurately, one necessary habit. Only because Dupin, who regularly reads every single item in the daily newspaper, happened to have filed away, in the vast archive of his brain, a small item about a lost orang-utan, is the mystery finally solved. Along similar lines, Sherlock Holmes too is often shown as being able to retrieve from a vast storehouse of information the one little bit which has suddenly become useful. Scientific information is important, but it does not help with all the crimes; the stories involving diplomatic and royal-family mysteries, in particular, show Holmes dipping into a huge storehouse of arcane military and political information.

Again, this way of proceeding is not scientific. Scientists do not look around their environment or around the lab and note every little detail just in case it might prove relevant later. They observe and record only certain kinds of data – experimental data, in many cases, or naturally occurring but highly selected data. What coat the lab assistant was wearing on the day of the experiment, or whether it was raining when the chemical crystallized, is precisely the sort of fact that the notoriously distracted laboratory scientist does not notice. Scientists are always focused on the small part of their world that is by general agreement deemed to be scientifically relevant. The work of detection, by contrast, requires the constant exercise of the kind of archival sensibility that is the opposite of the proverbial absent-mindedness of the great scientific genius. Detection requires building up vast physical or mental filing cabinets of every kind of raw, unprocessed information about people, substances and events, with the detective's brain emulating Bertillon's clerk's ability to retrieve the particular index card that is needed at a particular point in the investigation.

The reaction against clues: Agatha Christie's Hercule Poirot

In *Five Little Pigs*, an Agatha Christie story first published in 1942, a young woman contemplating hiring Hercule Poirot to solve an old mystery says:

> I've heard about you. The things you've done. The way you have done them. It's psychology that interests you, isn't it? Well, that doesn't change with time. The tangible things are gone – the cigarette end and the footprints and the bent blades of grass. You can't look for those any more. But you can go over all the facts of the case, and perhaps talk to the people who were there at the time – they're all alive still – and then – and then, as you said just now, you can lie back in your chair and think. And you'll know what really happened. (Christie, 2003, p 76)

Agatha Christie's Belgian private detective Hercule Poirot sometimes makes fun of his predecessor Sherlock Holmes by ridiculing the idea of a leisured gentleman spending his time doing experiments with cigars so as to generate a complete archive of ashes for potential future use in criminal investigations. Poirot does have an archive, of course, or he would not be a detective, but it is an archive of human feelings and motives, not an archive of physical clues.

Like many other female crime writers of the first half of the twentieth century (e.g. Dorothy Sayers), Agatha Christie only has a passing interest in the chemical and biological traces left by criminals in the wake of their crimes. Her mysteries – both those featuring male crime-solvers and female self-appointed detectives – stimulate the reader's interest not in applied biochemistry but rather in the psychology of love, hate and greed. And, in marked contrast to most crime writing today, it's the psychology of ordinary people that is the relevant knowledge for detectives like Christie's Miss Marple and Sayers' Lord Peter Wimsey. Abnormal psycho killers were not of interest to mystery writers or their readers until much later in the twentieth century – as we shall see in a later chapter when discussing Hitchcock's pioneering representation, the 1960 film *Psycho*.

Agatha Christie's interest in everyday psychology and consequent turn away from Holmes's extreme objectivism, it could be argued, is closely related to her preference for locating her murders almost exclusively in upper-class environments. The isolated aristocratic country house, the steamboat on the Nile catering to rich European tourists, and the first-class train car in the Orient Express are some of the best-known examples of her favourite venues. These venues were portrayed in the travel literature and the fiction of the time as always containing a certain risk of invasion. The European upper classes of the period in which Christie wrote her classics (the period between World War I and World War II) were haunted by the fear of being overrun by the much more numerous underclasses at home and/or the teeming millions of colonial subjects abroad. Upper-class anxiety about invasion had fuelled the plots of numerous popular tales, from Wilkie Collins's *The Moonstone*, in which Indians are shown as striking back against the Empire by travelling to England to regain the Koh-i-noor diamond, to the numerous sensational novels featuring local urban thieves and anarchists concocting plots against the rich in the Paris, London and New York of the 1880s and 1890s.

Agatha Christie's distinction as a crime writer is precisely that she carefully eschewed the conventional plot featuring barbarians invading the great bourgeois metropolis. Similarly, she avoids psycho-killer tales of the Jack the Ripper variety. Killers who kill at random without a specific motive, and who are understood only by specialized psychiatrists, would not have helped to show off Miss Marple's or Hercule Poirot's psychologically oriented but non-medically trained 'little grey cells'. While her books are highly racist, anti-Semitic, and often classist as well, she nevertheless avoids explicitly fanning the flames of imperial and bourgeois anxieties: she very rarely casts dark foreigners or resentful servants as the villains. Instead, Christie rose to fame by focusing on the evil that lurks in the heart of the upper classes, an evil that – like homosexuality – could not be directly seen. The 'locked room' plot device routinely used in her mysteries – reiterated in the format of the popular board game 'Cluedo' ('Clue' in the US), in which, significantly, neither professional criminals nor other outsiders are given playing positions – serves precisely to exclude from the outset any investigation of the conventional criminal elements.

Accordingly, the first thing that the police and/or the detectives in a Christie mystery will do is to note, often in painstaking detail, that no outsiders could have gained access to the crime scene in question during the relevant times. Typically, the Orient Express was held up during the relevant time period by a major snowstorm which not only paralysed the train but made it impossible for anyone to come in or go out without leaving tracks in the snow. In country-house mysteries, some 'insiders' – maids and butlers mainly – carry a certain taint by virtue of their inferior class position and often emerge as early suspects. But generally speaking, Christie's stories end up revealing that the butler did not do it, and that most respectable middle- and upper-class ladies and gentlemen are indeed capable of murder, given the right motivation.

To refer back to the distinctions drawn in the previous chapter, for Christie, the criminal is always a particular individual, not a representative of a type (since the upper classes don't count as a type, they are just 'normal' people, us). And particularity and individuality, for Christie as for many other later mystery writers (especially in the UK), is much more mental than physical. The mental processes of the killer, however, are generally normal mental processes, ordinary rational-choice reasoning. The peculiarities of the insane or the psychotic are not within Christie's purview.

The approach to detection that Poirot represents, which was developed over the following few decades in the more complex mysteries authored by PD James, Ruth Rendell and others, is signified by Poirot's trademark sign: his egg-shaped head, often mentioned as the first thing that people notice about him. Heads are often synecdoches for brains (think of the famous photo of Einstein's head, in which the wild hair seems to be erupting directly from his powerful brain). And 'egg shaped' is of course connected with 'egghead'. It is the contents of Poirot's brain, his 'little grey cells' as he calls them, which represent his special powers. In contrast, Sherlock Holmes's trademark sign is the magnifying glass, which is not only a tool of the trade but also a symbol representing his, uncanny ability to see and decipher physical objects.

Poirot's egg-shaped skull and Holmes's magnifying glass are simultaneously physical entities and allegorical images. They represent, in one convenient pictorial sign, the main two approaches to detection. Subsequent crime writers have used various combinations of these two to generate new subgenres, but, it seems to me, without creating any radically new embodiment of the forensic gaze. Physical clues and verbal/emotional clues are the two basic categories of clues, and close observation of the scene of crime and of the people involved in it are the two main ways of exercising the detective trade.

The notable differences in regard to what to observe and how to reason from the observations, which divide Holmes-type objectivist detectives from amateur psychologists like Poirot, should not, however, prevent us from seeing the commonalities found throughout detective stories as a genre. The key common assumption, the unstated premise from which the whole genre flows, concerns the importance of finding the truth about crimes, with that truth being defined rather narrowly as 'who did it'. Other inquiries into crimes – about the effects on survivors, for example, or concerning the general sociological reasons why a certain demographic commits more crimes than some other group, or the potential deterrent effect of apprehension on other criminals – do not hold appeal for fiction writers. 'Who done it' is virtually the only question. The reader accustomed to the genre's conventions accepts this without thinking, and so does not question why so much more energy (in life as in fiction) is put into finding out who did it than into helping victims or preventing future crimes.

But there are great variations in the role and function of the detective's truth, the truth that is revealed in the final scene of the novel or movie. In the Holmes stories, the discovery process is mainly an opportunity for intellectual gymnastics. As the film critic Thomas Leitch puts it, 'crime is no longer a danger to individuals and an affront to society, but the pretext for an entertainingly recondite mystery that can be solved by readers willing to suspend their emotional commitments to the characters' (Leitch, 2002, p 174). In Agatha Christie's books, mystery solving is largely a pastime like playing chess. And yet, there is also an intimation of a general moral/social lesson – namely, that evil lurks in the hearts of the most respectable members of society as much as in the lower orders.

Avoiding moral-social issues, the chess-game feel of the early mysteries shows us a world in which finding who done it has little or nothing to do with larger social issues, or even with justice itself. The exclusion of ethical questions about justice is in part effected through a common plot device that distinguishes early detective fiction from today's mysteries. In a surprising number of the stories authored by Conan Doyle and Christie, the perpetrators are not brought to justice at all – either because they are dead already, or because the evidence accumulated by the detective does not amount to legally admissible evidence, or, as in *Murder on the Orient Express*, because the murder is shown to be a justified act of revenge, which Poirot suggests (with others agreeing, including the reader) should be kept from the police.

Nevertheless, the criminal justice system is never directly criticized. Poirot decides not to turn over to police the 12 first-class passengers who avenged the death of a little girl by stabbing the murderer 12 times, one person at a time, but this is not because he does not trust the system. In fact, the English legal system is vindicated in an odd way, through Colonel Arbuthnot's insistence that the 12 criminals are actually acting as 12 jury members and convicting someone who deviously escaped justice. And Sherlock Holmes works in co-operation with Scotland Yard, even though many of his mysteries do not turn out to be legal crimes.

Direct criticisms of the criminal justice system, however, appear in a remarkably open and direct manner in the American so-called hard-boiled mysteries discussed in the next chapter. In that genre, and also in the related filmic genre of 'film noir', one finds a cynical view of criminal justice. More radically, even the detective is sometimes himself driven by greed and lust rather than by a pure desire to know the truth and to identify the criminal. Even truth is not always reached; some endings are ambiguous and leave the reader/viewer with unanswered questions. Thus, truth, justice and goodness are all put in question.

With this general theme about truth and justice in mind, we now turn to the hard-boiled detective story and its close relative, the crime stories of film noir.

Chapter 6
From the Hard-Boiled Detective to the Pre-Crime Unit: American Representations of Justice

Early English detective fiction generally upholds conventional bourgeois morality. Sherlock Holmes famously uses cocaine and morphine, but this is not often mentioned, and in any case, these drugs were not as demonized in the 1890s as they are today. Most other early detectives, while often eccentric in their habits, are firmly on the side of the law-abiding and respectable. Even when evil is shown to lurk in the hearts of respectable housewives, as in Agatha Christie's fiction, at the end of the story the harmony and order of the class-divided English village is fully restored to its pre-murder condition.

In contrast to this conformist message, the US authors who developed the 'mean streets' genre (Dashiell Hammett and Raymond Chandler, most famously), revelled in shocking their bourgeois readers by revealing deep corruption not only in the heart of conventional society but even in the hearts of the detectives themselves. Hammett, who had worked as Pinkerton's private detective/bodyguard in the 1910s – an occupation in which brute violence was often used – rose to fame and fortune with books featuring a detective, Sam Spade, who in the 1930 classic *The Maltese Falcon* is revealed very early in the book as a complete and utter blackguard. Like most other so-called 'hard-boiled' private eyes, Sam Spade is not only capable of committing evil deeds, but actually does commit such deeds regularly. Cheating people, callously seducing and rejecting women, and shooting the odd minor character, all activities in the daily agenda of Spade and his successors, are portrayed not as sudden eruptions of raw emotion but rather as calculated acts. The detective's little grey cells now seem to be wholly devoted to pursuing their owner's self-interest, not the truth.

Sam Spade and Philip Marlowe, the two most famous hard-boiled detectives of all time, both suffer from an excess of masculine toughness. It is thus not coincidental that it was only after second-wave feminism, in the 1980s, that American detective stories written by women and featuring female sleuths became popular. In the original version (developed in the 1930s and 1940s), the hard-boiled detective had to be a man, a super-masculine man in fact, because controlling his emotions at all times was part of the job description. Only the constant, compulsive lighting of cigarettes – performed most memorably on the big screen by Humphrey Bogart – subtly suggested that the private eye might have some emotional needs.

The Maltese Falcon, written not as a conventional narrative but as what it would later become – a script for a famous movie – quickly introduces the main characters, and then, in Chapter 2, goes on to describe how the unflappable tough guy Sam Spade is told of the death of his employee Miles Archer:

> A telephone bell rang in the darkness. When it had rung three times bed-springs creaked, fingers fumbled on wood, something small and hard thudded on a carpeted

floor, the springs creaked again, and a man's voice said: 'Hello . . . Yes, speaking . . . Dead? . . . Yes . . . Fifteen minutes. Thanks.'

The extreme objectivism of this writing style, in which ownerless 'fingers' are shown doing something, and in which a man's voice is said to be answering the phone without our receiving any information about how the man felt, or indeed about who he is, would remain the key feature of 'hard-boiled' detective fiction for decades to come. Typically, Spade's face is often said to be 'expressionless' or 'empty'. All we know about Spade is what he does. And what he does is show no emotion when hearing about the murder of his employee.

When he goes to the crime scene, he promises the officer in charge that he will tell Archer's wife about her husband's death – only to quickly phone his female secretary to pass the unpleasant task on to her. As if this were not enough, a couple of pages later we learn that Spade had been having an affair with Archer's wife. Learning of her husband's death, she immediately suspects Spade of having killed her husband out of jealousy: she imagines that he has some feelings, for her at any rate. But Spade rejects his mistress quickly and callously, and refuses to give her comfort or sympathy. Occasionally he is shown having a bit of trouble suppressing his feelings: for example, when attending the scene of his employee's murder, he blandly says that there is no need for him as well as the homicide detectives to look at the corpse, a statement which a hopeful female reader might construe as indicating that he does have a bit of a heart somewhere. But these hints of some kind of emotional or moral self are few and far between.

Spade is not in the business of sex for the sake of love, clearly. Of course, fictional detectives are, as a group, much more interested in pursuing the truth of crimes than in developing love relationships. Either they have no relationships at all (like Holmes and Poirot) or the women are expendable, like the girls in James Bond movies. But what is remarkable about the hard-boiled detective is that, unlike Holmes and Poirot, he is not shown experiencing pleasure even in the detective's calling, namely, in discovering the truth and solving the puzzle. Sam Spade, like many other fictional and presumably real-life private eyes, is in business not for the pleasure of unravelling mysteries but merely for the money. The narrative proceeds toward a closure that will involve revealing truths, and the reader is enlisted into the work of interpreting clues and solving the riddle; but unlike the reader, Spade himself is not particularly motivated by the search for truth. He has to constantly unmask deceptions in order to save his own hide and maximize his earnings, but on the hard-boiled detective's 'mean streets' (Raymond Chandler's famous phrase), the peeling away of one layer of deception after another does not result in any stable truths. Furthermore, Sam Spade, like most other American fictional detectives of the post-Agatha Christie period, thinks nothing of contributing to the general production of lies and deceit. He is neither more virtuous nor closer to the truth than the criminals he pursues; he is simply better at their own game.

The film noir style, with its sparsely furnished interiors, ordinary unembellished streets, stark lighting and bare-bones film sets, was partly a product of the severe restrictions on movie budgets imposed during World War II as part of the general practice of rationing. But it was also partly an aesthetic choice. The stark style can be seen as a reaction against the sentimental and showy productions of the 1930s. Gone were the elaborately constructed sets of gangster films and the masses of dancing girls of the classic musical. Instead, we see a very small number of characters acting tough, with as few words as possible, either on rain-slicked night-time streets or in interiors whose most notable feature is a set of Venetian blinds – through which the California sun shines but only in menacing, arrow-like shafts of light. The film noir aesthetic provided the ideal format for bringing hard-boiled detective stories to the screen.

One of the earliest film noir movies was the earlier cited *The Maltese Falcon* (1941), directed by John Houston and starring Humphrey Bogart as Sam Spade. This featured most of the 'signs' of film noir: a beautiful and immoral femme fatale; night-time settings in which even the main actors' faces are left in the dark; relentlessly pared-down dialogue, through which few facts and almost no feelings are conveyed, leaving the spectator grasping for meaning, any meaning; anonymous and ugly 'mean streets'; and, last but not least, a constant procession of glasses of whisky and cigarettes. The sharing of whisky and cigarettes, as critics have pointed out, is in many Bogart crime films the only sign of human warmth (Klein, 1993).

Another influential film of that period that can be seen as emblematic of the cynicism about truth and justice shared by film noir and hard-boiled detective stories is *Double Indemnity* (1944). This does not use the film noir aesthetic consistently: there are a good number of scenes shot either in the sunshine or in well-lit interiors. But the amoral, meaningless, always childless, and exaggeratedly ugly California of film noir is particularly well portrayed in this classic film, which also features the archetypal femme fatale, played by Barbara Stanwyck. She is shown using her sexual wiles to inveigle a not overly moral insurance salesman into helping her to fraudulently take out a life insurance policy on her husband and to then kill him, in a complicated, 'perfect crime' scenario. Partly because the only character shown as having an interest in the truth is an insurance employee (there are no police in the film, in keeping with the cynicism about the state and the justice system that marks the novels of Hammett and Chandler), insurance fraud ends up appearing as a worse crime than murder.

The Maltese Falcon has a similarly negative relationship to criminal justice. In that story too a formal, legal crime is at the heart of the story; but the crime (the theft of a unique ancient historical artifact, the Templars' falcon) appears mainly as an offence against its private owners, who do not call the police but rather employ private personnel to recover the statue of the falcon. Thus, in both of these classic films, the criminal justice system has been replaced by the profit-seeking private sector. And crime has been displaced and overshadowed by fraud – as if to return to the eighteenth-century English criminal justice system, which only worked if and when victims themselves prosecuted.

In both films, murders and scams are deviously complex. In *Double Indemnity*, the femme fatale gets the insurance agent to first kill and then impersonate the hapless husband: an unlikely plot that relies for its plausibility on film noir's general premise that no identity is knowable and stable. In *The Maltese Falcon*,

The film noir aesthetic was the perfect format for the 1940's 'hard-boiled' detective story.

whose plot is not easy to follow, especially in the film version, much confusion is caused by the fact that there are several parties involved in shootings and other violence, not just the cops and the bad guys. But in both cases it is the fraud story and not the crime that is the most elaborate, requiring the reader to get thoroughly involved in the fine details of the history of the Templars (in the Hammett story), or in the equally arcane details of accident and life insurance policies in the case of *Double Indemnity*. Sam Spade solves the complicated puzzles, but he is not interested in either formal legal justice or substantive, equity-style justice. He is only interested in surviving and getting paid. And order and reason never prevailed on the 'mean streets' of San Francisco and Los Angeles before the murders and scams, so they cannot be restored at the end.

In *Double Indemnity*, as in *The Postman Always Rings Twice* (1946), audiences see that the private sector devotes resources to truth seeking and order restoration, but only because this helps the insurance companies' bottom line. Telling audiences that only insurance companies (or other private interests) care about the truth and have the means to discover it is a more subtly radical message than showing incompetent, flat-footed bobbies. Major movie studios would have been unlikely to produce films overtly criticizing the criminal justice system. However, the ubiquity of money-driven private eyes and insurance investigators in the crime novels and films of the period carried a certain subtle message that was at odds with the patriotic official ideologies prevalent during World War II and the Cold War period. The cynicism about truth and about justice that is evident throughout the film noir genre has never been matched in mainstream American representations.

In keeping with this displacement and downgrading of the classic questions of truth and justice, crime films of the 1940s and early 1950s, like *The Maltese Falcon*, *Double Indemnity*, *The Big Sleep*, *Mildred Pierce*, *Dial M for Murder* and *The Big Heat*, are united more by the kind of urban scenario they show and the kind of evil women they feature than by the presence of a detective or quasi-detective. In the absence of a reliable, Poirot-style protagonist, the spectator is presented by the camera with various objects and actions whose meaning needs to be deciphered. Novels can encourage readers to play detective to some extent, but it is film, as a format, that works best to devolve the forensic gaze on to the spectator.

With the notable exception of guns, most of the objects that turn out to be clues in film noir about fraud and crime are perfectly ordinary – a car, a tyre, a telephone, a calling card. But the spectator familiar with the conventions of crime films will know that if the camera lingers, however briefly, on an apparently trivial object, such as a handkerchief or a shoe, the camera action is itself a sign. It is telling the spectator: look at this closely now, file it away in your mind, as later on you'll realize it was a key clue. We don't need an author like Arthur Conan Doyle to write a full sentence such as, 'Sherlock Holmes then scrutinized the markings on the wall': the camera puts us in the place formerly occupied by the detective.

In all crime stories and films, a truth about crime/evil is always provided at the end, and the quest for that truth keeps the spectator engaged. In more conventional stories, and in most of today's detective mysteries, the revelations at the end generally serve to restore and uphold the social order. By contrast, in hard-boiled detective stories and in the related genre of film noir, the truth about a particular crime always turns out to also be a truth about the essential selfishness of the alienated individuals shown wandering aesthetically but without moral purpose through a menacing urban scape. It is evident that the film noir aesthetic fits the writing style of Hammett and Chandler perfectly: given the peculiar lighting and the odd camera angles favoured in film noir movies, even a row of palm trees swayed by the California breeze can look like an omen of doom. The style and the cinematography thus fit the content perfectly. When at the end of the film the truth about this or that crime or fraud is revealed, the city remains a place of greed, alienation and meaninglessness. In the English mysteries of the 1930s, once the murderer is found out and quickly removed, the world returns to its happy pre-crime state. But hard-boiled detective stories are thoroughly pessimistic. There is no road from the truth about a crime to the larger question of justice, and so closure does not bring about contentment and satisfaction either for individuals or for the larger social body.

The criminal justice system as protagonist: from *Perry Mason* to *Law & Order*

In the 1950s Hollywood developed two types of films that would have enduring appeal: the lawyer film/courtroom drama and the 'cop film'. These genres also existed on television: in the days of black-and-white, two-channel broadcasting, *Perry Mason* was the most popular show on American television. Of course, lawyers and cops had played key roles in many earlier films. But it is possible to see the period after film noir – from the late 1950s to the 1970s, roughly – as concerned to dramatize not so much individual criminal behaviour and individual feats of detection, but rather the legal and ethical conflicts and dilemmas of the criminal justice system as a system. The play-based movie *Twelve Angry Men* (1957), which took the unusual tack of spending the whole film in the jury's deliberating room, thus focusing audience attention on a usually invisible, taken-for-granted wheel in the cog of criminal justice, is part of this broader trend toward making the system into the protagonist.

In keeping with the trend toward making the criminal justice system's inner workings and contradictions into the main source of narrative interest, the cop films of this period, as Thomas Leitch notes, generally feature a policeman at odds with his own colleagues and his own bureaucracy – sometimes even at odds with the law itself. Because they are not really officers of the state even when they are employed by police departments,

> loose-cannon cops from *G-men* (1935) to '*The Rock*' (1996) typically pursue suspects in chase sequences with guns blazing on both sides, leaving in their wake a high body count and impressive property damage; and suspects, instead of being taken into custody, are last seen snarling their defiance or getting carried out in a body bag. (Leitch, 2002, p 216)

The figure of the sheriff – that combination of law and lawlessness, order and arbitrariness, popularized by Westerns – is not far below the surface of many American representations of police work.

Early detective stories, from Edgar Allan Poe to Agatha Christie, featured private individuals who, rather implausibly, were allowed full access to the crime scene and every facility to interview suspects, thus blurring the line between the private and the public. So too, US police films and television programmes blur the public–private line from the other side, by showing cops who act as if they were private eyes, that is, without much regard either for superior officers, or the letter of the law, or the usual procedures of police work. And, as stated above, it is the system that is on trial as much, or more, than the suspect.

Identifying with the in-between figure of the cop at odds with the system, the man who is the law but seems to enforce it only by breaking it, audiences can have their cake and eat it too. The honest cop working in the corrupt police department is inside and outside the system at the same time, and if he ends up taking the law into his own hands, this act is both fulfilling the law, at least the general spirit of the law, and breaking it. Audiences can continue to believe that the system will in the end be made to work, while simultaneously maintaining the cynical view that all bureaucracies are rotten and that American masculinity has to include the unregulated use of guns because one can never rely on the State.

This fertile contradiction was taken in different directions by countless films and television series that helped Americans (and people around the world who watch American television) to maintain the contradictory attitude with respect to the criminal justice system that is documented in criminological public-opinion polls. People admit that there are serious flaws in the system but still retain faith in it, often calling for more law or stronger laws to deal with the supposed failures. When cops are shown as being hampered by law's requirements to achieve the prosecution and punishment of bad guys (as in the 1987 film *The Untouchables*, in which Sean Connery and Kevin Costner play police officers defeated by the clever tricks of Al Capone and his gang), the failure of law appears to the audience as a demand for more, stronger law. *The Untouchables* is perhaps emblematic because the well-known fact that the 1930s police could only gather enough evidence to charge Al Capone with a tax offence encapsulates this (perhaps typically American) story about the constant failure of law.

But in police films and television programmes, the failure of law does not mean that police work as such is discredited. The trustworthy authority that in *The Untouchables* issues, as it were, directly from Sean Connery's face envelops within its halo the recurring figure of the honest cop, the heroic cop who has to deal not only with criminals' power and wiles but also with the weakness of a legal system overly concerned with due process, evidentiary rules and the rights of suspects. It is typical of Americans, political scientists have noted, to worry much more about the personal qualities of leaders than about the soundness of institutions. And cop films too reassure Americans that an honest and courageous individual can bring about justice, even if the system remains essentially ill-designed or even corrupt.

The system as drama: *Law & Order*

In the previous section we showed that the most common plot of cop films is the good cop's struggle against a corrupt or malfunctioning system. Because of this focus on the individual honest cop, in cop films, figures like judges and prosecutors usually appear only to delay or frustrate the progress of justice. The system is only presented from one point of view: and from the police point of view, prosecutors and judges undermine the work that has been done to apprehend the suspect (suspects, in the police view, being automatically criminals). By contrast, courtroom dramas and lawyer films, which also show the system from only one point of view, but one in another location, pay no attention to police work, or else feature it only as an obstacle (e.g. a bungled investigation).

The brilliance of the long-running series *Law & Order*, which shows no sign of exhaustion after 14 seasons and which has given rise to two spin-offs, is embedded in its distinctive half-and-half format. The cops are the main characters in the first half of each show. As a suspect is apprehended, the prosecutors then become the protagonists of the second half. This makes the show somewhat confusing to the uninitiated: accustomed to the single point of view of conventional narrative, the first-time viewer ends up spending the whole second half wondering what happened to the stars introduced in the first half. This unusual format, however, allows for endless variations on the theme of the conflicts between the two parts of the system, a conflict that is usually taken for granted and put in the background in both cop-centred films/TV series and in lawyer-focused representations. And after one has become familiar with the format, the show appears as much more interesting than other crime shows precisely because of the change in point of view at the half-hour mark.

The creator of the series, Dick Wolf, explains that the unusually complex structure, which necessitates having two sets of 'separate but equal' star actors, was the product of a certain business climate as much as an aesthetic or political choice. In the fascinating 2003 coffee-table book *Law & Order Crime Scenes*, featuring black-and-white artsy stills of the same crime scenes that were shown in colour and in moving images at the beginning of episodes, Wolf writes:

> The split-format structure of *Law & Order* was initially predicated on a business, not an artistic, idea. While producers incur a deficit in creating the original episodes, syndication is where the profit is made in television. It was therefore thought to be advantageous to have a product that could be sold either as a half-hour or a full-hour show. I was fishing for various possibilities to meet this demand and tossed around several ideas, among them, 'Day & Night' and 'Cops & Robbers'. But, ironically, when I hit upon 'Law & Order', I felt that I had come up with a series that would be creatively enhanced by the use of the split-format. (Wolf, 2003, p 8)

The show always opens with a crime – almost always graphically represented by a dead body – which quickly becomes the object of the New York homicide detective gaze. The cops are shown linearly following up on clues and on witness statements, and going from one address (shown on the screen in black and white lettering, in Brecht-like style) to another. Their time is mainly spent interviewing witnesses and suspects. Physical clues are duly sent off to the forensics lab, but forensic work itself is rarely shown on the screen; the show follows the cops, not the biochemists.

The second half follows the more legalistic story of how prosecutors evaluate the evidence gathered by the cops and decide whether to lay a charge, and if so, what kind of charge. Sometimes the prosecutors' work has the effect of proving the cops wrong and forcing them to follow up avenues of inquiry that had been neglected earlier, a feature that, while undoubtedly reflective of 'real life', is rarely portrayed in mass-market representations of criminal justice. This complexity may be what explains the popularity of *Law & Order* among my academic colleagues.

While the cops always find a plausible suspect – otherwise the second half could not take place – the prosecutors are not always victorious. Occasionally the case unravels during the trial (though trials are not always shown, in keeping with the show's peculiar theory that the criminal justice system only has two consistent components). But more often, failure arises from the conflict between moral guilt and legal guilt. In one episode, the cops gathered evidence from the trash contained in a garbage bag left on the curb by a suspect, only to have the prosecutors inform them that since they only had a search warrant for the house, not the sidewalk or the garbage bag, this evidence was legally inadmissible. This meant that the prosecutors could only lay a lesser charge. And in a twist that is more typical of the early seasons of the programme than of recent, Republican-influenced content, the lesser charge turns out to be morally correct in the end, since the criminal in question turns out not to have been a typical criminal but rather a disinterested professional moved to violence by excessive zeal.

The show's half-and-half format has the highly political effect of formally precluding a third segment told from the standpoint of the defence. In contrast to lawyer films and books starring valiant defence counsel managing to obtain freedom for their (mainly innocent) clients (e.g. Scott Turow's novels), *Law & Order* completely excludes the defence bar. This is significant because it is symptomatic of a broader trend toward crime representations with conservative effects. During the years from Reagan to the second Bush administration, mainstream US crime television increasingly romanticized the capture and prosecution of villains. Occasionally, legal stories were told as tales of ordinary people managing to prevail over 'the system' and over powerful groups; but, significantly given the huge increase in harsh punishments and prison populations, the theme of the little guy up against an unjust system was generally explored in civil-law rather than criminal-law contexts (e.g. the extremely popular book and film *A Civil Action*). The criminal law and its enforcement, by contrast, became a field of dramatic events told almost wholly from the point of view of victims, cops and prosecutors. As critic Elayne Rapping puts it:

> What ever happened to the defense-attorney hero on television? Where are the Perry Masons? The TV versions of Atticus Finch, or the fictionalized Clarence Darrow of *Inherit the Wind* and *Compulsion*? A one-time staple of TV series about crime and justice, this staunch advocate for the poor, the powerless, the unjustly accused has slowly receded from TV screens to be replaced by heroic policeman and D.A.s [District Attorneys]. Even in pulp fiction and popular movies, it's the chasers and the

prosecutors of the 'bad guy' criminals who, with certain exceptions that prove the rule, have long reigned supreme. Defense attorneys, more often than not, appear as sleazy, corrupt, and unscrupulous, tainted by some suspiciously radical political agenda, or, at best, as hopelessly inept – the strawman foils of those who represent 'true justice'. (Rapping, 2003, p 21)

Although *Law & Order* plots sometimes undermine the law-and-order ideology by showing that the criminal law cannot address fundamental social problems, nevertheless, two further points can be made to demonstrate the links between *Law & Order* and the rising tide of conservatism in the US throughout the 1980s and 1990s. First, what might seem like a small point. In the 2003 season, shot in 2002, the desks of every New York homicide cop sprouted US flags, as did many lapels owned by various male characters. In addition, the show's website was changed to show a background in which the show's trademark colours, blue and red (the show's title as shown on the opening screen is half red and half blue) acquire a distinctly nationalist dimension as the US flag emerges from the background and wafts in an invisible breeze. Murder is not a national or federal matter in the US, legally speaking: murderers are prosecuted by the people of the State of New York, not the Queen or the country. But the literal flag-waving has the effect of undermining this longstanding legal doctrine and suggesting to readers that local homicide detectives paid out of local property taxes labour not for their municipality but for the nation. Prosecutors, while less likely to sport flag lapel pins, rarely mention the criminal code of the State of New York, and are shown as all-purpose, national crime fighters.

The emergence of flags – signs put in the background, but which carry a heavy meaning in post-September 11 America – can be shown to be related to the fact, evident from content analysis alone, that over the years the prosecutors depicted in *Law & Order* have become more conservative. To quote Rapping again:

Assistant [prosecutors] were first a race-conscious black male named Robinette and then a fairly liberal feminist, Claire Kincaid. Since then, each assistant, always an attractive white woman, has been increasingly less concerned with 'politically correct' morally troubling issues and more extreme in the pure pursuit of conviction at all costs . . . each successive woman has simply followed the tough-on-crime pattern now established by the series, with none of the ideological anguish typical of Robinette and Kincaid . . . (Rapping 2003, p 28)

The homicide side, for its part, has also changed over the years. The head white guy has here remained fairly constant, but his second in command – usually a man of colour – has changed. The Latino cop who held the role for the longest time was somewhat prone to violence, but usually only if subject to racial abuse. The current black cop, for his part, often beats up on suspects for no reason other than to subordinate them. That a high-class, artsy series with complex plots and excellent acting shows police brutality as a normal part of the job – rather than as a sign of the department's corruption, which is how it would have appeared in the 1970s – is perhaps a sign of the times. Criminals are evil, and the criminal justice system, while tough (the death penalty was reintroduced in New York State early in the life of the series) is sometimes powerless due to law's perpetual failures. What is conventionally regarded as falling within the sphere of 'torture' is never shown, and if shown would likely discredit the character engaging in it as well as the system. But when the black cop is shown throwing a chair at a suspect for no particular reason other than to vent his frustration at the whole population of youth gangs, no consequences follow, either for the cop or for the system. Repeatedly, the violent cop is merely told to 'cool it', and the plot goes on.

The normalization of police violence in the most popular police series on American television conveys a message on its own, quite apart from the messages about crime and justice contained in the plots. Showing police abuse of suspects going unpunished is perhaps not unrelated to the official US Government's response to the Iraqi war prisoner torture scandals. And needless to say, making the white characters (even when they are divorced alcoholics) appear as 'reasonable' by contrast to the violence-prone racial minority officers is also a powerful message of its own.

British television too has recently seen the rise of violence-prone police officers. Some of these are presented as the bent coppers in programmes featuring internal investigators as the heroes, in which case their tendency to violence is not normalized. But some of the tough-guy cops are romanticized, in series that seem designed specifically to lure viewers away from the much more violent offerings of US-made television shows and movies. The special undercover agents of *In Deep* are meant to be unusual – they are part of a small elite unit that infiltrates terrorist and organized crime groups, and the whole programme is based precisely on the fact that the world of the two tough-guy 'in deep' agents is totally removed from conventional crime fighting. But apart from the content, it is worth noting that the cinematographer of this show appears to have come straight from Hollywood – the camera often lingers on bloody faces and blown-up buildings, American-style, eschewing the much more restrained conventions of traditional British crime television. The popularity of programmes featuring armed special agents engaging in highly dangerous undercover work may be an indication of a certain normalization and indeed a glamorization of the violence committed by agents of British criminal justice, and perhaps also by British military personnel. The fatal shooting of an innocent Brazilian immigrant that took place in the London Tube after the July 2005 bombings would in a previous decade have looked to the British public like a scene from an American television programme. However, by 2005 scenes along those lines had already been featured in numerous British-made programmes featuring specialized law enforcement officers, such as bodyguards for foreign dignitaries and anti-terrorist specialists.

US-style violence has also been featured prominently in Ian Rankin's bestselling novels, whose protagonist is the Edinburgh homicide detective Inspector Rebus. The novels borrow heavily from the film noir aesthetic; they take place almost exclusively at night in anarchic, ugly, violence-ridden neighbourhoods. And Rebus's drinking habits rival those of characters played by Humphrey Bogart in the 1940s. Apart from these constant elements, there have been some significant shifts in the content. The first Rebus books were more concerned to convey a dark aesthetic, an Edinburgh whose existence tourists do not suspect; but later novels have featured increasingly graphic descriptions of violence – something not found in film noir, a genre in which there are numerous dead bodies but almost no blood. The old-fashioned, Holmes-like, almost purely intellectual skills of Ruth Rendell's Inspector Wexford and Colin Dexter's Inspector Morse, whose avuncular screen images functioned for years as messages reassuring (older, middle-class) British viewers that the world was fundamentally safe, seem to have given way to representations of police work that combine punches and kicks with a remarkable fondness for that mythical signifier of masculinity that British police have notoriously lacked, in art as in life, namely guns.

It is worth pausing for a moment to note that American cultural products that are exported around the world come to have different social implications, indeed different meanings, as they are transported and shown to different audiences – as they are placed in different contexts of consumption (see Chapter 2). Guns of course are normal in US police work, and are also worn by non-police state agents such as customs inspectors and immigration officers. Ordinary people also own handguns in huge numbers. But in the UK context guns have a different legal history and hence a different meaning. Just as whisky had a particular meaning in films and books written during or immediately after US Prohibition, so too semiotic elements that recur in crime films, such as guns, require specific analyses that take the specific location of the audience into account. Analyses of the 'translations' of US movies and television series that take place in countries that are also English-speaking and thus require no dubbing are, unfortunately, extremely scarce. And so we now turn to another US cultural product, one that as far as I know has not travelled very much outside of North America but which has given rise to a curious Canadian imitation that can be scrutinized to shed some light on these questions of the context of consumption, namely, the geographically specific meaning of signs used in representations of crime and of policing.

The return of the barbarian invasion: *COPS*

Police films are less popular today than they were in the 1970s and 1980s. In the world of film, the late 1990s and the early years of the twenty-first century were dominated by the craze for fantastical, quasi-historical mega-productions that is common to the success of *The Lord of the Rings*, the *Harry Potter* movies, and to the earlier *Star Wars* as well. On television, however, big-budget shows with large casts and all the latest computer-generated effects are not financially possible. And in any case, at the level of format, the small screen lends itself better to face-to-face interactions than to grand spectacles. Thus, audiences use television not so much to gain access to other worlds but rather to see the 'real' world (Ellis, 2000): to imaginatively explore the small-scale dramas of real life, be it the life of the family explored in soap operas or the life of the city explored in police series. Because police are usually represented as travelling back and forth across the social divides of class and race, the act of following the police around (with the help of the television camera) enables middle-class and respectable working-class viewers to explore, from the safety of the armchair, the seamy side of urban life. For all these reasons, police-centred television series are extremely popular, in the UK as in North America.

A series that first appeared on marginal channels and only in the daytime, *COPS*, has now become more mainstream, and is shown several times per day on different channels across North America. This is a 'reality' programme purporting to give the viewer a sense of what it is really like to be a police officer patrolling the streets of urban (and often suburban) America. Each episode runs for 22 minutes, half an hour with commercials, and is composed of several independent mini-episodes. It is thus well suited to channel-surfing and short attention spans.

A different police department is featured in each *COPS* show, so the characters change constantly. Continuity is provided by a standardized format, including the use of a hand-held video camera (always located right behind or beside the protagonist cop), and, last but not least, the theme song – a catchy reggae tune, 'Bad boy', played at the beginning as a series of disconnected shots follow one another on the screen. Sometimes the opening sequence features cops doing typical 'cop' things – putting handcuffs on youths, drawing their guns and crouching behind their cruisers expectantly, etc. But, remarkably, some of the opening sequences contain quite unrelated material that seems to have been selected for its curiosity or entertainment value rather than for any message it may convey about criminal justice. A high-speed boat moving across a harbour; a scantily clad black woman zoooming along on roller blades; a surfer falling off the surfboard; and an officer engaged in the delicate task of grabbing a crocodile by the tail and putting it in a cage – these are just a few of the images that have appeared as part of the all-important opening sequence.

The combination of representations of policing with randomly collected scenes whose significance – or whose provenance – is never mentioned in the body of the programme has the effect of suggesting to the audience that this is not a serious documentary about police work, but a combination of amateur video footage of policing work and anything that might contribute to the entertainment of the audience. The theme song, which is extremely catchy, contributes to create an overall effect that one might describe as 'infotainment'. Sung with a Caribbean accent, the lyrics seem to empathize with the criminals and other low-life whose troubles are exploited by the show more than with the cops: 'Bad boy, bad boy, what'cha gonna do, what'cha gonna do when they come for you . . .' This song acquired a life of its own as it made it into the hit parade in 1993. Especially in the case of those opening sequences featuring roller bladers and crocodiles, not just 'bad boys', the powerful music combines with the images to suggest that we are in the world of fun and entertainment.

This fun-oriented opening, however, is rarely followed up in the body of the programme. Immediately after the opening sequence, we see a long shot of a city or town, with the name written out below – usually an unglamorous name like Indianapolis, not New York or Chicago – and we hear the incomprehensible but unmistakeable sounds of a dispatcher, usually a woman, calmly responding to emergency calls and organizing the response. The dispatcher's calm rational manner is misleading, however. Most of what follows consists of disconnected bits, through which respectable viewers sitting at home not only see life 'in the projects', among the underclasses, but are actually thrown into a semiotically confusing succession of badly lit video clips with noisy soundtracks that rarely amount to a coherent narrative.

Since the action is usually taking place at night, and the reality-TV format means there is no proper film lighting, it is literally impossible to really see what is going on. The visual confusion is compounded by the noises left in the soundtrack, among which it is often hard to distinguish any words other than those of the 'lead' cop, our guide to the underworld (Doyle, 1998). The inhabitants of the disordered world being policed appear to us as they appear to the largely white cops who brusquely enter their run-down apartments: unkempt and unintelligible. And due to the fact that the microphone goes with the police officers, the voices of those being policed are reduced to a babble of indistinct shouts and sentence fragments, even when the speakers are native English speakers and are not drunk or on drugs, which is probably a minority of situations.

It is important to note the marked political effects of 'technical' facts such as the location of the microphone. In class discussions in which I have asked students to reflect on film and television technical choices, I have learned that students are often quite informed about film conventions – lighting, cinematography, soundtrack – that are used in films and in big-budget television drama like *Law & Order*. When shown clips of *COPS* shows, however, students uniformly fail to note that the apparent artlessness of the home-movie reality-TV genre has its own formal conventions: conventions and technical features that have important political effects. Imagining that 'tricks' are only used in film and in professionally made television shows, they do not see that the fact that the camera goes with the cop from the cruiser into the apartment or house under investigation has the effect of presenting the 'underworld' as the cop sees it, that is, as a space of constant risk and potential danger. In the five years I have taught a course in which I ask them to analyse such footage, none of the students has realized, unaided, that the 'reality' soundtrack, full of unintelligible sounds, conveys a certain message about the world of crime precisely through the lack of coherent meaning (Doyle, 1998; Rapping, 2003).

The format of *COPS* episodes is as follows. A cop chosen to 'star' in the episode is introduced at the beginning – or rather, he introduces himself, for there is no narrator, in line with reality-TV conventions. 'He' is the operative word here; I watched 25 randomly selected episodes and none featured a woman cop except in secondary roles. The officer is immediately personalized and rendered sympathetic. 'I could have been a priest but I became a cop' is one man's story. Another one, obviously prompted (in a question later edited out) to highlight his race, tells us a long tale about having been one of the few well-behaved African-American kids in his neighbourhood. The tone is informal and wistful. As the cop reminisces, the video camera, located in the back seat of the cruiser, gives us a tight close-up and hence very sympathetic view of the archetypal 'cop on the beat'.

After a few minutes the biographical narrative is interrupted by a call from the dispatcher. The cop springs into action – which means, in this show as in real-life American policing, that he steps on the accelerator. The car then speeds along either to a particular address or in pursuit of a vehicle. If called to an address, the cops – who usually gather a couple of other cruisers along the way – pile out and get themselves organized to enter the house, guns drawn and shouting to one another in militaristic language.

The interiors shown on *COPS* are remarkable for their disorder. Beer bottles lie on the carpet, people who do not appear to form a 'normal' family emerge from the darkness (often into a space lit with an ordinary living room lamp unsuitable for filming), and broken fragments of conversation ensue. The people who appear are always poor, and usually Latino, black or generically 'ethnic'. Men wear undershirts and basketball tops. Women are scantily clad in bright polyester, usually overweight, and sometimes sporting curlers in their hair. Children are shown as being up very late at night.

That social and familial disorder is highly likely to have been compounded by the cops' entry – and that some of its features, such as the kids being out of bed, may have actually been caused by the cops' arrival, is not likely to occur to the audience, given that reality-TV is a genre that does not encourage, or even allow, examination of the social and political roots of what one sees. The visible disorder appears as the natural habitat of the disorderly, ill-dressed people one sees.

When the cops yell at the people in question and get only indistinct mumbles in reply, the dividing line between the forces of order and the uncivilized jungle is further underlined. The screen shows us rational, well-dressed, sober white men with well-trimmed haircuts trying to make sense of an inherently unintelligible world. And since watching the show inevitably enlists us too in the work of trying to decipher the sounds and the sights of a disorderly and confusing world – the semiotic work that seems to take up most of the cops' time – it takes an act of mental courage to avoid totally identifying with the cops.

The video camera often lingers painfully on the awkward speech and movements of suspects or witnesses who have clearly had too much to drink. Drinking is not an unusual behaviour for cops, of course, but since their leisure time is not represented on the show, what we see is that the disorderly classes are often drunk and incoherent, whereas the cops are always rational and sober.

Drugs too are shown as being normal in the environments being policed. Just about every car stopped is searched for drugs, and the rate of 'hits' is much higher on *COPS* than in real-life policing. One gets the impression that drugs must be everywhere even when the cops don't find them. And drug use contributes to the 'law-and-order' effect of the show because people who are caught having just consumed a mind-altering substance don't look very rational when filmed. Two of the episodes I saw spent as much as five minutes (an eternity in TV time) with the camera focusing on someone who was obviously on drugs and could not get a coherent sentence out. As our impatience to find out just what is going on grows, we the viewers come to empathize with the cops' own semiotic frustration: we are thus more likely to unwittingly adopt the cops' theories about disorder and crime.

Some of the people whose world is being invaded are clearly visible and identifiable – whether because they signed a consent form agreeing to be on television or whether a consent form was never brought to them, we don't know. Some of those apprehended by the police as suspects, however, have their faces technologically obscured. One imagines this protects their identity; but, given the general atmosphere of unintelligibility, the blurred face also adds to the general confusion.

Shots are sometimes heard, as well as other worrying noises – glass breaking, people running, etc. Rarely does the audience actually see what is going on, however. The lighting is simply inadequate, and there is only one video camera available, or so it seems. Thus, the audience is reduced to a purely passive state: in a mostly dark screen, we see a figure rapidly running in and out of the light, and we hear several noises that might indicate a crime being committed – but might also indicate someone running from the police. We thus cling to the communications among the police officers – the only ones we can hear clearly – for dear life. 'The subject is behind the house!', 'the subject is running down Thirteenth Street!' . . . and so forth.

At the end of the incident we are often still in the dark about who did what to whom and why. But as we climb back into the comforting space of the police cruiser, that haven of safety, we – the camera and the microphone, that is – finally have an opportunity to hear the real story. The cop introduced at the beginning now provides the narrative that interprets all of the chaotic detail just seen and heard, organizing it into a coherent story about crime and police, often with an explicit 'moral of the story'. We the viewers have just visited the 'scene' with the cops (even though the screen was mainly black for a good bit of time and the noises recorded were not obviously meaningful). Therefore we believe that from the comfort of our living room we have seen crime with our own eyes. We forget that we only know what is/was going on when the cop, seated at the wheel of the cruiser, finally interprets for us the alien world we have just visited. Needless to say, no microphone stays behind to record what the hapless inhabitants of the underworld think or say.

The bleak urban and suburban spaces in which COPS takes place – lonely roads going from one featureless grouping of discount stores, ugly houses and cheap diners to another – are presented in the show as naturally ugly and disorderly. That federal cutbacks to public housing in the 1980s have something to do with the poor state of apartments and project parking lots is hardly likely to occur to audiences immersed in the events of the show. In general, viewers who have lived in the US all their lives are unlikely to reflect upon the history of the spaces in which the action takes place.

But if it were possible to get American COPS-watching audiences to watch the Canadian imitation of COPS, which is a rather obscure programme called To Serve and Protect, perhaps they would begin to wonder about the 'background' signs.

First of all, more Canadian episodes are shot in the daytime, and in the sunshine at that. Watching Edmonton police cruise down a remarkably sunny street, a viewer might well discover that a good part of the bleakness of COPS is merely a product of the show's preference for footage shot at 2 or 3 am, a time in which most neighbourhoods and most people who are awake have a tendency to look bedraggled. The same people might look rather different on a sunny Monday morning. Second, while a few Canadian cities have some pockets of deep poverty – most notably, Vancouver's heroin/cocaine users congregate in a neighbourhood that rivals barbarian encampments in Chicago or New York – the programme is shot in Edmonton, Alberta, a city that has virtually no slums.

Some of the interiors that appear in *To Serve and Protect* are very similar to those in the US show. In one episode, the camera, handled by someone who has obviously watched many *COPS* episodes, lingers on the television set (which is on in the daytime, a sure marker of 'welfare bum'), on the beer bottles scattered on the floor, and on the way the cops get the suspect to put on a shirt – a plaid lumberjack shirt – over his otherwise rather indecently clad body. But even in this episode, the outdoor scenes take place in a respectable working-class neighbourhood, and there is no garbage or disorder anywhere.

When the cruiser is seen driving off with the suspect in the back seat, the basic message is that 'the Mounties have got their man', as the Canadian cliché has it, and that order has been restored to an urban space that looks crushingly normal. And in the episodes I saw, the persons apprehended did not look in any way frightening. None was black – and black skin, especially on young males, is a sure sign of potential disorder for most Canadian as well as American white viewers. One episode featured a clearly aboriginal man. But he was not presented as a dangerous Other. He appeared to be happily drunk, and spoiled the barbarian effect that is so successfully produced by the US *COPS* programme by joking with the officers and hamming it up for the camera, causing the cops to laugh along with him. Furthermore, he seemed known to the police by name, something which reflects police reality (beat cops do get to know many of the 'usual suspects' by name) but which I have never seen on *COPS*. Again, seeing the Edmonton cops chat with a regular client serves to highlight something that might pass unremarked. The fact that on *COPS* criminals and cops are strangers to one another serves to further the general impression of the 'combat zones' as spaces populated by people who are not individuals but rather instances of a general type – the criminal classes, the anonymous 'bad boys' of the theme song.

The urban-jungle effect created in the American *COPS* through a combination of slum locations, time of the night, poor sound quality and an abundance of drugged or otherwise unintelligible suspects just cannot be reproduced north of the border – in Edmonton at any rate. Despite using the same techniques – a handheld video camera, the focus on minor everyday disorder rather than major crime, the prominent display of the police cruiser as the vehicle in which civiliza-tion (briefly) enters the jungle to bring temporary order to it – the Canadian show just cannot create the same political message. This is in part attributable to naïve Canadian police cinematographers, who appear to have decided that they need to shoot footage in the daytime because night-time footage would be far too dark, without realizing that a mostly black screen is actually a useful sign. But it is also due to the fact that the neighbourhoods explored are just not bleak and poor enough. Their denizens sometimes look dishevelled and disordered, but somehow they just don't look like 'aliens and nomads' (Rapping, 2003, p 48).

The apotheosis of the forensic gaze: CSI

COPS allows Americans to engage in some vicarious slum travel. The fact that audiences are seeing these areas from the standpoint of those who are strangers there – the police – is not likely to come to the attention of most viewers, since the programme is marketed as 'reality-TV', that is, as not acted, not scripted, not manipulated, and so not promoting any particular point of view or theory. But as we have seen, the very fact that the camera and the microphone go with the cops, and record the goings-on as the cops see and hear them, has the 'law-and-order' effect of making the cops' particular view of the urban poor into the real, truthful view.

While certain representations, such as gangster films, spend much time familiarizing audiences with particular villains, *COPS* is distinctive, among representations of cops and robbers, in that only the cops are individualized (the main cop by name, the others by police department). The 'robber' side of the old cops-and-robbers dialectic is represented not by individuals but by a demographic, a type (see Chapter 4) – the type associated with the general social condition of 'disorder'. The vast majority of incidents to which the police are called do not amount to crimes that require detection – consisting mainly of domestic violence whose perpetrator is never in doubt or drug possession offences that only require routine searching of persons and vehicles to establish reasonable and probable cause. Criminals are never individualized for more than a few seconds; and neither are the crimes themselves. Unlike Sherlock Holmes, who is in some awe of his constant powerful enemy Professor Moriarty, these officers are not presented as in battle against a clever villain or in any way engaged in careful gathering of information to either charge specific criminals or to prevent crimes in the communities being policed. Prevention never enters their vocabulary, as if to tell the audience that nothing significant can be done to alter the future. The officers shown seem to think that their job is only to manage, temporarily, a series of unresolved or ambiguous situations whose common denominator is disorder.

Let us now turn to the tremendously successful forensic series *CSI: Crime Scene Investigation*. At first sight, this popular series does everything that is left undone in *COPS*. *CSI* – the most popular programme on American television in 2005 – is all about specific crimes and specific criminals, and the officers shown do use sophisticated knowledge. Interestingly, however, the criminals themselves are of little interest; and the victims and the witnesses are also given very short shrift. In general, people do not matter, either as criminals or as victims. Only the physical clues and the technical gadgets used to interpret those clues matter.

In keeping with this Sherlock-Holmes approach, *CSI* shows virtually no uniformed officers. Even homicide detectives play a surprisingly secondary role. The central characters are those that in other shows (e.g. *Law & Order*) are placed behind the scenes and taken for granted: the technicians who examine the clues and the bodies. In real life, forensic technicians ('criminalists', as they are known in some parts of the US) simply turn over their test results, with minimal interpretation, to the homicide detectives. The detectives have other information, e.g. witness statements and existing police records. It is the homicide detectives (and sometimes their more specialized friends in the FBI) who are regarded in real life as being in the best position to generate a reliable account of the crime, having several kinds of evidence at their disposal (what is called 'triangulation' in social science research methods).

On *CSI*, however, the homicide detective has receded into the background completely. It is the forensic technicians, trained in applied biochemistry and in the use of tools like the microscope and the X-ray machine, who not only analyse the physical evidence but even reconstruct the crime, to the point of assigning guilt strictly from physical evidence. This is the Holmes theory of truth taken to its extreme – or, more accurately, it is the Holmes theory narrowed and impoverished. Holmes did not use only physical clues: as shown earlier, he also used a vast personal archive of variegated information about historical events, current affairs and so on. Holmes also spent much time reading up on previous criminal cases, and used that information to analyse each new crime. The *CSI* technicians, by contrast, live only in the present, and they appear to have no information at all about the social world.

In one episode, the distraught father of a mentally ill young woman is revealed as the (unwitting) killer of his daughter – after one keen-eyed forensic technician, examining the woman's clothes closet, finds a recent stain on a dress that DNA analysis revealed to have been caused by the father's tears. What sort of relation the father might have had with his mentally ill daughter was not discussed at all. A devoted father's tears could have been a semiotically rich sign whose layers – love for the daughter, frustration about her outbursts during episodes of illness, anger at the lack of social supports, etc. – could have been explored to document the troubles afflicting families with special-needs children. But the social and psychological discourses that a programme like *Law & Order* would routinely include in the depiction of a family tragedy were simply left aside. The salty water with the father's DNA was treated as a very simple signifier with only one (first-order) meaning, the forensic meaning.

To further the theory that truth is always, and exclusively, to be found in the physical traces left by a crime, the producers of *CSI* have developed some clever innovations in both photography and sound. As for visuals, *CSI* seems to have been the original site of a practice now used in a number of other crime shows, including some British ones: shifting from shooting what the technician sees, either with the naked eye or through a microscope or other machine, to an enhanced image that locates the body part or the knife fragment back in its original, just-before-the-crime condition. An example might help here. In one show, a technician is shown peering into a microscope. Immediately afterwards, the screen fills up completely with an image that one supposes is what the technician saw (though it was probably computer-enhanced): a bone with a jagged edge. The viewer is then taken back to the scene of the crime: and a miracle then takes place before the audience's eyes. The bit of jagged bone is transformed, through computer-enhanced photography, into a whole bone, which is in turn magically placed back inside the victim's body, with the body slowly resuscitated and shown as it was just before the fatal moment. The audience hitches a ride with the image, as if on a magic carpet. We the audience bypass all human agency and are thus able to occupy God's own point of view.

In regard to the soundtrack, which is as cleverly innovative as the photography, as the image generated through the combined power of microscopes and computers performs its magic-carpet feat, we in the audience also hear plaintive sounds, somewhere between noise and music. The characters do not seem to hear them; the sounds are not presented as occurring in the lab. But the almost musical hissing and crackling is not mere background music; it is not like the doomsday music in a Hitchcock film, which reiterates the message being communicated both by the photographic format and by the plot or content. The sound is a sign in its own right. As the noise/music starts, one technician says to another: 'Let the bones whisper to you.' This underscores the point that the crackling heard by the audience is not mere studio orchestra work; it is, rather, the bones' own lines. Of course, it would provoke laughter and break all the codes of television drama to have the bones literally speak. But when the bones are given some lines of non-human speech, this does not come across as at all ridiculous, however implausible it may sound when an attempt is made (as I am doing now) to capture it in rational words and without images or sound effects. The overall impression at the point of consumption, the impression that the audience has, is that the bones do indeed hoarsely whisper the truth of the crime – and they do so not only to the technician but also to viewers directly. We know the true story of how the bone was broken even before the technician who is our guide has time to tell the story in words to his colleagues.

Thus we are lulled into believing that no interpretation or judgement is required, either on the part of detectives or on our part as an inquisitive audience. We are led to believe that the bones and other clues speak for themselves, literally, telling us in sound the same story that we also see in images as the pieces of the victim's body are taken back to their pre-crime state, resurrection-style, only to be immediately made to endure once again the trauma that caused the victim's death. The image of the clue (the broken bone) itself transports us, without any apparent human intervention, to the real (not deduced) crime. It then takes us briefly back to the pristine body before the crime – and then, as if switching from rewind to fast forward, it brings us back again to the present, to the body as clue.

The viewer is thus transported back in time – something that neither microscopes nor CAT scans can do, of course, but which conforms with the fundamental logic, the backward-reasoning logic, of any murder mystery or detective story. And the viewer feels as if he/she has seen the crime itself, with his/her own eyes. Who needs to hear Sherlock Holmes's long and tedious account of how he deduced what must have taken place? Who even needs a smart Sherlock Holmes actively using his brain as he peers through the magnifying glass to decide what is a clue and what is mere background? We are transported in time instantly and are thus able to see for ourselves the truth of the crime 'as it really happened', as the famous historian Otto Ranke said when describing the (impossible) ideal of history-writing.

The Pre-Crime Unit: seeing and changing the future

If *CSI* allows audiences to imagine that it is actually possible to see, not just deduce, who done it, by rewinding the video of a criminal event just as football officials rewind the video of a game to see who really touched the ball, technological fantasies about seeing the future and preventing crime before it happens cannot be far behind. After all, if time can be abolished in the 'rewind' direction, why can't it be fast-forwarded?

Video recording technology, which habituates audiences to thinking of temporality not as fixed and unilinear but as reversible and as subject to speed changes, is not the only factor encouraging television and film producers to experiment with future-oriented policing techniques. The technological fact of fast-forwarding – and the revolution in people's sense of temporality that it facilitates – happens to fit brilliantly with the age-old dream of total crime prevention and total orderliness that one can trace as far back as Plato and as recently as the establishment of a Department of Homeland Security in the United States.

Sir Robert Peel's vision of a constabulary devoted wholly to surveillance and impersonal crime prevention is often cited as the origin of the (modern-age) utopia of urban security; but this story gives the modern police far too much prominence in the genealogy of contemporary security systems. For example, some decades before Peel, the late-eighteenth-century Glasgow magistrate and intellectual Patrick Colquhoun had already devised a host of methods to render urban spaces, especially the London docks, transparent, and to render the urban working-class economy financially transparent, through such means as micro-managing crime-prone businesses by means of tightly regulated licences.

Colquhoun's inventive suggestions for how to cut down dockside pilfering by both workers and vagrants, which involved re-designing the physical space of the docks as well as cultivating virtuous habits among the poor, could be regarded as an early experiment which the twentieth century would call 'crime prevention through environmental design' (CPTED). CPTED is the art or science of organizing urban space and workplaces so as to deter people from committing crimes at all; its contribution to the representations of criminality and the representation of law and order will be taken up in Chapter 8. In general, there is a long and complex history of techniques of visualization and surveillance that overlap with but are not contained by the history of police forces.

The Steven Spielberg film *Minority Report* (2002), the final representation of crime and security discussed in this chapter, presents us with a very rich array of representations of security. The film covers just about every policing utopia and dystopia in the history of modern security technologies. It envisages a near future in which ordinary crime prevention measures have reached a fever pitch – eye-scanning technology, in particular, is constantly used to closely monitor who is using public spaces and private facilities. But the techniques of total surveillance and universal suspicion associated with private-sector security and financial risk management remain largely in the background of the film. In the foreground is a dramatic tale, verging, especially at the end, on sentimental melodrama. The main site for this melodramatic tale of tragic personalities is the 'Pre-Crime Unit', a special taskforce that is able to see crimes that haven't yet happened by means that are half-scientific and half-magical. (They do not themselves see the crimes, but they are able to tap into the brains of special 'seers', defective human beings with a special ability to know the future as if it were the past – an ability that is for unexplained reasons limited to seeing murders.) The gaze of the Pre-Crime Unit is, however, limited: only murders can be anticipated, and only the few brief moments before they happen can be directly seen. The Pre-Crime Unit does not therefore quite occupy the place of God, despite the fact that the architecture of its office reminds one very strongly of medieval cathedrals.

The gaze of the Pre-Crime Unit is clearly very different from that of the traditional detective, who reconstructs the past on the basis of clues. Clue interpretation is part of the unit's labour nevertheless. The 'seers' don't speak: they lie in a suspended state in some kind of pool and are hooked up to a machine that turns brain activity into incomplete pictures of the scene of the (impending) murder.

The pre-crime officers have to interpret the clues that appear in the fragmentary pictures (e.g. by looking up the municipal archive of building records to find out where a particular house might be located). Unlike Holmes, they have to do it very quickly; semiotic speed is essential. But even when the visual clues have been quickly and accurately interpreted, the cops still don't have the god's-eye view of the near future. An interesting, legalistic twist, rarely found in cop films or detective novels, is that the images of the future are produced not by one prophet-type figure but by three such beings. Even though these three seers don't argue with one another as judges on an appellate bench do (since they are mute, at least while they're lying in the pool in the basement of the Pre-Crime Unit), the open-endedness of legal judgement is graphically represented when the audience finally learns that, contrary to what the American public has been told, the three prophet-judges don't agree all the time. The film's title refers to the fact that once in a while one of the beings with the peculiar brain capacities will issue a non-verbal minority report, that is, an image that does not correspond to the other two.

The enforcement efforts of the Pre-Crime Unit are thus shown as undermined by the minority report option and, more generally, by the fact that the system's limitations are not revealed to the broad public. The American public is shown not as democratically involved in making decisions about law and law enforcement but rather as subjected to Orwellian political commercials (parodies of Republican election advertising) in which the Pre-Crime Unit's record of having brought the crime rate in Washington DC down to zero is used by a sleazy politician in his campaign to extend the pilot project to the whole nation and thus gain nationwide renown. The politician turns out to be corrupt. And he commits suicide at the end, an equally clichéd plot development. The system is thus shown as manned by honest, hard-working officers whose efforts are undermined by their political masters – a recurring theme across a wide variety of Hollywood films, not only cop films.

The main officer in the Pre-Crime Unit, played by Tom Cruise, is given a part that is also deeply rooted in mainstream Hollywood plot structures. Shown to be a fine upstanding officer at the beginning of the film, he ends up being pursued by the very system that he once led. This is not because his ex-colleagues are in the pay of corrupt politicians – which would probably have been the story in the 1970s – but because he thinks he has found out who had killed his young son some years earlier, and he proceeds in time-honoured American manner to take justice into his own hands. As he starts plotting the revenge murder of the person he thinks is his son's murderer, he of course comes into the radar of the all-seeing Pre-Crime Unit, and a classic chase ensues.

Combining gangster-movie plot devices and sci-fi means of transportation, the film, now focused wholly on Tom Cruise, goes on to show the hero learning what every information-technology security expert already knows, namely, that each new security feature leads to new inventiveness among the criminals. Most memorably, it turns out that a lively black market in used eyes has developed as a direct result of the system's success in perfecting eye-scanning technology. Provided with new eyes by a seedy surgeon who specializes in selling eyes in the same manner that conventional crooks sell passports, the disgraced cop can now foil the otherwise infallible gaze of the total surveillance system. In keeping with the *CSI* theme of security features that do not depend on texts or on human judgement, the audience watches an army of mechanical spiders being sent by the authorities to slither under doors and crawl over people to read their eye measurements. The mechanical spider that finds the hero in his lair is of course foiled by the eye transplant – a plot development that reinforces the old American story about how individual human ingenuity always triumphs over bureaucracy and technology.

Vision is the key theme of *Minority Report*. This is explored both in relation to the technologies of surveillance (which include 'smart' billboards that address passers-by by name and shopping preference, presumably by reading their eye measurements at a distance) and in relation to that ancient tool that is the human eye itself. The eye is taken for granted in Sherlock Holmes-type detective stories as well as in *CSI*. Here, however, the human eye is problematized in a number of ways, not only by showing us eye transplants but also by imagining spiders with mechanical eyes that in turn read human eyes.

That the human eye is becoming an object to be examined – through biometric scanning techniques – rather than remaining what it has traditionally been, that is, an emblem of intelligence, rationality and power, is a very important shift, not only in the governance of security but in relation to the basic Western sense of self. As art historians have noted, since the Renaissance, European culture has privileged vision both in real life (e.g. inventing microscopes and telescopes to study nature) and symbolically (e.g. the divine disembodied eye featured on every US dollar bill.) But the power to see, Spielberg tells us, is not an unequivocal good. That having eyes makes us not only governable but also vulnerable is made graphically apparent at the beginning, in the first almost-murder depicted in the film, in which a husband almost murders his unfaithful wife and her lover by almost plunging a pair of scissors into their eyes.

At the beginning of the twenty-first century, the very organ that allows us to see and hence to know, either with the naked eye or through technical inventions, is turning out also to be the thing that allows near-perfect, Stalin-like surveillance to take place. To underscore this paradoxical message, the film briefly shows us a minor character who has no eyes: he has blinded himself to escape the coercive power of both state and corporate surveillance. His robe-like dress and oracular manner recalls the long line of real and fictional blind truth-tellers that goes back to Homer. Being blind has its advantages, in the land of constant biometric surveillance at any rate. This is something that could not have occurred to the optimistic

Enlightenment philosophers and inventors who dreamed about technical enhancements for the human eye that would allow science to develop and humanity to prosper.

Along with vision and its contradictions, the other main theme concerns temporality. If vision is paradoxical – a way of gaining power over nature and other humans but also a source of vulnerability – so too temporality is paradoxical. The film explores some of the dilemmas and contradictions created by the development of technologies, mostly fictional but not wholly implausible, for rewinding the film of crime and fast-forwarding the film of life.

The choice of these two venerable themes makes the film a good emblem for the dilemmas of security in our time. If vision is the key theme of writings about security, from Plato's *Republic* to the CCTV camera, temporality is the second main theme of writings concerned with long-term security, especially state security. The inability of the sovereign to directly see all his subjects at all times throughout the whole territory is the fundamental reason for the development of the criminal law and all other systems of internal security. And as the philosopher Thomas Hobbes noted centuries ago, the inability of individuals to visually secure their property and their physical safety over time, not just now but into the future, is the essential precondition of all systems in which free and equal human beings subject themselves to a sovereign to whom the task of ensuring future security is entrusted. Modern state security systems are all more or less inadequate answers to the problem of how to ensure that the sovereign can see not only over mountains and into buildings but also into the future. Reading the intentions of the citizens and acting before they are able to carry out their subversive plots is the utopian dream both of ordinary city policing and of state security.

The Spielberg film can thus stand here as an example of how even mainstream mass representations of law enforcement and of security problems are much more than just 'images of law and order'. Even when the overt message about law and order is rather bland, as is the case even in *Minority Report*, whose conclusion simply tells us that too much political ambition can wreck the state, complex representations do offer ordinary people a chance to explore the basic problems and dilemmas of law enforcement and of security. While some of the available representations certainly oversimplify – e.g. *COPS*, which lacks the complexity of programmes like *Law & Order* and only gives us the cop perspective on 'combat zones' – it is important to avoid academic snobbery. Criminologists need to recognize that most commercially successful representations, including Hollywood cop films and television lawyer dramas, provide viewers with an opportunity to explore the tensions and contradictions created by our longstanding and constantly failing search for order and security – a search that is also a constantly failing semiotic search for stable meanings, for intelligibility. Citizens who find it difficult and tiring to make sense of the 'real' world of politics, and who turn to television and other mass media for simple meanings and escape, are perhaps not escaping after all. They are experiencing all the inherent complexities of the problem of security in a democratic society.

Chapter 7
The Invention of the Psycho Killer and the Rise and Fall of the Welfare State

Criminologists routinely complain that there are far more murders on both large and small screens than in real life. The realities of crime and crime control are not being properly represented, they lament, either in news coverage or in film or television drama. Such criticisms fail to see that murders have to be over-represented. The deliberate killing of another human being, that most ancient of moral prohibitions, captures the public's attention more than other crimes. A murder trial is inherently more newsworthy than a trial for assault or robbery. And in fiction, murder is – as we have seen in the last two chapters – a most useful plot device. The dead body with which murder mysteries and police procedurals generally open is a multi-layered sign that acts to trigger a wide variety of representations that allow the public to explore, from the safety of the armchair, the depths of human evil – and the heights of human forensic ingenuity.

Fiction writers, television producers and film directors, however, always need a new angle on the old story of the dead body and the quest for truth about murder. They thus have to come up with new twists in the old plots – new methods of murder, new places for murders, new familial or business structures that structurally encourage homicide, new forensic techniques, different kinds of law enforcement personnel, and so forth.

The two previous chapters have covered many of the developments in the history of (fictional) detection. In this chapter we turn from this broad-sweep approach to a detailed analysis of one subgenre of crime fiction, namely, the 'serial psycho killer' film that has fascinated North American and international audiences for about four decades now. While psycho killer characters have much in common, what will be highlighted in this chapter (in keeping with one of the book's key themes) is that throughout this time, the construct of the 'psycho killer' has given rise to different kinds of authority figures. The types of knowledge thought to be most authoritative and most effective in regard to this specific kind of criminal have shifted over time, and they have done so in ways that tell us much about what institutions we trust to know and to deal with risks and dangers of all sorts, not just psycho killers. In the changes taking place in the psycho killer subgenre, I argue, we can see the outlines of one of the most important political stories of the last 50 years, namely, the rise and fall of the welfare state.

The invention of the serial killer

'Serial killer' is somewhat of a misnomer. As used in both true-crime writing and in popular speech, 'serial killer' does not include all murderers who kill several times. Those who kill only for economic motives (e.g. drug dealers) are rarely considered to fall within the category of 'serial killer'. And soldiers who kill the enemy, on or off the battlefield, are also excluded. So too are terrorists, regardless of how many people they kill. Men who murder their wives and children but leave strangers alone are also generally excluded from the 'serial killer' discourse. As Philip Jenkins points out in his thorough study of the emergence of this particular criminal type in the United States, the term 'serial killer', as used both in law enforcement and in popular speech, covers very few of the numerous individuals who have killed numbers of people (Jenkins, 1994). Criminals who murder people to steal their goods or to support or undermine a political regime are excluded, as are the large number of murderers whose anger is turned only toward their own family members. Only criminals who kill strangers for devious psychological reasons are regarded as falling within the 'serial killer' category. The history of the serial killer is thus intertwined with the history of psychological knowledge used in the criminal justice system.

Just as every new illness stimulates new medical practices, every new form of crime and deviance fosters new forms of knowledge. For example, the rise of computer viruses encourages a new forensic gaze, trained not on clues left on the ground but on electronic clues left along the fibre-optic pathways of the internet. What about the serial killer? What knowledge practices have been developed to define and to control this threat? Jenkins's careful study shows that the category of the serial killer, which emerged in the late 1980s, not only encouraged new law enforcement practices, but, more radically, was to a large extent a product of changing law enforcement practices. Of course there had been killers before who murdered a series of perfect strangers without deriving any economic or political advantage from their crimes – Jack the Ripper being perhaps the most notorious of these. But the serial killer of 1980s America was a historically and geographically specific type of repeat murderer.

Jenkins's detailed analysis points out that in the late 1980s the FBI was an organization in crisis. With the decline of communism there seemed to be little point in looking for 'reds' infiltrating American organizations. Moreover, Congress was making noises about serious budget cutbacks. Facing this dual crisis, the FBI had to reinvent itself. Murder is always useful to boost police budgets: but since in the US, garden-variety murder was and is a local or state responsibility, the FBI could only succeed in its attempt to reinvent itself as a crime-fighting force rather than as the protector of the US political system if it managed to find and define a new kind of murder that, like communism, could be regarded as a national rather than a local threat. As the new threat (the serial murderer) took shape in the public imagination, the solution or remedy to this specific new problem took shape as well. The new, supralocal criminal seemed naturally to demand the expensive expertise that only a national high-tech institution with the latest crime-fighting weapons could provide. Thus was the Behavioral Sciences Unit of the FBI born – a unit featured and glorified in the film *Silence of the Lambs*, which we shall analyse in detail later in this chapter.

The story of the rise of the serial killer is also a story about how forms of knowledge – and the personnel that monopolize them – see their authority waxing and waning in keeping with broad political and socio-economic change. The fictional character that many commentators regard as the first on-screen 'serial killer', Norman Bates (in Hitchcock's classic 1960 film *Psycho*), was neither apprehended nor studied by any police force. Once apprehended by the representatives of victims (rather than by police or even a private eye), he is immediately transferred to a holding cell and quickly and accurately interpreted for the edification of police and victim representatives by that paragon of 1950s prestigious science: a psychiatrist.

Psychiatrists of course still exist, but their monopoly on the soul, and in particular the criminal soul, has been definitively broken. Given the important role played historically by psychiatry in producing authorized accounts of criminals, a study of the marked shifts in the authority and the power of psychiatry – using *Psycho* and *Silence of the Lambs* as our main sources – can shed much light on this book's theme.

The case study presented in this chapter makes a much more general point. Analysts of 'crime in the media' or of 'law in film' usually proceed by taking for granted a self-contained justice system, in which the only tensions worth examining are those between police and prosecutors, between juries and lawyers, and so on. But the justice system is not self-contained. From prison chaplains to social workers to psychiatrists, non-criminal justice personnel have played and continue to play a key role in the real-life criminal justice system, and are also often key if neglected characters in fictional representations. The nun who is the protagonist of the capital punishment film *Dead Man Walking* is virtually the only such figure to have received attention in the relevant literature, and this is probably due to the fact that execution films have received a huge amount of attention among American commentators in recent years. But while the special ethical dilemmas of capital punishment do of course mobilize non-legal and non-forensic knowledge brokers in important ways, more routine criminal-justice situations often also depend on a variety of other kinds of personnel, volunteer and professional.

In general, the rise of criminology as a separate field of study has had the unfortunate effect of silently encouraging students to take the criminal justice system for granted as a focus of study. By contrast, this chapter encourages those interested in crime and criminal justice to look at specific problems with an open mind and to map some of the shifts in representations of all manner of authoritative producers of knowledge about crime and about law-and-order.

Psychiatrists are a useful case study because for a good part of the twentieth century they represented the most authoritative challenge to law's own knowledge of crime and deviance. But the approach and method used here would also work for studies of religious figures and their shifting status as knowers of crime and deviance – or for that matter for studies of the representation of academic criminology in novels, films and on the nightly news.

But if the criminal justice system cannot be understood as an autonomous organism, neither can psychiatry be discussed without a broader consideration of the changing fortunes of medical and scientific knowledge more generally. Thus, after a discussion of the pre-history of the serial killer (focused on Jack the Ripper) and a look at selected chapters in the history of the Hollywood psycho killer, the chapter draws some conclusions showing that the shifts in dominant psychology and psychiatry reflect much more general shifts in authoritative accounts of crime and deviance.

Jack the Ripper and Mr Hyde

The Ripper's fame, paradoxically, was built on his anonymity. Because Jack the Ripper was never located (perhaps because he did not exist), the murder and mutilation of several women of easy virtue in the East End of London in 1888 sparked a large number of theories and representations that can shed much light on the general processes by which individual criminals and criminal types take shape in the public imagination. A story with no closure, no final truth, and hence no privileged authority, is a richer site for the study of cultural constructions of criminality than one with a clear-cut ending. And criminologists are fortunate in that the brilliant social historian Judy Walkowitz has provided us with a detailed analysis of how the figure of Jack the Ripper was shaped by the cultural, racial and sexual tensions of late Victorian London, and of how the shifting ghostly figure of the Ripper in turn shaped everyday experience – especially women's experience – of the city and its dangers (Walkowitz, 1992, ch. 6).

The discovery of the mutilated corpse of a prostitute on one of Whitechapel's famously seedy, dirty narrow streets would not have caused a nationwide panic had it not been linked by local police to two previous local murders. This link – which may have existed only in the minds of certain police – was the necessary condition for the involvement of Scotland Yard. The involvement of this famed force in turn caused the media, both local and national, to report on the otherwise unremarkable murder in as much gory detail as the police would permit, and to quickly create the immortal character 'Jack the Ripper' – so named because some of the victim's internal organs had been literally ripped out (or dissected, in some accounts). In subsequent weeks three other women's bodies were found, also mutilated, in the same general neighbourhood. The fact that Scotland Yard began to receive a steady and growing stream of anonymous confessions and suggestions by post is an indication of the way in which the Ripper case captured the English imagination – including the imagination of some who were probably quite deranged. This is important in hindsight: while late twentieth-century homicide detectives are trained to be very sceptical about the 'tips' and the confessions that every widely reported murder seems to generate, those who have researched these crimes suggest that at this early point in modern police history, Scotland Yard treated these volunteered statements far too seriously, possibly taking the investigation in the wrong direction.

Be that as it may, in the absence of suspects, local opinion (as reported in the newspapers) focused initially on the immigrant Jewish working-class community of East End London. 'Jacob the Ripper' came to the fore, and black-and-white engravings in the popular press featured 'reconstructions' of the crimes in which the criminal had stereotypical Jewish features. There were a number of reasons for this sort of racial profiling, but xenophobia was certainly one of them: 'it was repeatedly asserted that no Englishman could have perpetrated such a horrible crime', Walkowitz reports (Walkowitz, 1992, p 203). Allusions to centuries-old Christian tales of Jews murdering people, especially children, in quasi-satanic rites circulated widely. But what is most interesting, for purposes of comparing the Ripper to today's psycho serial killer, is that when the Ripper was represented as a

Jew, little if anything was said about any sexual motive or sexual meaning. Jews as a group were represented as a culture prone to murdering and butchering Christians in the dark of night, in the deep European subconscious at any rate. But such mythical images of a threatening group, elaborated as far back as the Middle Ages, are constructed differently than images of individual deviance built out of modern psychological knowledges.

The Jacob the Ripper theory fuelled the fires of anti-Semitism so quickly that hundreds of police had to be brought in to prevent a pogrom. But perhaps more important in relation to preventing pogroms was the fact that the most notable popular journalist of the time, WT Stead, famous for his exposés of child prostitution, began to promote an alternative theory. While anyone familiar with East End life would think that a murderer would pick prostitutes as victims because of opportunity – they were out at night, they were unlikely to have influential friends, etc. – Stead's theory began by assuming that the criminal sought out prostitutes for specifically sexual reasons. Stead, who in earlier journalistic campaigns had stirred up working men's resentment against upper-class seducers, exhorted Londoners to stop looking for ordinary criminals with crooked noses and wild hair, and instead to contemplate the possibility that the culprit might be an educated gentleman who was the 'victim of erotic mania' (quoted by Walkowitz, 1992, p 207).

'Mania' was a very popular word in the 1880s, conveying a more strictly medical meaning than it has today – kleptomania and nymphomania were some of the numerous manias 'discovered' at that time by the new science of sexology. Since mania was a mental state, a disease of the mind, a maniac might commit murder for sexual reasons, even if the bodies did not show evidence of ordinary sexual relations. Thus, as the crime became sexualized, it also became psychologized. This was in marked contrast to the culturally focused image of Jewish ritual murder, in which evil deeds are seen as emerging directly from a deviant culture and religion, not an individual psyche. And psychological sexual deviants were, experts thought, just as likely to be found in the educated upper classes as in the traditional breeding grounds of social deviance. (Oscar Wilde, at the height of his fame/infamy around this time, was an important cultural sign of the late Victorian figure of the educated degenerate.) In Stead's influential account, the killer was now located in the West End – or more accurately, not in the West End as a whole, but rather in the sick mind of a unique gentleman who did not look like a criminal and who was suffering from an invisible individual mental illness.

To back up a theory that was somewhat at odds with mainstream middle-class views about crime as issuing directly out of poor neighbourhoods' vice and degeneration, Stead resorted to the evidence of fiction. The best-selling book *Dr. Jekyll and Mr. Hyde*, published two years earlier in 1886 and turned into a popular stage play, showed, Stead claimed, that well-educated respectable gentlemen might well be responsible for some of the city's worst murders. An ordinary Englishman would not commit such a crime: but an English gentleman suffering from mental alienation, and specifically what was then called 'double consciousness' (Hacking, 1995), while unlikely to commit burglary, might well be the guilty party in the case of murders whose clues pointed to a deviant psyche. When

Scotland Yard finally released the previously secret details of one of the autopsies, which showed that internal organs had been carefully cut out, not 'ripped' out, the upper-class rake theory quickly merged with the 'mad doctor' figure famously articulated in another bestseller of the time, Mary Shelley's *Frankenstein*. Only a doctor would be able to 'dissect' corpses so cleanly, it was said. And of course, as luck would have it for Stead's theory, the respectable alter ego of the dreadful murderer Mr Hyde was none other than a medical-scientific man, Dr Jekyll.

Even today tourists can sign up for Jack the Ripper tours of East End London, and apparently irrational serial killers are in our own time routinely compared to the 'original' Ripper, most notoriously in the 'Yorkshire Ripper' case. It seems that the absence of a final definitive truth about the Ripper's identity encourages such references. But our concern here is not to trace the cultural history of the Ripper figure; it is instead to use the Ripper as a sort of foil to more clearly specify the historical and cultural contours of the present-day figure of the psycho serial killer. Let us thus then move on to a consideration of two very famous twentieth-century representations of psycho killers, and of the authorities that generate knowledge about them.

Hitchcock's psychiatrist and the rise of the postwar welfare state

American criminology often puts forward, as a truth about humanity in general, a binary opposition contrasting 'instrumental' crime with 'expressive' crime. A Mafia enforcer killing someone to preserve the organization's wealth and power is committing an instrumental crime; a lady who compulsively steals from department stores more shoes than she could possibly ever wear is a different, non-rational criminal. Expressive crime is all about emotion; instrumental crime is all about cold-blooded calculation and profit seeking. Of course, these criminologists would admit that a Mafia enforcer might be a sadist as well; but if individual crimes are acknowledged to contain some hybridity, the categories – the types – are kept very separate, almost pure. This questionable criminological cliché, which ignores the contradictoriness of most behaviour and assumes that the rational is somehow separable from the irrational, is the starting point of Hitchcock's famous 1960 film *Psycho*.

The psycho killer that grew up in the bosom of a neurotic family, especially a neurotic mother, is repeatedly separated off from 'ordinary' criminals by Hitchcock precisely by deploying the cliché about instrumental vs. expressive crime. Norman Bates is wholly defined and dominated by his deviant psyche, a psyche that is wholly Freudian, and is thus fully occupied by the dialectic of eros and thanatos, lust and the death wish – leaving no room for ordinary greed. By contrast, the hapless victim-to-be, presented at the start of the film as a perfectly normal secretary, sets off on her journey to death precisely because she has just stolen $40,000 – a huge sum in 1960 – from her employer, who had trusted her to deposit it in the bank. Her stealing somehow makes her normal: nobody calls her a criminal. A private investigator is sent to find her and recover the money, but there is no discussion of criminal prosecution.

Norman Bates's deviance, by contrast, is illustrated precisely by showing that

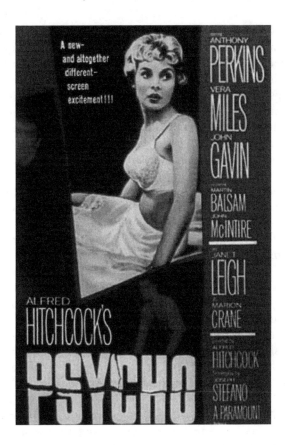

unlike normal Americans, he cares nothing about money. The motel he runs is empty and the family business is in obvious decay, but he seems not to care. And more importantly, much is made of the fact that at the end of the film, the victim's bundle of money is found, well after her death, still sitting in her car. The boy-friend who arrives at the Bates motel looking for his runaway girlfriend (who has been murdered in the shower, as even people who have not seen the film probably know) makes the fatal mistake of assuming that Bates is interested in the money – he assumes Bates is a normal American. And so do the police officers.

But the viewer knows right away that Bates is not normal. Weird stuffed birds occupy prominent spots in his motel; the family home up the hill from the hotel, shot in the evening, looks menacing even before we know what it conceals; and of course, Hitchcock's famous 'scary music' is used to convey to the audience that we are in the presence of a grave threat, even if he looks like a harmless skinny guy wearing an ordinary white business shirt. The signs of 'horror' are all there, doing their work in advance of the narrative.

Anthony Perkins's considerable acting ability is deployed to compound the general impression of danger and horror. In this film, allegedly based on the story of a real-life murderer, the young Perkins gave such a memorable performance that the 'psycho' persona assumed for this film spilled over into other films. For example, in the urbane and witty period film, *Murder on the Orient Express*, Perkins, playing a Hungarian count, exhibits the same nervous tics and painfully awkward manner of his earlier character, Norman Bates, even though the film bears none of the characteristic Hitchcock marks of danger/obsession/horror. That Perkins's psycho performance influenced both his subsequent acting and subsequent audiences' experience of his acting is acknowledged in the film studies literature. But what these scholarly studies do not discuss is the extent to which Perkins's performance influenced people's understanding of what a 'psycho' looks like. Familiarity with the rather unpleasant genre of 'serial killer' literature (e.g. the coffee table book *Encyclopedia of Serial Killers*) shows that the on-screen Norman Bates bears a striking resemblance to the photographs (and not just mug shots) of later real-life notorious killers. One might ask whether the photographers taking the shots, including police photographers, were somehow unconsciously influenced by having seen Perkins on screen; or whether there is a physiological family resemblance among American white male serial killers that Perkins somehow captured. Yet the fact is that the slim, middle-class, clean-cut, well-spoken, efficient and yet unsettling character produced by Hitchcock and Perkins together has served as a kind of paradigm or model for later representations, including representations of real serial killers.

When Bates is exposed and caught, it is revealed that he had kept the corpse of his mother as if she were still alive and had sometimes dressed in her clothes and even spoken in her voice. Neither police nor amateur sleuths are able to decipher the signs of Bates's psycho brand of criminality. As the press and the public gather around the local court house in the wake of Bates's apprehension, the local cop, who had known Norman Bates and his family for years but had taken their white, middle-class status at face value as a sign of normality, ringingly declares: 'If anyone gets the answers, it will be the psychiatrist. Even I couldn't get to know him, and he knows me.' Personal knowledge and cop knowledge are thus both demoted, to give way to the knowledge of experts.

The psychiatrist then stands up to deliver a whole lecture on the Oedipal complex (without calling it by name) to the awed cop and the equally awed victim's family, pacing the room as if he were lecturing to a large undergraduate class. Having psychoanalysed Bates in world-record time, he is able to give a full account not only of the murder of the secretary but even of earlier murders for which there were no physical clues. His inspection of Bates's mind suffices to generate the deduction that Bates must have killed his own mother earlier on, as well as having murdered two other young women that the police had treated as missing persons cases. The existence of these missing persons cases was not previously known to the psychiatrist, so his deduction – 'Have you got any unsolved missing persons cases?' – shows off his brilliance in classic Sherlock Holmes style.

In keeping with the prevalent sexist psychology of the day, the most important truth about Bates's deviant psyche concerns his overbearing mother. Bates's mother was a 'clinging, demanding woman', the psychiatrist explains. She and her son lived 'as if there was nobody else in the world' after the early death of Bates's father. With an absent father and a clinging mother, the son was bound to grow up to be pathologically attached to his mother. Thus, when she dared to go outside the neurotic mother–son duo to establish a romantic relationship, the young Norman murdered the lovers. The psychiatrist speaks as if this crime had to happen, given Bates's psychological make-up. But 'matricide is the most unbearable crime', the police and the victim's friends are told. Carefully avoiding the technical terms 'repression' and 'unconscious', the psychiatrist, who is Hitchcock's mouthpiece, nevertheless educates the audience in psychoanalytic theory as he suggests that Bates felt so (unconsciously) guilty about having killed his mother that he 'gave her half his life'. Bates pretended that she was still alive and started speaking to her corpse, eventually hearing her voice in his mind and even beginning to speak aloud in her voice.

The audience thus gets a quick tour of every Freudian 1950s cliché: unconscious desire for the mother, repressed guilt and shame about that desire, extreme but unconscious jealousy, and the transformation of desire into hatred as eros turns to thanatos. This well-known Freudian argument culminates in the deterministic creation of a psychotic murderer who, due mainly to bad mothering, has acquired many (though not all) of the features of what later would come to be called multiple personality disorder (MPD).

That the split personality theory – first mooted by WT Stead in relation to the Ripper, albeit relying more on Stevenson's fictional Mr Hyde than on medical science – would be prominently displayed at the conclusion of the most famous film ever made about psycho killers is no accident. As Jenkins's study shows, the figure of the serial/psycho killer is inextricably linked, in the American imaginary, with that of 'the multiple' – although to be classified as a 'multiple', strictly speaking, a patient needs to exhibit more than two personalities. As it became the subject of countless popular books and real-life court cases in the 1980s, multiple personality disorder was usually linked to child abuse. By contrast, the 1880s theory of 'double consciousness' or split personality tended to emphasize the way

Anthony Perkins' performance as the protagonist of Hitchcock's *Psycho* (1960) shaped popular understandings of crime.

in which a criminal or sex-crazed personality co-existed with a respectable one, but without much psychologizing about childhood.

Because in 1960 'multiple personality disorder' was not a household term, Hitchcock's shrink has to explain in some detail how the son introjected the (dead) mother. 'The mind houses two personalities', he explains. To show that the psychiatrist's knowledge is new to the listeners, the cop interjects that since Bates was dressed in his mother's old dress while attacking the heroine with a knife, he must be a 'tranvestite'. The shrink, however, corrects this misinterpretation as a lecturer corrects a student – or as Sherlock Holmes routinely corrects Dr Watson's sensible but incorrect conclusions. Bates is not a garden-variety, red-light district transvestite. His unique psyche requires a more sophisticated form of psychiatric knowledge than that gained by cops on the beat about transvestites and homosexuals. In a long and patronizing speech that presages later developments in real-life forensic psychiatry, the psychiatrist works hard to detach Bates from the vast mass of low-life petty criminals and everyday deviants that are the daily fare of police knowledge. This killer is different from those encountered by police. Only psychiatry can understand his motives and his identity.

It is crucial, in this context, that on the screen Norman Bates does not look at all like a criminal. He is tidy, his shirt is clean and pressed, and he is quite capable of running a business all by himself. He does of course commit murder, but that's because he has a double personality. In keeping with this psychiatrization, at the end of the film he is shown in a holding cell – but there are no other criminals around, and the cops in charge treat him very kindly, as if he were a patient in a nursing home.

So if he is not a conventional criminal, what is he? And who is to provide the American public with the knowledge necessary to identify and guard against this new risk, the psycho serial killer? Bates is a psycho killer who is more of a psycho than a killer. We see this particularly clearly when we note that the space usually allocated at the end of detective novels to revealing the meaning of clues and narrating the details of the crime is devoted instead to a psychiatric explanation of the dynamics of the criminal's twisted mind. The truths that are of interest and that allow the psychiatrist to deduce crimes that are not known to the police are not scattered on the ground: they are found in the inner psyche.

In sharp contrast to the Sherlock Holmes style of narrative, in which each physical clue is a link in the chain of a narrative culminating in the reconstruction of a specific act, here the crime with which he is being charged itself becomes a clue – a symptom. Having heard the psychiatrist's speech, we have the truth we need, the truth about the type of psycho who is overly attached to his mother. The details of how he murdered specific individuals do not seem to be of any interest to anyone. The only detail that is shown as 'The End' appears on the screen – the private investigator's car being dragged out of a swamp – is important only because it proves that the psychiatrist can deduce the existence of crimes previously unknown to the police. How Bates managed to push the car into the swamp would have been of great interest to Hercule Poirot and to Holmes, but it is of no interest to Hitchcock and to an audience fascinated not with clues but with the psycho's mind.

As the film ends we see Bates, wrapped in a blanket like an old woman, gradually adopting the raspy voice of the mother as well as her self-serving explanations of the murders. This full-fledged psychotic descent into the 'alter ego', the personality of the mother, is exactly what the psychiatrist had predicted only a few minutes earlier. His speech to those who courageously apprehended the criminal but who are now portrayed as ignorant students began precisely by predicting that Bates would never regain his own personality, and would slide into total madness by fully assuming the personality of the murdered mother. Thus, when we see Perkins's mobile face being subtly transformed into that of his dead mother, we experience the same awe in regard to the psychiatrist's knowledge that Dr Watson felt while listening to Holmes's lengthy chains of deductions. The difference, however, is that Holmes actually works hard to get to the truth – he concocts elaborate disguises, prowls London by night, performs chemical tests in his home laboratory, and in addition spends a great deal of time smoking a pipe or playing the violin, thinking. The psychiatrist, by contrast, neither collects clues nor undertakes a chase. He is not even shown interviewing Bates or reflecting on Bates's statements. He appears to the other characters, and hence to the audience, as a classic *deus ex machina*, providing the final truth without having done any work. He can do this because his truths come not from empirical observations or physical exertions but directly from the psychiatric texts.

In the US as in other advanced capitalist countries, the high-water mark of the welfare state idea was reached in the 1960s. Conditions previously left to religious orders or to philanthropic inner-city settlements – alcoholism, for example – suddenly came into the domain of psychiatry in the 1950s. And psychiatric social work and psychiatric nursing spread psychiatric knowledge beyond the confines of both hospitals and consulting offices and into unemployment centres, school guidance offices and immigrant-settlement organizations. In 1960, the educational systems of most English-speaking countries were undergoing an unprecedented expansion; and many social assistance programmes were devised and implemented as the decade wore on. Hitchcock's psychiatrist can thus be seen as an emblematic welfare-era authority figure whose power and prestige were immense – but short-lived. Subsequent filmic and novelistic representations of criminality, even those focusing specifically on the psychology of mad killers, do not feature authority figures comparable to the unnamed doctor (the generic psychiatrist) who gives the definitive closing truths in *Psycho*.

Medical expertise on crime was of course not new. For example, the Jack the Ripper phenomenon had made some space for medical expertise – Dr Forbes Winslow, a well-known specialist in diseases of the mind (an 'alienist', in the language of the time) had offered many explanations and suggestions, walking about Whitechapel so much that he began to be considered as a potential suspect (Walkowitz, 1992, p 213). And as we saw earlier, a second-hand version of the new medical theory of 'double consciousness' (Hacking, 1995) was put forward by Stead, though his account was a hybrid of music-hall stock figures (the hapless female victim, the aristocratic rake) and scientific concepts. The late Victorian period was certainly interested in the sciences of the mind, as numerous histories of psychiatry have shown; but in the 1880s – particularly in the case of murders without apprehended suspects – anti-Semitic fears rooted in medieval anxieties about purity and religion, as well as populist resentment against aristocrats seducing young working-class women, had as much if not more power than scientific theories and explanations.

By 1960, however, populist theories and explanations of 'psycho' crimes, while still in existence, could not rival the prestige of biomedical science, and psychiatry in particular. It is important to note that the prestige of psychiatry was not merely a matter of 'expert discourse' somehow prevailing by sheer semiotic power. Psychiatry would have had little influence had it not managed to leap out of the asylum and sink deep roots into the myriad institutions developed in many countries in the post-World War II era to provide health, education and welfare to all. The fact that the shrink whose truths conclude the film *Psycho* looks ridiculous to post-welfare audiences (when I show the film in class, my students always giggle when he begins to pontificate) is perhaps a small indication that the whole postwar dream of expert-led social security and social healthcare has faded.

The fragmentation of psy knowledges of psycho killers: *Silence of the Lambs*

Neither the welfare state in general nor psychiatric hospitals in particular have disappeared. They have, however, been downsized, transformed and restructured. And a major component of the restructuring has involved making way for other knowledges, some of which are new and some of which are old but have acquired a new lease of life. Health insurance plans now cover chiropractors, massage therapists, and sometimes Chinese medicine practitioners and other purveyors of previously marginalized knowledges. And while medical schools continue training psychiatrists using largely traditional frameworks and methods, a whole host of alternative practitioners of mental health have arisen to cover both middle-class and working-class demand. Middle-class people can and do go to 'life coaches', to non-medical psychotherapists, and to yoga classes. Alcoholics Anonymous, marginal low-prestige religions, and astrologers all flourish today in my own city, Toronto, as they do across North America and parts of the UK. As social theorists have pointed out, the father-knows-best model associated with Hitchock's all-seeing psychiatrist has given way to a neoliberal marketplace in which consumers are overwhelmed with information intended to 'empower' us to make our own informed choices, constructing a 'personalized plan' from a dizzying array of possible regimes, healers and helpers.

What about forensic psychiatry? This speciality has never been consumer driven, for obvious reasons rooted in the coercive nature of the criminal justice system. In this field the sort of 'informed consumer choice' that is now found in other areas of health services provision can hardly be implemented. But we do see the other features of neoliberal healthcare, and neoliberal knowledge production generally. We see the development of a quasi-market, in which various institutions vie with one another both for prestige and for contracts. And we also see knowledge being borrowed and adapted by all manner of untrained or differently trained practitioners much more rapidly than in the past. In the 1960s psychiatric nurses of course used 'borrowed' psychiatric knowledge, but they did not directly compete with MDs; there was a clearer hierarchy, among knowledges as among practitioners. And while physicians in the 1960s sometimes referred clients to non-medical services, Alcoholics Anonymous was pretty much the only widely available self-help group. Now, however, the provision of mental health services involves a large array of 'survivor' or self-help groups, as well as an increase in the number of para-professionals, often specializing in a particular condition or a particular type of patient and using ad hoc combinations of knowledges from a variety of sources. Devotion to a single theory is rare today, among healers of the soul as among academics.

This new fluidity of knowledge production and knowledge use reaches a high-water mark in the 1991 blockbuster film *Silence of the Lambs* directed by Jonathan Demme. The film's plot is unusually complex: instead of one hero/ authority pursuing the truth about one evildoer, we have multiple competing authorities and two separate but equally horrid murderers. And there are two psychiatrists: one imprisoned in a high-security dungeon and one in charge of the dungeon. Since the key interest here is not to see how criminals are represented, but rather to understand how the prestige of various authorities waxes and wanes, let us first note how the psychiatrists are portrayed, noting the use by the director of certain signs that convey authority or lack of it, and then go on to analyse the representation of second-hand psychiatric – or more accurately psychological – knowledges held by the FBI. Precisely because they exist not in their pure state but are thoroughly mixed with police experience, gut feelings, physical prowess and a passionate devotion to finding criminals, the second-hand psy knowledges held by the FBI turn out to be much more authoritative than the knowledges held by certified doctors.

Before the first 15 minutes of the film are over, the audience is introduced to two psychiatrists. One is an unctuous MD in charge of a Baltimore institution for the criminally insane, who is quickly discredited by being shown to be (a) a sexual harasser and (b) concerned more with his ego than with scientific findings about psycho killers. He makes a clumsy pass at the Jodie Foster character (FBI trainee Clarice Starling), and once his advances are repelled he stops feigning interest in the psychological scientific project that is the (ostensible) reason for her visit to his institution. Even before we meet his sleazy self, however, he is already discredited. (Hollywood films always use a great deal of 'redundancy', in that several signs, mainly non-verbal, shown in quick succession all convey the same message). The building housing the psychiatric-criminal unit he heads up is referred to, ana-chronistically, as 'an asylum', a word that has the effect of discrediting the dir-ector as well as the place. To compound this, the architecture as well as the furnishings are pure nineteenth century, as if to underscore the point that the old welfare state institutions are literally in tatters. The psychiatrist's desk does not even have a computer on it.

Having repelled the greasy advances of the non-authoritative psychiatrist, agent Starling proceeds to the Dickensian basement of the institution in question, which houses the notorious Hannibal Lecter (played by Anthony Hopkins). He is said to have been in prison for a very long time, having been found guilty of several horrible murders and acts of cannibalism. And yet, he seems to have preserved what WT Stead would have called his West End distinction. The other inmates of the dungeon-like unit are shown as stereotypical criminal madmen, but Lecter is still a gentleman. He speaks in the most educated of voices, using a peculiar mid-Atlantic accent. Furthermore when we first see him, he is busy producing very sophisticated architectural drawings in which he relies on his old memories of European travel. As he puts it, these make up for the fact that his cell is in a dank basement and 'has no view'. Like Stead's Ripper, he combines the most abject of crimes – including cannibalism, often regarded as a worse breach of moral codes than murder – with the ability to fully participate in a cosmopolitan world of refinement. With his own rather good drawing of the Florence skyline in the background, he describes to the horrified Starling how he killed someone and ate his victim's liver 'with fava beans and a nice Chianti'. Lecter is thus the most uncivilized of men – a cannibal – but also a man who, unlike most Americans, knows how to cook fava beans, and would open a good Italian wine to go along with his savage meal. He is thus totally unlike the ordinary, slobbering mad murderers who populate the back wards of hospitals for the criminally insane and who appear in the film as the background and the foil for Lecter's unique form of criminality.

As one could predict from the moment one sees the psychiatrist in charge return to his computerless study, it is the other psychiatrist, the one who is himself a psycho murderer and cannibal, who ends up helping the FBI to find the serial killer ('Buffalo Bill') who has been terrorizing communities. In one of the many reversals of knowledge authority in the film, it turns out that the psychological test that was the FBI's excuse for approaching Lecter – which would have objectified Lecter and helped the FBI to classify him better – was just a ruse. Starling's boss, Jack Crawford, knew full well that Lecter would refuse to be measured or studied in any way. But he thought that Lecter might be able to provide some suggestions that could help the FBI to catch their current serial killer at large. Crawford could not ask directly for Lecter's help, in part because he would refuse, and in part because the FBI's credibility would be endangered if they were known to be seeking help from such sources of psychological knowledge. But Lecter's knowledge could be mined nevertheless, Crawford has decided – especially if the agent who brings the test to him is not informed about the deception. Since Lecter is shown to be able to read motives as ordinary people read newspapers, it is more effective to set up a situation in which he might unwittingly reveal some useful clues. The mind game being played between Crawford and Lecter puts Starling in the role of duped intermediary, but she quickly grasps Crawford's real plan and takes it on as her own quest.

As the quest proceeds, Starling has to jump over a whole series of obstacles, psychological and literal, to find her target, in the time-honoured style of detective thrillers. But the quest has a more complicated structure than most thrillers due to Lecter's dual role, as a threat to the public and to Starling herself and also as a valuable source of knowledge about the killer who is at large. In the end, while the FBI's accumulated knowledge of psycho serial killers is useful in relation to the killer at large, whose 'profile' is presented as something well within the knowledge

of Crawford's behavioural science, the unique Dr Lecter cannot be either apprehended or understood with the FBI's combination of psychological science,
forensic skill, and physical courage. Lecter eludes them physically, having managed to escape; but more importantly, he eludes the FBI's agents as a knowledge
object. He is both the most dangerous criminal and the best authority on deviant
criminality, both the perfect object and the perfect subject. But his authority
comes in part from personal experience, which in the realm of crime is never
regarded as properly authoritative. The FBI's knowledge is certainly romanticized
and glamorized in this film, and they do catch their main prey: but whether they
can recapture the escaped Lecter and subject him to their specialized gaze is left to
the sequel. Serial killers as a category are definitely within the FBI's purview, as
knowledge objects and as criminals to be apprehended. But Lecter constantly
escapes their gaze and even turns the forensic gaze back on itself – he is shown
surreptitiously following Starling.

For our purposes, what matters most is that the only source of psychological
knowledge about serial killers that is not discredited does not emanate either from
psychiatric doctrine or from actual psychiatrists. Rather, the source of knowledge
that proves most authoritative is located inside the FBI building (which was actually used as a set). The FBI is glamorized from the very beginning of the film.
Before the opening credits roll, agent Starling is shown valiantly sweating through
a difficult obstacle course, and the building that she returns to – large, expensive,
ultra-modern, full of earnest looking young recruits, and located in the woods, not
in a seedy downtown – appears to the audience as the exact opposite, the antith-
esis of the Dickensian Baltimore 'asylum'. Thus, while at the start of the film
audiences have not yet learned which characters are most trustworthy and authoritative, the sharp contrast between the two buildings and their occupants already
communicate to the audience, via a series of carefully calibrated binary opposi-
tions, the message that it will be the forces of contemporary law-and-order that
will not only apprehend the suspects but provide the authoritative account of the
'type' (serial/psycho killer). The whole apparatus of welfare-state psychiatry is
discredited from the moment we see the dilapidated 'asylum' building and meet its
sleazy occupant.

As the camera follows agent Starling into the FBI building, we see large numbers of fit, capable-looking agents engaged in target practice and other traditional
law-and-order pursuits. But we also see that the building incorporates certain
elements borrowed from university-based science. We meet Jack Crawford, head
of the Behavioral Sciences Unit. And we find out that he not only knows some
psychology but even teaches courses in Psychology at the University of Virginia.
This detail is important, since it shows that the FBI's scientific credentials are
recognized even in prestigious public universities (not only in police training
academies).

As Jenkins explains, Jack Crawford is modelled to some extent on the FBI's
John Douglas, who successfully borrowed various bits of psychological knowledges of deviance and combined these with existing forensic techniques to create
the new science (or art) of 'profiling' (Jenkins, 1994). The story of John Douglas's
contribution to psychological science had first been told by novelist Thomas

Harris, whose novels (*Red Dragon* and *Silence of the Lambs*) were the basis for the film *Silence of the Lambs* and its sequels.

Jenkins notes that in the novel that was turned into the film under discussion:

> The BSU [Behavioral Sciences Unit] was portrayed as an elite team of superdetectives called in to assist local agencies facing the threat of savage roaming killers, while there was at least the [incorrect] impression that the unit had a special jurisdiction over serial murder cases wherever they occurred ... Intentionally or not, Thomas Harris provided the FBI's violent-crime experts with invaluable publicity and unprecedented visibility. (Jenkins, 1994, p 73)

This publicity could not have come at a better time, since the FBI was facing major cutbacks from a Congress that had become highly critical of the FBI after investigating their mishandling of a major act of sabotage in the US Navy.

The FBI has never had jurisdiction over murder. But after the public relations coup scored by the Thomas Harris novel and the subsequent film, local communities and municipal police forces were unlikely to resist the pressure to seek help from the specialized 'superdetectives' of the FBI's Behavioral Sciences Unit, particularly since calling in the feds would alleviate pressures on municipal police budgets. It is important to note, however, that the unit was not merely a passive recipient of good publicity. John Douglas, in particular, became very adept at actively using the media to promote his books and his own consulting career.

Luckily for Douglas, just as *Silence of the Lambs* was being released, a cannibalistic serial killer was apprehended and brought to justice, in real life that is: Jeffrey Dahmer. Dahmer was not a psychiatrist and was not heterosexual; nevertheless, the slippage between the real-life Dahmer featured in the nightly news and the Hannibal Lecter of the movie (who in turn is loosely based on the Ed Gein 1950s case) helped the FBI's public relations a great deal. In turn, the FBI's unique knowledge tool – 'profiling' – was disseminated to other police forces and other countries (such as Canada), by the real-time travel of FBI agents and ex-agents consulting with other police forces and by other, often commercial, avenues through which agents past and present were able to share their expertise.

Some former FBI agents were able to develop a lucrative career by becoming consultants to 'reality' television programmes, mainly on Court TV. Their post-retirement consulting work with television programmes closes the circle that links 'real-life' law enforcement to on-screen images, the circle created as the prestige and the emotional appeal of well-known films rub off on real-life police institutions – and vice versa.

Conclusion

The representations analysed in this chapter are obviously not a random sample. But neither are they obscure or marginal. The Jack the Ripper phenomenon can be regarded as a sort of paradigm case or original model for a whole series of representations of crimes and criminals, among which the films analysed here are two of the most memorable and popular. Many analyses of the 'psycho killer' phenomenon exist; but, while paying some attention to shifts in how criminal mad-men or mad criminals are represented, the main concern of this chapter has been to focus not on the psycho himself but on the authorities who apprehend and study this particular 'type'.

The figure of Jack the Ripper gave rise to a whole panoply of competing author-ities, partly because science had not yet established a firm grip on either madness or criminality, and partly because the Ripper's very anonymity fostered open-ended debates. Hitchock's *Psycho*, by contrast, presents us with a frightening figure who can be understood by the psychiatrist and only by the psychiatrist. But later representations (and later real-life cases too, although we did not examine any here) show the monopoly of medically trained experts being challenged from other quarters. In some situations psychiatric expertise is rejected altogether in favour of a populist discourse of 'monsters' (as in British and American public discussions of sex offenders released into the community). But in other situations what we see is not so much a return to pre-scientific populism but rather the success of second-hand psychological and psychiatric knowledges held mainly by specialized police units.

The evident prestige, in American life and on the screen, of the FBI's Behavioral Sciences Unit, which claims to be able to apprehend serial killers by the use of 'profiling', is linked, we have argued, to a broader shift in the formation of authoritative knowledges. The fact that the FBI combines physical prowess, mili-tary skills, psychological knowledge of deviance, the gut feeling that good detect-ives have always laid claim to, and a computerized database that holds many more data than Sherlock Holmes's famously capacious brain, is in keeping with general developments in the production of knowledge. Today, combining sources of authority and kinds of knowledge is seen to add to one's prestige, rather than de-tracting from the purity of science. In the domain of criminal justice, risk assess-ments using psychological categories are generally combined with 'everyday' or common-sense knowledges in the practical work involved in managing offenders. In my own city, for example, scientific psychology is used to devise drug treatment programmes for federal offenders, but the Salvation Army's important role in organizing community service orders, homes for ex-offenders and parole supervi-sion has not been supplanted. My local halfway house for male federal parolees offers quasi-scientific drug treatment (provided by young women with a com-munity college degree, not by psychologists) alongside old-fashioned Bible meet-ings. Mixing second-hand science with non-scientific traditional types of know-ledge seems to be the recipe for success within the criminal justice system today.

The medical project to monopolize knowlege of crime and deviance, which is represented in almost pure form by Hitchcock, has not failed, since forensic psy-chiatrists still ply their trade and carry a certain authority. The medicalization project, however, has certainly been transformed almost beyond recognition. In our own era, representations of madmen and of criminals do not necessarily gain in prestige or authority if they are certified by a high-status professional. Mixed knowledges appear to be the rule. We shall see in the next chapter that the mixed-knowledges formula is also at work in a very different area, namely, representa-tions not of humans but of spaces – criminogenic spaces and safe spaces.

Chapter 8

Chronotopes of Crime: Perceptions of Danger in Urban Space

Previous chapters have critically examined how certain people – either unique individuals or types – appear, in various regimes of visibility, as inherently bad or dangerous. They have also examined how the authority to know crime and danger and to protect society has come to be embodied in certain authoritative persons or institutions. Visualization is key to the social construction of both crime/danger and of its opposite or its remedy, namely, safety and order.

But messages and myths about crime and danger are not restricted to representations of persons, human types and institutions. Spaces too, especially urban spaces, are experienced as either safe or unsafe somewhat independently of the persons who happen to be located there at any one time. Of course certain spaces come to have a certain reputation, mainly because they are thought to be inhabited by questionable or dangerous types of persons. But once a certain kind of space has been repeatedly associated with bad people or bad events (either through real-life events or through repeated representations), the characteristic features of such a space become signs in and of themselves. This insight has been exploited for law-and-order purposes by the 'broken-windows' school of applied criminology, which developed precisely from the premise that a broken window and litter on the street were signs in and of themselves, regardless of actual crime rates in the area. These signs, it was said, needed to be acted upon and changed so as to send a different, more welcoming message to the urban middle classes.

This insight about the semiotic importance of apparently minor visual cues gave rise, from the mid-1980s onward, to a whole series of community-policing and community safety projects designed to change signs, meanings and myths. The Toronto Police Service, for instance, developed in the 1990s a programme to eradicate graffiti. The website for this programme shows 'before' and 'after' pictures of walls and alleys. The impression is given that changing the paint will improve the moral tone of the neighbourhood. The website's photographs also show convicts in their distinctive orange jumpsuits doing the painting – as if the convicts' own souls were being scrubbed clean through the same forced labour that changes the semiotics of the walls.

One does not have to share the right-wing politics of the police force's graffiti eradicators and other promoters of 'broken windows', zero-tolerance policing to recognize that there is some truth in their fundamental premise. That truth is that even when there's nobody around, we all interpret little visual cues, such as broken windows or litter, in such a way as to make instant judgements about the safety or lack of safety that prevails in a particular space – and we do this whether we are seeing the space directly, with our own eyes, or whether we are seeing it represented in a film or a news programme.

This chapter examines some of the ways in which particular spaces come to be imbued with a sense of danger. It also initiates a reflection on the fact that, just as each perception of criminality helps to generate an image of a particular form of crime-solving authority, so too, each idea about what makes urban spaces look dangerous generates a kind of shadow representation, namely, a visual image of safety and peace. This is very important: while most criminologists could easily show that certain perceptions about dangerous spaces – e.g. thinking that graffiti on the walls of an alleyway always mean danger – are based on nothing but prejudice and myth, few criminologists study beliefs and myths about safety. Ian Taylor's analysis of his neighbours' feelings about crime and space is one of the few detailed empirical studies to help us think critically about why it is that a street with single-family detached homes surrounded by neatly clipped hedges appears as inherently safe and crime-free (Taylor, 1995).

The basic semiotic insight that meaning is always relational and contextual, which was developed in Chapters 1 and 2, is here used to analyse some examples of the dialectic between safe spaces and dangerous spaces. We can better understand how and why certain places (graffiti-covered alleys, badly lit parking lots) seem 'bad' if we analyse why certain other places (well-kept, single-family homes) seem instantly 'good'. And while certain signs of order or disorder are interpreted in much the same way by a variety of subpopulations, it is important to note at the outset that the general dialectic of good places/bad places, signs of order/disorder also depends (as do all semiotic systems) on the particular context in which the signs are 'consumed' or interpreted. To give an example from my teaching experience: I once had a student, who worked as a call girl, organize a focus group of sex trade workers to canvass their views about safe vs. unsafe places, for an assignment on perceptions of urban space. For these women, hotel lobbies and hotel elevators were safe – if any client got out of hand, help was near, they said. But making out-calls to isolated single-family homes in the suburbs was regarded as very risky. A photo of a 'nice' suburban home evoked feelings of danger among the group participants. Thus, the dominant culture's binary opposition (unsafe downtown, safe suburbs) was turned upside down: the experiences acquired in the course of their work resulted in the women developing a different semiotic code for interpreting visual cues of safety and danger.

There is a large literature on (mainstream) public perceptions of the visual cues that surround us and that act as signifiers of disorder or danger. Most of that literature takes public perceptions at face value and seeks simply to give advice to urban planners, community groups and parks departments about which visual cues will further people's feelings of safety. This advice literature assumes that it does not matter whether people's perceptions are actually justified in terms of real crime risks, or whether the semiotic codes act to reinforce class, race or other power dynamics. One of the main tenets of mainstream crime prevention and urban design literature is that public perceptions are self-fulfilling prophecies: even if they are based on prejudices, they end up becoming true just because people believe in them. People will stay away from spaces perceived as dangerous, an action that will have the effect of making those spaces actually dangerous – whether they originally were or not – as respectable folks flee to and stay in spaces that display more familiar and more comforting visual cues.

Sometimes the generally accepted semiotic codes for deciphering urban visual cues are simply mistaken. Some important US court decisions on zoning rules applying to sex shops assume that the areas around the sex shops will end up being populated only by questionable characters, such as beggars and men with no fixed address. But neither judges nor the gentrifiers living in downtown US cities seem to be aware that recent research shows that in American cities, sex shops are actually better lit, better guarded, and hence more crime-free than comparable locations (gas stations, small grocery stores) that are not burdened by negative cultural associations but which are in fact more dangerous (Linz et al., 2004).

For practical purposes of urban design, it is important to try to introduce accurate information – such as the study just cited – into urban planning deliberations. However, this is not the goal of this chapter. In keeping with the general approach laid out in the initial chapters, we will not engage here in the debate about whether the public's fears are justified, or try to give advice about how to replace prejudices by rational argument and correct information. Instead, we shall offer some analytical tools that both criminologists and the general public can use to understand better the complex cultural, political and psychological processes by which certain associations are routinely made between visual cues on the one hand and feelings of safety or danger on the other.

In order to encourage this kind of critical analysis of the cultural and semiotic processes underlying the often heated debates about urban safety, it will be useful to provide a brief overview of different ways in which sociology, urban studies and criminology have themselves used visualizations of space to represent (aggregate) danger and safety. As we shall see, urban sociology and criminology have often failed to adopt a critical distance in regard to public perceptions and prejudices, and have instead added a scholarly gloss to common-sensical, middle-class ideas about the link between signs of poverty, on the one hand, and crime on the other. But before we go on to the historical overview of sociological and criminological visualizations of urban space, a note about the importance of temporality is in order.

The temporality of space: Bakhtin's 'chronotope'

Urban studies, urban sociology and most crime prevention literature on urban space and perceptions of danger treat spaces as having a relatively fixed identity. A qualifying comment might be made about the fact that a given space might be or might look more dangerous at night than during the day, but other than such passing comments, temporality is often ignored. Literature on crime prevention through environmental design (CPTED), for example, is replete with diagrams and photographs, but very rarely is there a mention made in the caption of the relevant time of day. Indeed, while photographs have a particular temporality embedded in them (even if the caption does not highlight it), the black-and-white diagrams popularized by 1960s and 1970s crime prevention specialists – diagrams that purport to show urban dwellers the virtues and defects of certain kinds of design arrangements – are presented as timeless. Diagrams showing such things as a housing complex designed with a courtyard of optimum dimensions – optimum here meaning dimensions that facilitate the informal, unpaid surveillance of the courtyard by residents who have windows along the courtyard – have no reference to time. The fact that during a portion of the day most residents are at work or in school, and thus unavailable for this kind of informal surveillance, is not mentioned. Neither is the fact that in the middle of the night people are mainly sleeping, and are thus unable to observe intruders.

The general problem of ignoring temporality is exemplified in the crime prevention phrase attributed in the literature to urbanist Jane Jacobs ('eyes on the street'), one of the most influential pieces of criminological knowledge of all time. The idea put forward by Jacobs and taken up in crime prevention literature was that instead of asking for more uniformed police patrols, neighbourhoods would be better off encouraging architectural designs and patterns of behaviour that further 'natural surveillance', that is, surveillance carried out by non-specialized personnel as an adjunct to their everyday lives. Jacobs's rather idealized portrait of her Greenwich village daily life, with neighbours walking rather than driving to shops, and with small shopkeepers interacting daily with numerous people known to them by sight, has been repeatedly used as a model of how to improve safety without increasing police numbers or hiring private security. In Jacobs's view, safety is the product of everyday informal relations of trust (Jacobs, 1961).

This is sensible enough; but the phrase 'eyes on the street' does not take temporality into consideration. The phrase, coined at a time – the 1960s – when most middle-class and many working-class married women did not go out to work every day, encourages the naturalization of a historically specific family form marked by a distinct daily and weekly temporality. Kitchen windows that look out on to an inner courtyard acts as a crime-prevention mechanism only if someone – the traditional housewife, mainly – is actually washing dishes and casually looking out during her working day. The 'breadwinner' family that was the norm during the postwar era had a particular temporal organization as well as a

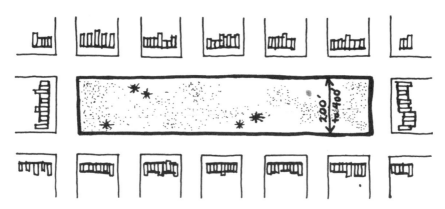

Architect Oscar Newman developed the criminological concepts 'defensible space' and 'territoriality' and advocated for urban design strategies involving what urbanist Jane Jacobs famously called 'eyes on the street' (in Oscar Newman, *Defensible Space*, New York, Macmillan, 1972).

distinctive arrangement of gender roles. Most women were home in the daytime; and small children were much more numerous in that baby-boom generation than they are in many of today's urban neighbourhoods. A dual-income couple without children, especially if they frequently go out in the evening, will be unlikely to be involved in the sort of informal interactions that generate trust exemplified by the famous phrase 'eyes on the street'. Their temporal rhythms do not facilitate informal surveillance.

If temporality is a crucial feature of 'normal' social relations, so too is it a hugely important dimension of criminality and danger. Certain kinds of crimes are committed almost exclusively by day – from corporate fraud to bank hold-ups, to property damage committed by children playing truant. Other crimes, such as thefts from automobiles, are committed mainly under cover of darkness. The truly horrific crimes – child abduction and rape, for example – do not have specific temporalities. But the most common, run-of-the-mill crimes do have certain temporal cycles, partly because they are less likely to be planned in advance and are more dependent on opportunity. And opportunity is usually temporally specific. Brawls outside of pubs and bars, to mention only the most obvious example, take place almost exclusively within fairly narrow temporal parameters, and are highly concentrated around closing time. Drinking and driving is similarly concentrated temporally: no doubt there are some cases of drunk drivers at 9 am, but local police data virtually everywhere in the English-speaking world show a marked temporal concentration of this crime. Weekly and seasonal variations are also important. Friday and Saturday evenings are different from other evenings, and the weeks before Christmas, when office parties and other social occasions abound, pose particular risks. Safety and disorder are thus as much dependent on time as on space.

It would not be helpful, however, to focus on the temporal distribution of crimes and risks – and on perceptions of the criminal propensities, so to speak, of various times of day or times of the year – to the detriment of analysing spatialization. It is more appropriate to try to address both spatialization and temporalization at the same time in our analyses. This can be done, I argue, if we borrow from the great Russian cultural theorist Mikhail Bakhtin the term 'chronotope', which means, roughly, a particular way of combining temporality and spatialization.

In work carried out in the 1920s and 1930s, Bakhtin used the term 'chronotope' to describe differences among literary genres (Bakhtin, 1981). Without going into detail, it is easy to see that a Greek mythological epic has a different temporality and a different way of spatializing events than those found in, say, a Jane Austen novel. When the novel was first invented, the temporality of family life – particularly of that bit of family life that precedes marriage – was thought to be intrinsic to the novel form, and readers would have complained if their novels had not ended in at least one and preferably two or three weddings. Later on the novel form was employed more creatively. Today one subgenre of the novel is science fiction, in which a distinctive temporality – the future – enables the author to construct spaces that are not only fictional but implausible and fantastical. Similarly, soap operas are distinguished from other dramatic television series by a certain temporality: the open-ended story with multiple subplots that branch off indefinitely, without any final closure – just like real family life. This temporalization is the opposite of the closure-centred, much more linear temporality of the detective story. In keeping with Bakhtin's notion of the chronotope, the unique temporality of the soap format is closely linked to certain typical spaces. Some scenes might be shot outdoors, or in a boardroom; but the soap opera's paradigmatic spaces are the kitchen and the living room, the sites of perpetual, open-ended family conflicts. Thus, if Bakhtin had lived long enough to analyse television, he might have produced an analysis of the chronotope of the soap opera.

So what does this have to do with crime and urban space? The answer is that it is important to remember that each space appears to us not abstractly (cf. the crime-prevention drawing of the ideal courtyard) but rather embedded in a particular temporality. Particular urban experiences are always temporally as well as spatially specific. To give an obvious example, the pub at 11 am is just not the same place as the pub at 11 pm. And a park is not the same place on a sunny Sunday morning as on a rainy winter night. If we are documenting either actual changes in crime and disorder or people's feelings and views about crime and disorder, it is thus essential to be specific about time as well as about space. And Bakhtin's key point is that time and space are not independent from each other. While there is always flexibility – someone could be drinking and driving at 9 am – there are certain culturally specific links between the temporality and the spatialization of all activities, including crime.

Our urban environment is thus best regarded as made up of chronotopes rather than as made up only of spaces or even of spaces + times. Certain chronotopes feel and look 'scary' and full of potential crime; other chronotopes feel safe. When we go about our daily business, we constantly take unconscious mental notes regarding our own temporal location, as well as taking unconscious or conscious notes about the visual cues – spatially located signs that we think tell us whether we are in a safe place or not. To give another everyday example, most women will take certain precautions at night that they would not employ for the same space at 10 am. And they will do so without consciously articulating elaborate theories about danger and temporality.

Early social mapping of urban poverty and crime

The ancient binary opposition of good vs. bad places did not become the subject of scientific study until late in the history of Western cities. Certain social reformers, particularly those interested in public health and in factory-related poverty, began quasi-scientific studies of urban slums in the 1840s. But it was mainly in the 1880s and 1890s that socially concerned, middle-class writers and philanthropists in both England and the US developed tools, presentation devices and semiotic codes to visually represent, in a scientific manner, the spatial differentiation of cities. Schematic maps and diagrams, in particular, provided the reading public with something that their own eyes could not reveal, however much they walked around the city: a bird's-eye view of the city.

In England, the most innovative bird's-eye mapper of urban poverty was

Charles Booth, an independent researcher who was neither a civil servant nor a university teacher. He undertook a huge study of social and economic conditions in London, especially the East End (Booth, 1891). His important role in the history of visualizing urban space is partly due to the fact that he decided to focus not on individual households, or on the city as a whole, but rather on what he thought was the experientially basic unit of city living: the street. Over a period of several years he gathered detailed information about work and poverty on each and every street in East End London. He did this not by entering households and asking directly for information, but rather by talking with local ministers, doctors and other worthies, who in those pre-survey days were thought to be the most authoritative sources of knowledge about urban ills. Having gathered information from what he thought were the best sources, he obtained an Ordnance Survey map and proceeded to translate his vast collection of data into a classification scheme aggregating information about households – wages, drinking habits, truancy among the family's children, etc. – into a rating for the street as a whole. He then used colour to show street-level differences in poverty and 'vice'.

The now standard technique of using colour-differentiated maps to show the spatial distribution of social, geophysical or economic facts was then novel; colour printing was very expensive and generally reserved for art books. Booth, who had a private income, paid his publisher to append a large coloured map to the final volume of his multi-volume study of the East End, a map that had to be printed separately and folded and glued to the back cover.

The colour scheme used in Booth's map reflected long-standing mythological associations: light colours such as yellow were used for the 'better' streets, and the two worst social conditions were represented by purple and black. Forgetting that he himself chose the rather symbolically laden colours, Booth admired his own map in the following terms: 'the eye readily notices . . . those black spots which betoken a miserable combination of poverty, vice, and crime' (Booth, 1891, p 335). 'Black spot' is here a very useful word because it has several signifieds: the black ink used to colour in the actual map; the soot; filth and unsanitary conditions of the London streets; the immorality and vice traditionally associated, in Christian culture, with the word 'black'; and the primitive ignorance associated with the 'dark' continent (Africa), regularly compared, at that time, to the equally primitive ignorance of metropolitan tribes.

The urban map with coloured streets was an innovation in the inscription techniques of sociology that became instantly popular. An influential Edwardian urban reformer, Charles Masterman, copied Booth's technique. Like Booth, Masterman drew the attention of his middle-class readership not to the actual poor people of the East End but rather to the map. He exhorted his readers to pay close attention to the 'blotches of black and dark blue that arise now in the midst of the red artisans' quarters' (Masterman, 1907, p 20) – as if the artisans' houses were actually red and the poorest of the poor lived in physically black houses.

Masterman's habit of treating the representation (the map) as more real than the houses it represents foreshadows later American urban sociology, which exhibits a similar tendency to treat the texts and the maps as more real than the families and neighbourhoods that they schematically represent. Tellingly, as

Masterman thinks he is describing social processes, it is obvious to the reader that he is actually just looking at his map:

> The black aggregations disappear from the chart of poverty . . . But . . . the effect of scattering is clearly traceable in the surrounding areas. It is as if one washed out an inskpot on a picture with water; the blot vanishes, but the whole neighbourhood sensibly becomes coloured a darker hue. (Masterman, 1907, p 21)

Techniques to visually represent the differentiation of urban spaces in black and white, and specifically as schematic maps, were also pioneered, more or less at the same time, on the other side of the Atlantic, especially in Chicago. The social reformers associated with Jane Addams's Hull House – the first of many 'settlement houses' providing social services, recreation and labour market information to immigrant and poor families, mainly on a philanthropic basis – also developed their own techniques for localizing poverty and crime and rendering this knowledge visually apparent on a two-dimensional piece of paper. The Hull House maps of a multi-ethnic Chicago neighbourhood, whose large-scale originals are on display today on the walls of the House itself (now a historical site), used similar mapping techniques. The borrowing of Booth's semiotic innovation – the detailed coloured map of the city – is highlighted in the introduction (Residents of Hull House, [1895] 1970). But the data sources were different: instead of asking clergymen and school inspectors to relay their own knowledge of poor households, the inhabitants were directly interviewed.

Nevertheless, the rise of the new formats did not immediately result in a decline of older, unscientific formats. Even in the Hull House documents, ethno-centric cultural assumptions are visible. The colour black, long associated with danger, ignorance and sin, was unproblematically chosen to represent African-American people and households. The equally symbolically loaded colour white was in turn used to represent white Americans – and English, Scottish and English Canadian immigrants. Irish-American households were, in turn, coloured green.

Seeing aggregate deviance: the Chicago School's mode of visualization

The late nineteenth-century international movement focusing on urban reform that generated scientific studies such as Charles Booth's work and the Hull House *Maps and Papers* was not university based, and its key concerns were practical even though much effort was spent on social science research. It makes sense that a movement that did not see science and practical reform as mutually exclusive endeavours would be fairly eclectic in its information formats and its modes of visualization. But as social science began to differentiate itself from social reform, and to set up academic institutions such as the London School of Economics and Political Science and the University of Chicago department of sociology, the creative mixing of formats and sources of authority gave way to more rigid and standardized formats. Melodramatic tales about individuals were excluded from the texts produced by the new university-based experts on urban ills and social deviance – experts who began to call themselves 'sociologists' – and colour was both literally and metaphorically purged from the new textbooks.

In the United Kingdom, sociology took longer to find a firm foothold in the universities than it did in the US and in France. Even outside the academy, however, modernizing researchers such as Sidney and Beatrice Webb produced fully scientific texts that strictly avoided both sensation and human interest. The Webbs's numerous and impressive-looking volumes – compiled with the help of a group of research assistants paid out of Beatrice's private fortune – marked a new standard in English social scientific prose and social scientific formatting. Gone were the emotional engravings found in magazines and in evangelical texts. Instead, one finds page upon page of black-on-white, small-font type, relieved by nothing except columns of numbers. And the tone of the writing is equally monotone and dry.

Most of the Webbs's voluminous publications were generated in the context of government or private inquiries leading to policy change, so they were what would later be called 'policy documents'. But however politically committed, the Webbs worshipped the scientific method. Most tellingly, they took the trouble to publish detailed instructions about how exactly researchers should take notes from archives and other sources of primary data. Write down one fact on a single sheet, they advised, and on the top right-hand corner put a symbol indicating what topic or topics this fact belongs to: in this way, when using the data to write a book, the sheets can be shuffled and reshuffled so as to collect together all of the facts bearing on a particular topic, but allowing that the same fact might be used in different sections for different purposes. The Webbs's researchers must have collected literally millions of these single sheets of paper, a collection that could rival any contemporary database. (The Webbs helpfully included a sample of such a sheet, one of the few visual aids contained in their publications.) This standardized sheet of paper was an advanced form of information technology, at a time when neither photocopiers nor computers, or for that matter coloured highlighters, had yet been invented. But in the long run the English-speaking world's array of tools and codes to visualize and map urban deviance and crime would be more influenced by the University of Chicago department of sociology – the home of the first fully academic urban sociology research projects – than by the Webbs.

Key to the self-defined mission of the new departments of sociology was a strict separation between knowledges of individual deviance – assigned to the older profession of psychiatry and to the newer discipline of psychology – and the knowledges of aggregate deviance, which sociology saw as its own distinct contribution. In earlier chapters we touched upon some of the medical knowledges of deviance and crime that constituted individual criminals and types (e.g. forensic psychiatry), particularly focusing on the representation of these knowledges in crime films. Urban sociology, by contrast, has not played much of a role in Hollywood or in other popular representations of either deviance or its remedies. And yet, sociology's tools of visualization were not without influence, particularly in regard to how we see the city.

While French sociology developed as a science of 'societies', meaning national societies, in the United States sociology had a particular affinity for the city. And among the Chicago School's innovations – at the level of format and presentation

– there is little doubt that the one that stands out for its longevity is the simple black-on-white diagram of concentric circles that purports to represent the ideal-typical or paradigmatic structure, not of 'society' (that Durkheimian object visualized in national statistics) but rather of the city – the city as such (cf. Chapter 4).

The concentric circles diagram was developed out of data gathered in Chicago by Robert Park, Ernest Burgess and Roderick McKenzie, all at the University of Chicago's sociology department (see Figure 4.2). The data gathering was in turn driven by a pre-existing theoretical commitment to an organic and functionalist vision that emphasized slow and unplanned evolution and underplayed conflict. Loosely applying the conceptual structures of evolutionary biology to the social, and using the biological term 'evolution' first as a metaphor but then as a 'real' descriptor, these sociologists looked at the city as a macro-organism. They sought to reveal the ways in which different environmental conditions (e.g. economic activity, demographic structure and geography) generated different city forms, in the same way that among natural organisms environmental conditions facilitate the rise or decline of certain species.

In relation to crime and deviance, the most important claim made by the Chicago School was that the process by which different ethnic and socio-economic groups came to occupy different neighbourhoods and streets was a natural one, akin to the process by which different bird populations come to dominate this or that wetland. Even African-American segregated housing, a direct result of slavery, appeared in this way of seeing the city as somehow natural and normal. As the popular text *The City* put it: 'Personal tastes and convenience, vocational and economic interests, infallibly tend to segregate and thus to classify the populations of great cities. In this way the city acquires an organization and distribution of population which is neither designed nor controlled' (Park et al., 1925, p. 7).

Just as Charles Booth did not think it necessary to explain why he chose the colour black to represent the worst poverty and vice, so too the Chicago School's famous circles are naturalized through neutral-sounding descriptions that make it seem as if race and class were 'natural' groupings:

> Business and industry seek advantageous locations [inner circle] and draw around them certain portions of the population. There spring up fashionable residential quarters from which the poorer classes are excluded becuse of the increased value of the land. Then there grow up slums which are inhabited by great numbers of the poorer classes who are unable to defend themselves from association with the derelict and vicious. (Ibid, p 21).

The circles diagram does not apply to many American cities: the diagram cannot be superimposed on Manhattan, to give just one example. And even a passing acquaintance with the great European capitals would have shown that the middle-class preference for the outer suburbs, in the 1920s, was US-specific. The grande bourgeoisie of Europe lived, until perhaps the 1970s or 1980s, in large apartments on major avenues near the downtown core. In general, in the Chicago School account, the cultural, economic and legal specificities that gave rise to urban forms in which the bourgeoisie preferred to live in single-family homes at a certain distance from the centre were swept under the carpet. Similarly, the concentration of African-Americans and Asian immigrants in certain inner-city neighbourhoods was imagined as an organic 'natural' process rather than as a political fact.

Critical geographers and sociologists of knowledge have long analysed the political manoeuvres accomplished through the apparently politically neutral activity of drawing maps and bringing those maps – often across empires – to some centre of power which then uses the map to carry out various governance projects at a distance. They have also analysed how it is that the map or the statistical chart acquires a reality of its own and comes to be talked about as if it were more real than the events it purports to represent, with its users often forgetting that the tools they use are just tools, not perfect embodiments of the world. The longevity of the Chicago School's circle diagram (still found in sociology textbooks to this day) shows that the history and the features of technical tools, including presentation tools like drawings and charts, needs to be closely analysed. Only by paying attention to formats, codes and presentation conventions can we gain a full analysis of how crime and deviance – aggregate crime and deviance, in particular – have been visualized and understood.

CPTED: visual cues of disorder and of safety

Today's social science texts do not feature illustrations of criminal faces or skulls such as those that graced the works of the criminal anthropologists of the 1890s. Neither do they contain anything like the drawings and photographs of 'degenerate' bodies that gave interest to the works on 'feeble-mindedness' of the 1910s and 1920s. Quantitative studies are of course full of tables, and these are now often coloured (especially on PowerPoint presentations). But these illustrations are nothing but visual renditions of relations among numbers. The average quantitative sociological article is extremely unlikely to contain any depiction of persons, human types or urban spaces.

For their part, qualitative and critical writing about 'the underclass' and about the links between poverty and crime usually lack illustrations of any kind, even tables or graphics. In books, as opposed to journals, one may occasionally encounter some journalistic photographs illustrating qualitative sociological works. An unusual example of the use of photographs of actual people is the ethnography of Manhattan street vending by Mitchell Duneier, entitled *Sidewalk* (Duneier, 1999). Duneier's representational choice, probably influenced by contemporary anthropological ethics, which prompts researchers to acknowledge their informants by name, is not common in academic texts. It is not coincidental that Duneier's book was not published by a university press. Even analyses of crime films or police television shows often appear without any pictures (e.g. Sparks, 1996). It is as if, in an overreaction against the old stereotypical images of criminal types and dangerous individuals popular in earlier decades, progressive social scientists have become afraid of imagery as such.

But in less academically oriented settings, innovations in visual tools for representing crime, danger and deviance have flourished. Conventions vary widely, and so, to avoid the dangers of generalization, the discussion here will be limited to one of the main current literatures addressing the theme of this chapter: 'Crime Prevention Through Environmental Design' (CPTED). Not coincidentally, this is a literature that is mainly non-academic.

It is not inappropriate to consider US public housing architect Oscar Newman's 1972 book *Defensible Space: Crime Prevention through Urban Design* as the key early text setting out the main tenets of CPTED. These tenets can be reduced, for simplicity's sake, to two: 'natural surveillance' (which is much the same as Jane Jacobs's 'eyes on the street') and 'defensible space'.

Natural surveillance

An important reason for the popularity of 'natural surveillance' is that the high property crime rates of the 1960s and 1970s encouraged municipal officials, social housing architects, planners and police forces to find ways of enlisting ordinary people in the work of crime-prevention surveillance, since it was clear that police officers could not possibly watch every space at all times. It was also found by consultants specializing in such crimes as pilfering by company employees that ongoing informal surveillance of employees by other employees and by management was more effective in minimizing losses than trying to catch and punish wrongdoers. This led to a veritable boom in office renovations. Receptionists' desks were moved to spots where the clerical staff could watch the elevators and entrances; supply cupboards were moved so that sightlines would not be blocked by corners or filing cabinets; and to supplement and reinforce the security features embedded in the architectural and furniture arrangements, all employees were encouraged to exercise vigilance at all times.

The concept of natural surveillance takes crime prevention out of the specialized domain of police and private security and embeds it into the daily routines of everyone who lives or works in a particular place – people who are not paid to 'do security', but who are somehow persuaded to add security to their existing obligations. Making everyone responsible for surveillance and security obviously has effects on the labour force and on unions; but for our purposes, what is important is that 'natural' surveillance involves a transformation of the everyday citizen's gaze, a whole new way of seeing.

Conscientious employees and responsible apartment block householders who take on natural surveillance to deter potential criminals will begin to see their immediate environment as rife with potential dangers and criminal possibilities. This crime-centred way of seeing one's workplace or neighbourhood is not explicitly taught with facts and arguments. People come to this new way of seeing not by formal education but through practical participation in crime-prevention activities, e.g. being involved in 'safety audits'. The safety audit, a very popular technique on university campuses and in housing complexes, involves walking slowly through a workplace or neighbourhood and noting every physical arrangement that may be providing opportunities for crime. Bushes now become hiding places for rapists instead of aesthetic objects beautifying urban space.

Defensible space

The rather paranoid gaze that is embedded in and generated by micro-practices of natural surveillance is reinforced by practices undertaken under the banner of the other key tenet of CPTED, 'defensible space'. Naturalizing capitalist social relations in ways that are similar to what was discussed in relation to the Chicago School of urban sociology, Oscar Newman's pioneer work – and the whole 'designing out crime' movement that arose in its wake – assumes that people will care about and protect only those spaces that either are their private property or that feel as if they are their property. Large lawns surrounding public housing (council) blocks are nobody's property, and hence nobody's responsibility, Newman argued, and so they become literal breeding grounds of crime and disorder. Ignoring all of the other reasons why tenants living in ugly tower blocks might feel alienated and disinclined to look after communal spaces, Newman's design-centric argument was that if housing blocks were provided with small courtyards and well-designed front lawns, and were clearly separated from the public street by hedges or some other marker, then the residents would automatically, without being told, come to look after the common spaces.

Newman and the other pioneers of 'designing out crime' (e.g. Poyner, 1983) did not explicitly state that they had given up on the postwar 1950s welfarist ideal of democratizing the city – the social democratic utopia that built the public housing which is now universally condemned but which at the time was seen as a vast improvement over the dirty streets and the 'blight' (a favourite 1950s word) of the slums. Their highly influential works simply took it for granted that it was no longer worth giving any thought to the social democratic ideal of a fully public and fully democratic city. This pessimistic view of the basic dynamic of urban space, taken to an extreme in the American programme *COPS*, discussed in Chapter 6, is also evident in British Home Office policies, Blairite as well as Thatcherite. Making everyone feel at home is no longer the goal. Crime-prevention authorities speak as if urban life were nothing but a battle: either the football hooligans and rowdy drunks are in charge, or we are. And if the city is by nature a battlefield in which professional couples engaged in approved consumption fight for space against groups of youth who do not seem to shop or work but merely 'hang out', then the only question that is worth posing is: Which side will win? Which group will set the tone? Who is going to physically and symbolically occupy and dominate the city?

Newman was writing well before the Thatcher-era move to sell council houses to their tenants, but he laid the cultural preconditions for the legal privatization of public real estate by putting forward, as a common-sense truth based on purely technical features, that the only way to achieve security and safety in public housing settings is to re-design both interior and exterior spaces such that all spaces, whatever their legal status, look as if they are private. The technical drawings that take up a very large proportion of the pages in Newman's text communicate this neoliberal, post-welfarist message more effectively than any political tract. Newman himself was not a right-winger: he was interested in improving the situation of poor families living in public housing. And CPTED tools have been used by poor communities to improve their own safety and by women's organizations to minimize the risk of sexual assault. Design strategies are not hard-wired to a single political project. But the technical proposals Newman put forward had embedded in them the most bourgeois of all messages, namely, that safety is found only in private property.

That spaces that are public or are perceived as public are inherently more dangerous and unsafe than private or private-looking spaces is one the most fundamental assumptions of contemporary urban design. It can be directly seen in newer public-housing projects, which work very hard to look as if they are not public. It is also found in the advertising produced by gated communities. Many gated communities do not actually have private streets; but by putting up fancy ironwork, low brick walls, gas lights and other traditional markers of property divisions, designers communicate a clear message to potential buyers: 'This is an exclusive space.' The same signs communicate a rather different message to racialized and poorer citizens who may be passing by, namely: 'This is a club, and you don't belong to it.' The dual message communicated by the ubiquitous ironwork fixtures and brick columns dotting the city outskirts is an excellent example of the point made in Chapters 2 and 3 about the importance of the context in which signs are interpreted. The same signs manage to welcome one group and exclude another. People will more or less automatically read the signs differently, depending on their demographic characteristics.

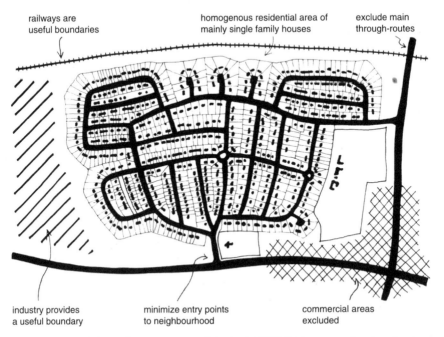

'Crime Prevention Through Environmental Design' (CPTED) is a way of seeing the city and its dangers, as well as a crime prevention strategy (in Barry Poyner, *Design Against Crime*, London & Boston, Butterworths, 1983).

The CPTED literature – much of which is readily available online from a variety of sources in the UK, the US, Australia, Canada and Europe – is full of suggestions encouraging worried citizens to put up what are called 'symbolic barriers': gates that can't be closed, for example, but that look as if one is about to enter a wealthy estate or a golf club. Flower beds, cobblestones, fancy pavements, and decorative street lights are some of the other signifiers that are regularly recommended in the CPTED literature.

Signs of symbolic privatization can be readily seen in my own university campus, which is located downtown in a large cosmopolitan city. When I first started teaching at the University of Toronto in the mid-1980s, there were no markers dividing the campus from the rest of the city. Only small blue signs with the building's name and the university crest distinguished 'the university' from the city. In the 1990s, however, the university began to build fake gates, to put up flower beds in (public) sidewalks, and to experiment with various architectural signs marking off the campus as a distinct and exclusive space. At the bottom and at the top of the four blocks of St George Street which the university occupies, large concrete markers with the university's name and crest were installed, with iron columns rising up from the concrete. This architectural innovation made it seem as if one were entering an exclusive private college rather than a public university in a public and very busy downtown street.

Of course, this type of marker, like other signs, does not always work to convey the intended meaning. The four blocks of St George Street that have university buildings were re-paved at great expense, with wide swaths of brickwork replacing much of the asphalt. This innovation, which is extremely common in gated communities, actually decreased safety. First, it became clear to those of us who use the space that the architect must have been imported from California or some other warm climate: winter ice makes the bricks buckle up, increasing the danger to everyone, especially the hapless cyclists who had been encouraged to use this street rather than another one by the painting of bicycle lane signs. In addition, I and every other user of the street made a half-conscious assumption that each swath of brick represented a pedestrian crossing, and so began to cross the very busy street using what we thought were pedestrian crossings. This caused confusion and constantly brought cars screeching to a halt. Confronted with this unexpected consequence of the use of Newman's principles, the university authorities ended up putting up a sign by the bricked portions of the street warning pedestrians that 'This is not a crosswalk.'

Failures and unexpected semiotic consequences aside, however, the key point is that the CPTED literature never mentions the fact that the new fetish objects (cobblestones, fake gates, flower beds) convey the 'keep out' message because of a culturally and historically specific contingency, namely, that in most British and American urban settings public property is not as well maintained as private property. This was not always the case: but since the 1970s it has definitely been true that privately owned spaces have in general been better kept than publicly owned ones. Lower taxation, decreased central government funding for public inner-city spaces, higher corporate profits, and an increasing disparity between the fancy physical structures built for the rich and those run-down buildings in which the poor live, work and shop are the background economic facts – the social context – that enable the cobbblestones or the flower beds to be perceived as indicators of a sudden increase in the level of safety. The recent history of the deterioration of public urban spaces is suppressed or repressed in advice literature that takes it for granted that private property is inherently nicer and safer. As a CPTED specialist puts it:

> A sense of territoriality is fostered by architecture that allows easy identification of certain areas as the exclusive domain of a particular individual or group. This feeling is enhanced when the area involved is one the individual can relate to with a sense of pride and ownership. It is not enough for a person simply to be able to defend his environment, he must also want to defend it. That 'want' results from territorial feelings of pride and ownership. The term ownership when used in this context does not necessarily mean actual legal ownership. It can be, and very often is, a perceived ownership resulting from an individual's relationship to the environment. (Robert Gardner, 'Crime Prevention Through Environmental Design,' *www.vcnet.com/expert*)

Like CPTED literature generally, Gardner avoids asking the hard question, namely: If the contested space in question is nobody's legal property but rather the common property of a public body, why does it have to belong to only one group? Why do the middle-class, white homeowners have an automatic right to treat the local park as theirs and to demand that the city put up signifiers that will help to deter others – say, black youth – from using the park? Because this kind of question is never asked in crime-prevention literature, the absence of answers goes unnoticed. The CPTED literature merely assumes that urban space is a semiotic and social battlefield.

A good example of this warlike depiction of urban chronotopes is found in one of the most influential texts on crime and urban disorder of the past 20 years, namely, the original 'Broken Windows' article that gave rise to a book and a whole movement by the same name (Kelling and Wilson, 1982). The distinct right-wing politics of the 'broken windows' approach is not necessarily shared by everyone who favours CPTED. But the risk-driven and crime-centred gaze that CPTED encourages citizens to develop is the same as that honed by the 'broken windows' criminologists.

In the original article, George Kelling and James Q. Wilson famously argued that even if broken windows and other visual cues of disorder and neglect are not correlated with higher crime rates, nevertheless it is crucial to replace them by signs of order, since American inner cities suffer not only from crime but also from 'disorderly people' and disordered objects. The Kelling/Wilson argument has been challenged and critiqued by numerous academic criminologists. But to my knowledge, none of the critiques has mentioned the fact that the famous 1982 article did not just have words: it also had five good-sized, black-and-white drawings that made an argument of their own, quite independent of the text.

A quick social semiotics analysis of these images reveals a few points of interest. First, the respectable people – a man wearing a hat, a lady with a shopping bag – seem to be living in the 1950s, or at any rate, seem to be wearing 1950s clothes. A car shown in one drawing is also very old-fashioned and could be a 1950s model.

Cartoon-style depictions of urban disorder illustrating Kelling and Wilson's 1982 'Broken Windows' article encouraged simplistic views of social problems. (Artwork reprinted by permission from The Pushpin Group.)

The disorderly youth, the beggar and the prostitute, by contrast, are wearing clothes that are more contemporary and far less dated. Whatever the artist's intention, the allusion to a previous decade and the fact that the allusion is much stronger in depictions of the respectable citizens than in depictions of the under-class, combine to construct the 'proper' reader of the article – the subject position – as a middle-aged or elderly respectable person.

Second, given that *The Atlantic Monthly* is a glossy magazine replete with full-colour advertisements and photos, the odd choice of black-and-white, child-like drawings is noteworthy. Whatever the artist's intentions, the effect of this choice of artistic tool is greatly to oversimplify the semiotic complexity and ambiguity of downtown urban spaces. A candid photograph of a downtown street corner might show a human figure that definitely looks like a beggar; but it would be very difficult to take an unposed photograph that neatly divided up the urban popula-tion into 'rough' and 'respectable'. The choice of a very simple artistic medium (cartoon-like drawings) is a format choice that greatly influences content, since it simplifies the urban scene by dividing people into cartoon-style caricatures. Each cartoon-like figure is either rough or respectable. There are only two camps in the war about urban space.

In real life it is often difficult for middle-aged people to know whether a 15-year-old wearing baggy pants and a baseball cap is engaged in disorderly activity or is merely showing off the latest fashions. But the caricatures admit no ambigu-ity. Disorder can be readily seen and immediately identified: the signs of disorder are unequivocal, uncontested and apolitical. Of particular importance in the US context is the fact that race, unavoidable when photos are used, is swept under the carpet in line drawings. If a photo showing black or Latino disorderly youth were used, 'racism' might come into the mind of the reader. But line drawings help to erase race, and thus to erase politics.

Furthermore, because the signs of disorder are so readily apparent, so apolitical and so 'obvious', it is equally obvious what has to be done: just erase them. The removal of 'disorderly people' from inner cities thus appears not as a particular political project based on particular cultural preferences and economic interests, but as a common-sense solution. The frequent use of the term 'clean-up' to refer not only to physical cleaning but also to getting rid of undesirable people has a similar semiotic dynamic, in that a seemingly unpolitical sign – cleanliness – with powerful mythical connotations is used both to signify and to promote a political campaign with demographically specific targets.

The general point here is that popular campaigns about crime and disorder are also cultural battles, semiotic wars. Precisely because the contests about safety in urban spaces are as much about meanings as about power, breaches of the respectable family-based inhabitants' semiotic code rate as much attention in the CPTED literature as crime. Not coincidentally, the Toronto Police anti-graffiti squad (mentioned earlier) has produced a coffee mug with an illustration – little red blocks falling down – that seems to be telling the coffee drinker that the walls of the city are literally crumbling down.

But erasing signs of disorder is not an end in itself: it is a means to a much more semiotically ambitious end. The European *Designing Out Crime Newsletter*, just to give one example, informs us that the European Crime Prevention Award for 2002 was given to a Belgian anti-graffiti project: 'The project was a combination of a clean-up operation, removal of new graffiti within 48 hours and severe reprimanding of offenders. At the same time artistic graffiti was tolerated on specially appointed objects.' Encouraging replacement activities that are semiotically agreeable to those who feel they own the city, and that are confined to 'specially appointed objects', is in keeping with the general CPTED approach. CPTED seeks not only to get rid of broken windows and unsupervisable large courtyards but, more ambitiously, to encourage activities felt to be appropriate. CPTED's dream envisages the complete transformation of urban spaces and the re-population of inner cities by happy respectable families picnicking in parks that were previously the haunt of the homeless and the gangs. This dream is signified and nurtured through the deployment of a whole array of signs that have proliferated around us without attracting much criticism. Even progressive politicians and urban activists who are challenging the gentrification of cities rarely challenge the semiotic dimension of the battle for control over public space. But battles are not won by money alone; they are also won with signs and symbols.

Chapter 9

'Gruesome' Pictures: Images and their Effects in Criminal Justice Practice

This final chapter deals with some debates on the circulation of shocking or graphic images in criminal justice contexts. When and how it is (a) ethical and (b) legal to show images of actual bodies and their suffering is a vexed question in the criminal justice system, particularly now that home videos and digital cameras encourage everyone to record their own or other people's crimes. The representations of actual dead or injured bodies which the American legal literature calls 'gruesome pictures' present complicated ethical as well as legal dilemmas for judges asked to rule on the admissibility of such evidence, and on whether the images will be made available beyond the courtroom. These legal dilemmas are simultaneously semiotic, since in deciding on admissibility and on publication bans, judges are making certain assumptions about the effects of signs, that is, about the impact that representations will have on juries and on victims.

We will begin with two events that highlight the diverse and conflicting roles played by images in and around criminal justice contexts.

Case study 1 The most notorious Canadian criminal of recent years, Paul Bernardo, is a graduate of Scarborough College, one of the University of Toronto's two suburban campuses. A hallway in the main building of the pleasantly situated, leafy university complex features a set of bulletin boards, one for each year, crammed with rows of small photographs of students in their graduating gowns. The unremarkable photograph of Paul Bernardo – who was convicted and jailed indefinitely in 1995 – was at some point defaced by heavy scratches that were obviously designed to eliminate Bernardo from the group. Whatever emotional outlet making these scratches might have provided to offended or angry students, the result is that the heavy scratches draw increased attention to his literally shadowy presence among his fellow graduates. As censors everywhere know, trying to erase or delete a representation often results in further publicity for the representation in question.

Case study 2 A former homicide detective now in charge of the Toronto Police's photographic service told me in a phone interview that in a 2003 preliminary hearing on the murder of a young girl whose body had been found cut into pieces inside garbage bags, the judge had ruled that the colour photographs of the remains that were going to be entered into evidence had to be replaced by black-and-white sketches that captured the necessary detail. The officer was unsure whether the judge objected to the colour or to the fact that the images in question were photographs; but, after complaining about the amount of work created for his staff by this request, he contextualized it by remarking that judges often feel that they have to protect juries from 'gruesome' evidence, including graphic photos. He opined that this unnecessarily infantilized the jury members.

It is clear that a host of complicated ethical issues, and a whole range of philosophical assumptions about the meaning and the effects of different kinds of visual images, swirl around these two events: (a) the decision of a student to scratch out the pictorial representation of another student, and (b) a judge's ruling to exclude what American law standardly calls 'inflammatory' images and to request representations in a different, less inflammatory form. By contrast with the topics covered in other chapters, which all have extensive relevant literatures, there is no scholarly literature that I have been able to locate dealing with the complex issues regarding representations not *of* but *in* criminal justice. Therefore this is necessarily a preliminary account, offered in the hopes that some readers will take up the baton and go on to pursue more detailed studies.

The chapter will proceed in three parts. First, an overview of the legal history of the admissibility of photographic evidence will be presented: this will highlight legal challenges regarding what are known in law as 'gruesome' pictures, especially of dead bodies, in jury trials. An examination of American case law on this by way of the law of evidence suggests that fights about admissibility are grounded in, and help to construct, large-scale philosophical theories about the relation between images and human behaviour. That only jury members have passions to be controlled or managed – passions which are routinely assumed to be 'inflamed' by graphic pictures – is only one of the interesting, more specifically legal assumptions shared by all participants in these fights. That police officers, prosecutors and judges also have 'passions' is never contemplated.

The case law on gruesome pictures has been largely driven by defence counsel's efforts to keep prejudicial evidence from the jury, as would be expected. But in very recent years, a different type of dispute has come to the fore. The second part of this chapter, discussing debates on the semiotic issues involved in claiming a right to privacy of victims and their families, focuses on an area of law that has developed very recently along a wholly separate line, with barely a mention of the cases on the right of the accused to a fair trial. A study of the repeated efforts by some of Paul Bernardo's victims' families to keep the home-made videos of his crimes out of the public courtroom – and, later, to have the videos physically destroyed – will help to illuminate the wrenching emotional and ethical issues involved in these newer legal disputes about the status and the circulation of evidence. Contrasting this new, victim-centred type of legal dispute with the more established rules governing the 'inflammatory' effects of pictures on juries leads to a broader issue. This concerns the abysmal lack of opportunities, within the legal process, to name, discuss and debate the competing theories about reason and the passions, and about representations and their effects, which shape the legal fights about images but which remain implicit and unnamed.

Nowhere in this chapter do I dare to suggest that I have the answer to any of the difficult dilemmas that emerge in specific cases. The argument is simply that a broader and deeper understanding of the varying effects of representations can only help courts and criminal justice personnel to understand the roots, and the implications, of decisions that are often taken with nothing but gut feelings.

Photographic evidence in American trials

Media studies scholars have shown that people today generally believe that if they see some image on television, however blurry or ambiguous, they have come closer to the truth than if they have read any number of black-and-white newspaper column inches regarding the same event. Given the dominance and the prestige of the visual in contemporary culture, it is striking to discover that in the context of trials, it is only very recently that images have been allowed to 'tell their own story'.

→ Photographs have been used in court since at least the 1880s. But for many decades, photos were only admitted as what the law calls 'illustrative' evidence. That is, the photos had to take a back seat to the orally presented evidence of a live human witness, with the oral evidence enclosing the photo, as it were, and determining its value: any failings in the credibility of the witness would automatically be seen as affecting the legal value of the image in question. An article in the *Kentucky Law Journal*, published in 1958, put this curious inversion of the usual relation between visual images and truth as follows:

> A photograph . . . is simply nothing except so far as it has a human being's credit to support it . . . as a preliminary foundation for the admission of photographs, they must be 'verified' by a testimonial sponsor as correctly expressing his observation . . . (Quoted in MacFarlane, 1973, p 155)

A police doctor or a detective who had been at the scene of the crime could bring a photo into court while testifying, but the photo was supposed to merely 'illustrate' his oral testimony. The process of accrediting a witness in court, including obtaining a ruling from the judge that Mr X is indeed an expert for purposes of this trial, the subsequent presentation of oral testimony and the cross-examination that follows, are the three steps of the process known as 'laying the foundation'. In this process, the witness's own professional credentials and his/her credibility (that is, moral character) stands surety, as it were, for the legal value of the images presented. Out on the streets, a picture on a billboard does its work by itself; the impact of its message is not thought to depend on the truthfulness or the professional qualifications of the photographer or the designer. But in the legal system, in both civil and criminal trials, images could not, until very recently, speak for themselves.

This curious limitation is at one level just an effect of the adversarial system. Only live human witnesses can be cross-examined in an adversarial courtroom. Therefore, evidence of all kinds, from photos to bloody gloves to claims about having seen Mr A running down the alley, has to be generated in the form of human speech – specifically, that limited form of human speech that consists of answers to lawyers' questions. Legally, then, exhibits have to serve merely as visual aids illustrating what the speaker is describing, not as signifiers in their own right – although the tremendous cultural prestige of photographic or technologically created images is now often regarded as trumping other considerations, as was earlier discussed in relation to fingerprint and DNA typing images shown to juries (See Chapter 4).

Nevertheless, as one reads some of the court decisions about the admissibility and weight of visual images, one also discerns a more cultural or philosophical non-legal issue at work. Judges are text-driven creatures; law is a black-and-white, blackletter business. Visual images, by contrast, are associated with advertising, with movies, and with art: that is, with the passions. If, as feminist and psychoanalytic critics have both argued, Western culture is obsessed with the threat that 'the passions' pose for reason, law will fall on the side of reason and cold logic and against emotions and passions. There is thus more to the case law on photos than the particular features of the adversarial trial. Battles about the admissibility of this or that picture draw their force and their fascination from the deepest cultural conflict in Western culture – passion vs. reason; body vs. mind.

This is clear from the language of the decisions pertaining to the somewhat narrow question of whether 'gruesome' pictures should be shown to the jury, helpfully gathered (for the US) in a lengthy annotation in the *American Law Reports* (Veilleux, 2002). Typical of this case law is a 1991 decision by a Kentucky court to the effect that certain pictures of a murder victim's skull did not help to prove the crime, and thus had little 'probative' value: they served 'only to arouse passion and shock at the sight of a gory event'. Along the same lines, another court concluded that 'the gruesome color slides and videotape were not necessary to depict the victim's injuries but were inflammatory and served to arouse passion'.

The dozens upon dozens of cases summarized by Veilleux tend to use the same boilerplate language. The jury's passions are routinely said to be 'inflamed' by images that 'arouse' 'passion', and this is taken as a natural, pre-legal fact of life. The judge's role is thus simply to weigh the disadvantages (mainly in relation to the accused's right to a fair trial) of admitting this naturally inflammable evidence against potential advantages. The main advantage is taken to be that showing the jury the crime-scene signs and clues used by detectives and doctors to arrive at their conclusions about cause of death will help the jury to understand how the prosecution built its case.

The case law on this is shot through with questions that raise interesting issues about social semiotics, that is, about the effects of pictorial representations. For example, judges have had on occasion to consider whether colour videos have an inherently more 'inflammatory' effect on the jury's passions than black-and-white stills. The competing theories about representation, passion and legal reason that undergird these questions and arguments are, however, never explicitly formulated and discussed. As far as I have been able to determine, courtroom battles about the admissibility of this or that gruesome image are not settled by calling in visual studies experts or film professors. The battles are settled on purely legal grounds by judges who make what appear to be 'gut' decisions about whether the prejudicial effect (i.e. inflammatory potential) of image X is greater or lesser than its probative value.

The case law on 'gruesome' pictures thus serves to highlight a more general point regarding the legal fortunes of pictorial images in general. It is clear that the old legal requirement that called for enveloping an image or a video in the oral testimony of a witness – most often, a police officer, police photographer or a doctor, who are all trained to give the most 'graphic' testimony in the most dispassionate, monotone voice possible – achieves a broad cultural effect, as well as having the legal effect of allowing for cross-examination. The cultural effect is that the impact of the image is by mediated, managed and minimized through this highly dispassionate manner of presentation.

Around 1970, however, the law of evidence changed to allow certain images to walk into court by themselves, if not to speak for themselves. One might have thought that CCTV surveillance cameras, which record images automatically without any person having to decide how to frame the shot, and whose film thus cannot be introduced by someone who was there and saw what the camera saw, would be the crucial technological change motivating a change in court procedure. But the change in law allowing for photographs and video recordings to 'speak for themselves' was not wholly technologically driven.

A few cases that took place before the invention of video and surveillance cameras already paved the way for a new, more exalted legal role for images – a role as 'demonstrative' rather than 'illustrative' evidence. Interestingly, the two leading cases – one from the US and one from the UK – pioneering this new semiotic/legal doctrine both involved consensual sexual activities rather than ordinary crimes. In one case, a California court ruled that sexy photographs taken by the participants – a married couple – of an act of oral sex could be introduced as evidence used to convict them of sodomy, even though the photographer in question, being one of the two accused, could hardly be expected to testify for the prosecution about how the picture was taken (MacFarlane, 1973, p 153). A similar English case concerning pictures of sexual activity resulted in a Court of Appeal ruling that photographs did not need to become a part of someone's oral testimony (Ibid, p 158).

Pictures and video recordings can now walk into court as signs in their own right. This is a rather belated admission, on the part of legal actors, of the power and prestige that visual images have acquired in our culture. The most authoritative treatise on the law of evidence, *Wigmore*, describes this as follows, in the 1970 edition:

> [The illustrative rule] was advanced in prior editions of this work as the only theoretical basis which could justify the receipt of photographs in evidence. With later advancements in the art of photography, however, and with increasing awareness of the manifold evidentiary uses of the products of the art, it has become clear that an additional theory of admissibility of photographs is entitled to recognition . . . Given an adequate foundation assuring the accuracy of the process producing it, the photograph should then be received as a so-called silent witness or as a witness which 'speaks for itself'. (Cited in MacFarlane, 1973, p 160)

Thus, images are now recognized as signs in their own right rather than as aids brought by a human witness to help him/her present the testimony.

But as the law of evidence changed to include the situation of photos and other images acting as 'silent witnesses', what remained the same was the underlying assumption that the admissibility issue would be decided by weighing the potential legal (probative) value of the image against the possibility that seeing a gory picture would so inflame the passions of the jury as to result in a mistrial. Although some images have been given the hallowed status of 'silent witnesses', most images in today's trials are introduced merely to illustrate what the police officer or other professional is relating and describing to the court. And police officers who regularly testify in court are trained in how to describe both crime scenes and pictures in ways that help to turn 'graphic' photos into cold, hard evidence. Trials involving pornography, obscenity and indecency, for example, routinely feature police officers and other professionals testifying using objectivist language and refraining from laughing or showing any emotion, as if extreme coldness and professionalism in the witness were necessary to counteract the fiery effect of the images.

The reduction of the complex issues around representation, passion and legal process to the arbitrarily narrow question of the jury's tendency to let passion get the better of their reason has not been questioned in any relevant case, as far as I know. Defence counsel tends to develop arguments that assume that juries are irrational and child-like, and that their client will thus be disadvantaged by graphic images of damage or violence, but no evidence drawn from jury studies is generally introduced. By contrast, prosecutors and police have a professional investment in showing the court every bit of evidence and every gruesome picture. The old battle between defence and prosecution gets arbitrated by judges who seem to be similarly lacking in information about the actual effect of images on juries.

Evidence-free assumptions about the jury's emotionalism are not the only ones underlying these legal battles about the admissibility of graphic evidence. What is equally remarkable is that the emotions of the legal professionals involved are never brought into view, not even to claim that because they are professionals they don't let their emotions sway their judgement. The case law governing the admissibility of 'gruesome' pictures – a narrow area of the law of evidence, but one that nicely illuminates some important broad assumptions about the complex relation between representation and legality – proceeds as if only the jury has passions. Everybody else is thus placed, by implication, firmly on the side of cold reason. This has the effect of reinforcing the old legal ideology through which it is assumed that lay people involved in legal situations (juries) are much more prone to being (mis)led by their irrational feelings than legally trained personnel.

From the passions of juries to the feelings of victims

In very recent years, a new type of legal battle about admissibility has emerged, one whose protagonist is not the emotional or irrational juror, but rather the traumatized victim and the traumatized family member. These cases often pit the mass media – who push for evidence to be presented in open court rather than in camera and against publication bans – against the victims and their families, who argue that their right to privacy requires that certain images be kept from the public eye even if they are admitted in evidence. These new battles, then, are not about admissibility. The claim made by many victims – and on behalf of victims – is that some of the evidence that is required for a trial, and is thus shown to the jury, should not be reproduced or otherwise circulated.

These new legal battles are often three-sided or four-sided rather than adversarial, since the media's and the victims' legal interests do not necessarily coincide with those of either defence or prosecution. Thus, the multi-party battles about the circulation of images need to be understood in the context of the growing presence of victims within and around the criminal justice process. This growing presence has often been discussed in relation to sentencing, since in many jurisdictions, victim impact statements are now routine components of sentencing hearings. Victim impact statements can be accommodated within a largely adversarial and state-centred criminal justice system with little trouble, since deciding on the specifics of a sentence has traditionally required at least some attention to the actual harm caused. But victims' involvement in battles about the legal, physical and semiotic status of certain bits of evidence is more problematic legally, since victims have no obvious role in the trial process itself as distinct from the sentencing.

A highly publicized battle regarding the circulation of some home-made videos made by the notorious Canadian rape-and-murder couple, Paul Bernardo and Karla Homolka, can be used to show how these legal manoeuvrings shed some light on people's mainly implicit assumptions and beliefs about representations and their effects (see archived stories at www.canoe.ca).

In the early 1990s, Paul Bernardo raped a large number of women, mainly in Scarborough, a suburb of Toronto. The so-called 'Scarborough rapist' was never caught. He then moved to the nearby town of St Catherines, where he moved in with and later married Karla Homolka. The couple were involved in drugging and raping Karla's 15-year-old sister, who died on Christmas Eve of drug-induced asphyxiation shortly after she was raped by Bernardo in the Homolka family home. Some of the events immediately preceding this death were captured on a family home video that featured both 'innocent' images of a Christmas family party and also not so innocent pictures involving Homolka and her sister. A short time later, around the time of their wedding, Bernardo and Homolka lured two young women, on separate occasions, to their bungalow, and proceeded to sexually abuse and eventually murder both of them. It was these last two murders for which Bernardo and Homolka were tried and convicted.

Reportedly graphic, indeed horrific, videotapes of the two last murders were made at the time by the couple, and hidden away behind a ceiling light fixture. An incompetent police search that went on for months failed to uncover these videos. Eventually Bernardo told his lawyer how to find them, and the lawyer got them and held on to them for over six months, something which gave rise to both a prosecution for obstruction of justice and a professional law society hearing. When Bernardo's second lawyer finally turned the videos over to the prosecution, a long series of legal battles ensued about how the videos would be used.

In most of the case law covered in the previous section, it was defence counsel that tried to keep potentially inflammatory images out of the jury's eyes, and by implication, out of the public's eye as well, since it was assumed by all involved that the images would make juries more likely to convict. In this case, however, it was the prosecution, not the defence, that sought to limit both public and media access to tapes. Bernardo's lawyer wanted the videos shown. This was because Bernardo and/or his lawyer believed that the videos could be used to support the claim that there was no proof beyond a reasonable doubt that it was Bernardo rather than Homolka who had actually killed the teenagers, since she appeared in the videos as an apparently willing participant. The families of the two young murder victims joined the prosecution's battle to limit the dissemination of the horrific images, but with their own lawyer, who made his own submissions.

The victims' families of course wanted the jury to see the videos, since there was general agreement that no jury or judge who saw the videos could do anything except convict Bernardo of the first-degree murders of the girls. (Homolka had previously managed to plea bargain with the crown for a 12-year sentence; the videos were not yet available when this plea bargain, popularly referred to as 'a pact with the devil', had been made.) Thus, admissibility was not the issue.

But the victims' families did not want the videos to be shown in open court, that is, to the public galleries and the media. Videos shown in court cannot then be shown on television in Canada, since no recording equipment is allowed into criminal trials; but the families did not want reporters even to verbally describe the details of the videotapes. The prosecution had suggested that the videos need not be shown to anyone except the jury, the lawyers and the judge; but as good lawyers, the prosecutors went on to add that the court should not be emptied of spectators. In the interests of the principle of open justice in open courts, the prosecution suggested, the videos should indeed be played in open court, but with the monitors placed in such a manner that the public galleries and the press would not be able to actually see the images – only hear the soundtrack. This appears to have been suggested as a kind of wisdom-of-Solomon style compromise between total openness and total in camera exclusion, not out of any particular theory or information about the differential effects of sounds vs. images on either the legal participants or the victims and their families.

The victims' families hired a high-profile lawyer who attempted to stop the showing of the videos by appealing to the Supreme Court. This attempt to circumvent the usual appeal process was unsuccessful, and so the parties had to accept the ruling on the matter of the trial judge, Patrick LeSage. In a 40-page ruling, which bends over backwards to acknowledge the feelings of victims and their families, LeSage agreed with the prosecution's peculiar proposal, and ordered that the videos be shown in open court – but in such a way as to allow the public and journalists to hear but not see the by now famous videos.

In another effort to find a 'middle ground' between the feelings of the victims and the 'open court, open justice' principle, transcripts of the soundtrack were not actually released to the press, but were instead read out loud to the press by a court official. Apparently, the unlucky court reporter whose job it was to read aloud to reporters the typed transcript tried very hard to keep all emotion out of her voice as she read through a document that included the final words and sounds of the victims.

It is impossible to know whether the judge had any sense of the effects that the sound-but-not-image decision would have on the various parties concerned. And no research was done at that time to document the effects of this decision on legal personnel, on the friends and relatives of the victims, or on the public at large, so the effects are still unknown. However, anyone familiar with scholarly studies of television and film would have suggested to the judge that blanking out the image but proceeding with the live soundtrack could be more 'inflammatory' and upsetting than simply showing the video. When audiences are in the 'watching a video' position but they are prevented from seeing the screen, a familiarity with film techniques and with the general effects of censorship practices suggests that their imaginations will run wild, such that they might construct in their minds even worse scenes than those that are on the video in question. After all, when audiences know that a certain bit of a movie or a newspaper has been censored, the bit they cannot see acquires a certain fascination and interest, and is assumed to have an extremely inflammatory effect, simply because it has been censored.

Supporting evidence for the theory that suppressing the picture but leaving the sound in real time may have unintended 'inflammatory' effects is found in the notable effectiveness of the blank screen with live sound technique used by Michael Moore in his film *Fahrenheit 9/11* (2004). As the film moves toward the climactic moment that everyone in the audience knows is coming – the destruction of the World Trade Center buildings by hijacked airplanes – the screen goes blank. Then, soundtrack from the television and video footage taken that day is played in real time. After the film opened in North American theatres, film reviewers reported that audiences appeared to be more affected and moved by this unusual technique than if the expected photos of the collapsing towers had been shown.

This is not to suggest that the judge made a wrong ruling in the Bernardo videos case. A long series of very specific events and situations – e.g. the fact that the existence of the videos went undetected for over a year – combined with the particularly horrifying character of the crimes in question, created a situation in which any decision that the judge might take would be wrong, in the sense of having unintended negative effects of some magnitude. The detailed press accounts of the trial, and of the battle about the videos in particular, suggest that the judge was trying his best to accommodate the victims' families' feelings, while at the same time not wanting to sow complete confusion into the Canadian legal system by allowing victims to determine which evidence will be shown and how, or to call for and obtain in camera (non-public) proceedings.

But the point is not to take sides in the courtroom battles. Our purpose here is to encourage further reflections on the assumptions that are made every day in much more mundane trials about the meaning, role and effects of various representations – including but not limited to videos showing actual crimes.

If we compare the legal battles about the Bernardo videos with the other types of cases discussed earlier in the chapter, one notable difference is that in the Bernardo trial the potential effects of the videos (or the audio portion) on the 'passions' of the hapless jury members were never discussed. Perhaps this was simply because the defence had chosen to see the videos as helping to sow doubt in the jury's mind as to whether Homolka or Bernardo was the worse villain of the two, and so none of the parties had any legal interest in appearing to protect the jury's delicate sensibilities. But it is interesting nevertheless that the traditional judicial theory about graphic images as inflaming lay jurors' passions went completely unmentioned. Instead, the graphic images were discussed solely in respect to a rather novel doctrine, namely, the right to privacy not only of actual victims but also of their surviving family members. This right to privacy was assumed to involve some right to have limits put on the circulation of images depicting the victims in question.

Looking at all the cases together, it thus appears that the legal system only has room for the emotions of one stakeholder at a time. In most of the case law, it is the jurors' feelings and passions that are deemed vulnerable and inflammable, and only the jurors'. How victims, police officers or television news audiences are moved or inflamed by representations of crime is simply not a legally relevant question. Then, quite suddenly, we move from that situation – one in which the passionate, child-like lay jurors need to be protected from evidence that the more seasoned legal professionals are assumed to handle without consequences – to that typified by the Bernardo video issue, a situation in which it is the feelings and emotions of the traumatized survivors that matter – nobody else's. It is as if law, when forced to confront the fact that not everything and everyone is cold, logical and rational, can only bring itself to admit one set of emotions at a time.

Conclusion

In a long article summarizing statements made to a judges' conference by the judge who had presided over the Bernardo trial, Patrick LeSage, *Globe and Mail* reporter Kirk Makin eloquently described the visible emotions of the party that in the common law is most associated with the cold light of reason: the judge. Leaving aside the strictly legal issues of admissibility and open courts, Makin took the tack of emphasizing the occupational risks of being a judge, and especially, the emotional stress caused by 'gruesome pictures'. Reporting on the judges' conference, Makin wrote: 'The toll of one particular type of stress – wrenching trial evidence – was dramatically illustrated during a panel session yesterday morning, when Ontario Superior Court Chief Justice Patrick LeSage broke down in tears as he gave a speech' (*Globe and Mail*, 14 August 2002).

Makin interviewed LeSage after this speech. He reported that LeSage explained the difference between having on the one hand to serve as the emotionless referee in a battle between two impassioned parties, and on the other hand, being in the congenial setting of a judicial conference among peers who could sympathize. LeSage said, 'I can control myself pretty well in the courtroom when I'm on the podium . . . But when I'm in a surrounding such as this, certain things will trigger tears.' And instead of being embarrassed by this unmanly behaviour, LeSage decided to encourage his more junior colleagues to go ahead and feel their emotions: 'I told the judges that we all have emotions; don't be embarrassed or ashamed . . .'

LeSage also told Makin that he was so upset at seeing the three and a half hours of Bernardo videos that he wanted to step down and not preside over the later hearing at which Bernardo was declared a dangerous offender. However, because a deal was reached between the prosecution and about a dozen of Bernardo's rape victims to the effect that they would not have to testify in person but simply provide some facts in the form of written statements, he agreed to go ahead with the dangerous offender hearing.

The spectacle of a senior male judge breaking down in tears while admitting that after seeing some truly horrific representations of a crime his emotions so overwhelmed him that he seriously considered stepping down from the judicial podium is one deserving of careful sympathetic reflection. It is an image that can perhaps serve to end this book, since it illustrates very graphically and movingly the point with which we began – namely, that representations are not mere conveyors of specific information. Imagining what Justice LeSage was feeling as he broke down at the judges' conference can act for us as a useful reminder that representations move us, stimulating the passions – pity and compassion as much as fear or anger – and triggering powerful memories, fears, dreams and hopes.

This final vignette underlines the fundamental premise giving rise to this book, namely, that the domains of law, justice and crime are constituted in part through representations – and through people's responses to these representations. Signs, meanings and myths are integral components of all social processes, including those relating to crime and justice. This is why those who are interested in the workings of law and justice, either professionally or as citizens, would do well to sharpen their semiotic skills.

Bibliography

Allen, C, *The Law of Evidence in Victorian England*, 1997, Cambridge: Cambridge University Press

Bakhtin, M, 'Forms of time and the chronotope of the novel' in Bakhtin, M, *The Dialogic Imagination*, 1981, Austin: University of Texas Press

Barthes, R, *The System of Fashion*, 1967, New York: Hill & Wang

Barthes, R, *Mythologies*, Lavers, A (trans), 1972, London: Cape

Best, J and Horiuchi, GT, 'The razor blade in the apple: the social construction of urban legends', in Ericson, R (ed), *Crime and the Media*, 1985, 203–213

Blomley, N, *Unsettling the City: Urban Land and the Politics of Property*, 2004, New York: Routledge

Booth, C, *Labour and Life of the Pople of London* (series I), 1891, London: Williams & Norgate

Chinball, S, *Law and Order News: Analysis of Crime Reporting in the British Press*, 1977, London: Tavistock

Christie, A, *Poirot: the War Years*, 2003, New York: HarperCollins

Cohen, S, *Folk Devils and Moral Panics: the Creation of the Mods and the Rockers*, 1972, London: MacGibbon & Kee

Cole, S, *Suspect Identities: a History of Fingerprinting and Criminal Identification*, 2001, Cambridge, Mass: Harvard University Press

Conan Doyle, A, *A Study in Scarlet*, 2001 [1887], Harmondsworth: Penguin

Coward, R, *Female Desire*, 1984, London: Granada

Dean, J, *Aliens in America: Conspiracy Cultures from Outerspace to Cyberspace*, 1998, Ithaca: Cornell University Press

De Haan, W and Loader, I, 'On the emotions of crime, punishment, and social control', *Theoretical Criminology*, 2002, Vol 6, pp 243–253

Dean, M, *Governmentality: Power and Rule in Modern Society*, 1999, London: Sage

Donovan, P, *No Way of Knowing: Crime, Urban Legends, and the Internet*, 2004, New York: Routledge

Doyle, A, 'Cops: television policing as policing reality', in Cavender, G, and Fishman, M, (eds), *Entertaining Crime: Television Reality Programs*, 1998, New York: Aldine de Gruyter

Duneier, M, *Sidewalk*, 1999, New York: Farrar, Strauss & Giroux

Durkheim, E, *The Division of Labor in Society*, 1964, New York: The Free Press

Ellis, J, *Seeing Things: Television in an Age of Uncertainty*, 2000, London: IB Tauris Publishers

Ericson, R (ed), *Crime and the Media*, 1995, Aldershot: Dartmouth

Ericson, R, Baranek, P, and Chan, J, *Visualizing Deviance: a Study of News Organization*, 1987, Toronto: University of Toronto Press

Ericson, R, Baranek, P, and Chan, J, *Negotiating Control: a Study of News Sources*, 1989, Toronto: University of Toronto Press

Ericson, R, Baranek, P, and Chan, J, *Representing Order: Crime, Law and Justice in the News Media*, 1991, Toronto: University of Toronto Press

Garland, D, *Punishment and Modern Society*, 1990, Chicago: University of Chicago Press

Ginzburg, C, *Myths, Emblems, Clues*, 1987, London: Hutchinson

Glasgow University Media Group, *Bad News*, 1976, London: Routledge & Kegan Paul

Glasgow University Media Group, *More Bad News*, 1980, London: Routledge & Kegan Paul

Hacking, I, *Rewriting the Soul: Multiple Personality and the Sciences of Memory*, 1995, Princeton: Princeton University Press

Hall, S, et al., *Policing the Crisis: Mugging, the State, and Law and Order*, 1978, London: Macmillan

Hall, S, 'The toad in the garden', in Nelson, C, and Grossberg, L (eds), *Marxism and the Interpretation of Culture*, 1988, Urbana: University of Illinois Press

Henry, F and Tator, C, *Discourses of Domination: Racial Bias in the Canadian English Language Press*, 2002, Toronto: University of Toronto Press

Herbert, S, *Policing Space: Territoriality and the Los Angeles Police Department*, 1997, Minneapolis: University of Minnesota Press

Hodge, B and Kress, G, *Social Semiotics*, 1988, Cambridge: Polity Press

Jacobs, J, *The Death and Life of Great American Cities*, 1961, New York: Vintage

Jenkins, P, *Using Murder: the Social Construction of Homicide*, 1994, New York: Aldine de Gruyter

Katz, J, *Seductions of Crime: Moral and Sensual Attractions in Doing Evil*, 1988, New York: Basic Books

Katz, J, 'What makes crime "news"?', in Ericson, R (ed), *Crime and the Media*, 1995, Aldershot: Dartmouth

Kelling, G and Wilson, J, 'Broken windows', *The Atlantic Monthly* (March), 1982

Klein, R, *Cigarettes Are Sublime*, 1993, Durham NC: Duke University Press

Leitch, T, *Crime Films*, 2002, Cambridge: Cambridge University Press

Linz, D et al., 'An examination of the assumption that adult businesses are associated with crime in surrounding areas', *Law and Society Review*, 2004, Vol 38, (1), pp 69–104

Loader, I and Mulcahy, A, *Policing and the Condition of England: Memory, Politics, and Culture*, 2003, Oxford: Oxford University Press

MacFarlane, B, 'Photographic evidence', *Criminal Law Quarterly*, 1973, Vol 16

Masterman, C, *The Heart of the Empire*, 1907, London: Fisher & Unwin

McLuhan, M, *Understanding Media: The Extensions of Man*, 1964, New York: McGraw-Hill

Newman, O, *Defensible Space: Crime Prevention through Urban Design*, 1972, New York: Macmillan

Park, R, Burgess, E, and Mackenzie, R, *The City*, 1925, Chicago: University of Chicago Press

Phillips, S, Haworth-Booth, M, and Squiers, C, *Police Pictures: the Photographic Evidence*, 1997, San Francisco: San Francisco Museum of Modern Art

Poe, Edgar Allan, *The Fall of the House of Usher and Other Tales*, 1998, New York: Signet

Poyner, B, *Design against Crime: beyond Defensible Space*, 1983, London: Butterworths

Rafter, N, *Shots in the Mirror: Crime Films and Society*, 2000, New York: Oxford University Press

Rapping, E, *Law and Justice as Seen on TV*, 2003, New York: New York University Press

Residents of Hull House, *Hull House Maps and Papers*, 1970 [1895], Reprinted New York: Arno Press

Sekula, A, 'The body and the archive', *October*, 1986, Vol 39, pp 3–64

Sparks, R, *Television and the Drama of Crime: Moral Tales and the Place of Crime in Public Life*, 1992, Buckingham: Open University Press

Sparks, R, 'Masculinity and heroism in the Hollywood blockbuster', *British Journal of Criminology*, 1996, Vol 36, (3), pp 348–360

Taylor, I, 'Private homes and public others: an analysis of talk about crime in suburban South Manchester in the mid-1990s', *British Journal of Criminology* 1995, Vol 35, (2), pp 263–285

Thomas, R, *Detective Fiction and the Rise of Forensic Science*, 1999, Cambridge: Cambridge University Press

Valverde, M, *Law's Dream of a Common Knowledge*, 2003, Princeton: Princeton University Press

Veilleux, DR, 'Annotation: admissibility in homicide prosecution of allegedly gruesome or inflammatory visual recording of crime scene', 2002, Vol 37 *American Law Reports*, p 515

Walkowitz, J, *City of Dreadful Delight: Narratives of Sexual Danger in Late Victorian London*, 1992, Chicago: University of Chicago Press

Welsh, A, *Strong Representations: Narrative and Circumstantial Evidence in England*, 1992, Baltimore: Johns Hopkins University Press

Wolf, D, *Law & Order Crime Scenes*, 2003, New York: Barnes & Noble

Young, A, *Imagining Crime: Textual Outlaws and Criminal Conversations*, 1996, London: Sage